Ice Tea & Elvis

A Saunter through the Southern States

NICK MIDDLETON

PHŒNIX

A PHOENIX PAPERBACK

First published in Great Britain
by Weidenfeld & Nicolson in 1999
This paperback edition published in 2000
by Phoenix,
an imprint of Orion Books Ltd,
Orion House, 5 Upper St Martin's Lane,
London WC2H 9EA

A CIP catalogue record for this book
is available from the British Library.

ISBN: 0 75381 013 1

Printed and bound in Great Britain by
The Guernsey Press Co. Ltd, Guernsey, C.I.

Critical acclaim for Nick Middleton

'He keeps neither his curiosity nor his sense of humour in check. There have been several accounts of touring the American South over the past few years, but this one stands out for its wit and wisdom and for its ability to make even the strangest of regional peccadilloes seem understandable'
Sunday Times

'Middleton's razor-sharp prose is invaluable in explaining how and why the South is what it is' *Good Book Guide*

'Skilful enough to avoid the crass, while helping us with the obvious – one of the delights of armchair travel'
Financial Times

'Rattles along at a furious pace, reflecting on an endless catalogue of absurd signs, laws, customs and curiosities. Middleton has that rare gift of taking the most ordinary object, or abominable subject, and describing it with enticing prose' *Geographical*

'With his eye for detail and his ear for the absurd, Middleton could be funny on the Gatwick Express'
Guardian

'Vivid, insightful and hilarious. Nick Middleton is the perfect guide in this strangely mysterious, sometimes moving, and also wildly offbeat part of the United States. The author's fascination with the place is certainly contagious' Bol.com

'His tenaciously well-informed prose transcends traveloguery' *Observer*

'Nick Middleton writes with straightforward and relentless good humour. He is good on quirky detail and a nice turn of phrase' *Independent*

'A very funny book . . . His anecdotes are uniformly excellent' *Spectator*

'Middleton's experiences are delivered with sparky, quirky charm' *Mail on Sunday*

Nick Middleton was born in London. As a geographer he has travelled to more than fifty countries and teaches part-time at Oxford University, where he is a Fellow of St Anne's College. Among his many foreign assignments, he has reviewed industrial development in Mongolia for the United Nations, edited a report on washing machine efficiency in Denmark and written information boards for a Kenyan National Park. He has also assessed educational tours in Ghana, taught earth sciences in Oman and led wildlife expeditions to Namibia. Nick Middleton has written four travel books and numerous other publications for a wide variety of readers, from politicians to five-year-olds.

By the same author

The Last Disco in Outer Mongolia

Kalashnikovs and Zombie Cucumbers:
Travels in Mozambique

Travels as a Brussels Scout

For my mum, Rita

Acknowledgements

I'd like to thank the following people who helped me with this book in the ways they know how: David Adams, Cherry, Nasser and Claudine Chegini, Michael Slattery, Tammie Middleton, Tyler Jo Smith, Bonnie O'Brien, Charles Peters, Gordon Wells, Michael Williams, Doreen Montgomery, and Lorraine Desai.

Contents

1

Sock City

I wasn't sure whether I was flying into Miami or not. I'd heard that they were trying to abolish it.

'They're having a referendum,' my contact had explained to me over the telephone, 'the motion is to dissolve the city government.' It had become so riddled with corruption that they wanted to absorb Miami into the more salubrious Dade County. When I checked in my bag to the airline official at Heathrow, it seemed appropriate that the tag she taped to the handle read 'MIA'. The entire city of Miami was on the brink of going Missing in Action.

It has been heading that way for a long time. Back in the 1980s Miami was known above all else for one thing – drugs. Every Miami resident was implicated in laundering drug money and handling narcotics. In 1985, a local pharmacologist tested bundles of banknotes taken from seven of the city's most reputable banks. He found large amounts of cocaine on all of them. Statistically speaking, every man, woman and child was involved in the drug business.

With the drugs came a generous helping of violence, all served up on a hotbed of Cuban exiles. So the city was turned into a television series. While the Miami Metro vice squad chased villains on an annual budget of $1.2 million, a TV production company spent $1.4 million a week making *Miami Vice*. On television the result was a roaring success. Miami was New York with palm trees and automatic weapons. In the real city that is often likened to Paradise, it was business as usual. Sure, the Garden of Eden had a serpent problem, but it was the price they paid for gorging themselves on forbidden fruit.

I probably watch too much television at home, and it's hard not to be influenced by North American cop shows. Under the guise of entertainment, the message about American city streets is clear. It seems as though all the people carry firearms and they're not for decoration. Like everything else in the United States of America, violence has been neatly packaged and mass marketed to the consumer. They play out little wars every day on the streets, using real guns and real bullets and, just like in real wars, people get killed. If the cop shows are to be believed, it's usually the bad guys, but innocent bystanders often get caught in the crossfire. I was more nervous about visiting this corner of the USA than I had been about visiting Mozambique, a country fighting a real war.

Miami's dangerous reputation had been confirmed to me only that morning, on a radio news story I heard in the taxi on the way to the bus station in Oxford. A man had been shot by Dade County police on Southwest 200th Street and 117th Avenue. Several local residents had flagged down a passing police car, worried that the man was acting suspiciously and was in possession of a weapon. The squad car called more police to the scene. When fourteen officers were in position, they took careful aim, and started shooting. The man was hit twenty-three times. The radio report left the punchline until the end. After careful inspection, the victim's weapon turned out to be a sock.

Emerging from immigration, I picked up my bag from the conveyor belt, walked through customs and bought a copy of the *Miami Herald* from a newsstand. I stepped out of the air-conditioned arrivals hall into a muggy mixture of subtropical air and petrol fumes to buy a ticket for the airport shuttle bus. The story had made the front page of the local news section.

The bus hummed out of the airport complex and into the sunshine along the Airport Expressway. From the elevated ribbon of concrete I looked down onto bald baseball diamonds and luscious green golf courses dotted with palm trees. Below us to the left sat Liberty City, where by all accounts the most reliable form of liberty comes in a syringe. To the right we passed the Miami Jai-Alai stadium. The sock story made engrossing reading. Apparently the man, one Bobby Whipple, had stopped his car to change a tyre and had put his sock on his hand to keep it clean. Mr Whipple's attorney told the newspaper that he was 'puzzled how a sock looks like a gun'. If Mr Whipple had been conscious, he would probably have expressed similar sentiments, but he was in a critical condition in Jackson Memorial Hospital. The report said he was pumped full of morphine and confined to a rotating bed, which under different circumstances sounded like it might be fun. The police were concerned that the story sounded as if they had used undue force in dealing with Mr Whipple. An officer from homicide wanted to stress that Whipple had been shot fewer than twenty-three times. 'The amount of holes, injuries, wounds isn't necessarily indicative of how many times he was shot,' he was quoted as saying.

I stopped reading for a moment to work out how this might be the case. We were passing over sparkling blue water and the Airport Expressway had become the Julia Tuttle Expressway for the final stretch of Interstate 195 East. It struck me that under the bright sunshine the concrete highways looked quite smooth and pleasing – in Britain they usually looked dull and dreary. I gave up trying to imagine how bullets had been designed to loop-the-loop, to come back on themselves for another shot, and read on. Some of the police had been using shotguns, spraying pellets rather than bullets. This would no doubt make Mr Whipple feel a whole lot better when he woke up on his rotating bed.

My bus was now down at ground level in Miami Beach. We inched along through the road works on Collins Avenue more slowly than the guys on roller blades on the sidewalk. On Ocean Drive the driver stopped to let someone out at an Art Deco hotel that had seen better days (despite the name the ocean wasn't visible because there was a park in the way). Soon we were back on Collins heading north, to drop off an old lady who lived near the Caballero Funeral Home, and to continue to my destination – Sunny Isles.

While the city of Miami is full of Hispanics, mostly Cubans, and Miami Beach is characterised by its Jewish community (Broad Causeway between the two used to be called the longest bridge in the world because it ran from Cuba to Israel), Sunny Isles is rapidly gaining distinction as a 'Little Moscow'. Some of these new arrivals are happy to keep up the local traditions of this urban metaphor for drugs and violence. One of the Russian immigrants, a young man by the nickname of Tarzan, was rumoured to sell Soviet helicopters and nuclear submarines to representatives of Colombian drug cartels in the back room of his strip club, Porky's. But such activities were the domain of Dade County's younger inhabitants. Miami's population, and south Florida's in general, also contains a less violent element – the elderly. Unwittingly, I was deposited right in their midst.

I climbed out of the bus and picked up my bag as an old bird wearing a dressing gown and fluffy pink slippers shuffled up to the glass door to give me the once-over. Her eyes were watery and full of suspicion. The woman behind the reception desk looked equally doubtful when I told her that I had come to visit one of her residents.

The friend I was staying with lived in this condominium because he had a young family. Miami regularly topped the polls for the worst city in the USA to bring up kids so condos full of old people tended to be safer, although even David's next door neighbour had recently been indicted for money laundering. He and his wife and their small son appeared to be the condo's youngest inhabitants, by about fifty years. It was the sort of place where the average resident spent half a day pushing his wife's wheelchair across the acre or so of carpet in the lobby.

This part of Sunny Isles was all high rise and low rise condos, hemmed in by well-groomed lawns dotted with palms and neat slices of aquamarine swimming pool. The tarmac streets looked freshly laid, with new yellow road markings to guide your shiny motor car. They were deftly complemented by glassy waterways for your white motor launch. From the condominium balconies you could see mangroves in the distance beneath the clear blue sky with its single white fluffy cloud. It was a nice view if you like views that are orderly and not too threatening, and that of course was just the way the residents wanted it.

I only had a couple of days in Miami. Being the southernmost major city in the continental USA, it seemed like a good place to start a journey around the Southern states. The South interested me because I thought the region would have all the usual things one associates with the United States – I could drive-in, take-out, and have-a-nice-day to my heart's content – plus the idiosyncrasies of a mythical place apart. From the outside, the Southern mindset still owes much to the Civil War, itself an extraordinary facet. When you think of Germany and Japan, and most other countries which have lost wars, you assume that after a few decades the losers bounce back and start booming. Not so the Southern states, which remained a backwater for a hundred years after losing out to the Yankees. For a century the region had been so terminally sick with poverty and prejudice that these diseases appeared to be genetic. The South was an unfortunate mutation of the American dream, an antebellum skeleton in a steamy cupboard, the Heart of Darkness in the USA.

An American friend of mine laughed when I told him I was off to travel the Southern states. He advised me to stay in my car and only get out at motels. If I tried to speak to the locals I'd be asking for trouble. 'In Tennessee it takes them half an hour to say a sentence and in Alabama they just beat it into you. In Florida they throw you in jail if you say anything bad about the state.' My friend is from Chicago and he thought that his city would be much more interesting.

I was not so sure. I was fascinated by this place characterised by God and guns, heat and history. I wanted to soak up the jazz, the blues and the country music, to wander the homeland of Elvis Presley and see the cotton-picking machines that had replaced the slaves in the Mississippi Delta. I was keen to observe the tribal rituals, like eating grits and barbecue and drinking tea with ice in it. I wondered what had happened to all those nice verandahs, the gentle Southern folk and their polite black servants in *Gone with the Wind*. I wanted to see the low flat part of the USA, the bit usually coloured green on the map.

Despite its geographical position, Miami isn't really in the South. It missed out on most of the defining moments of Southern history because while they were building the plantation houses and importing the slaves, southern Florida was a backwater only fit for alligators. While they were fighting the Civil War, Miami didn't exist. By the turn of the century, the place had just three hundred residents and the post was delivered by a barefooted mailman who took three days to walk from Palm Beach. Today, Miami is a booming metropolis, the surrogate capital of Latin America where golfers use global positioning systems to cheat on the fairways. It's a young hybrid of a city, which might help to explain why it is still going through its cowboys and indians phase. Miami is a child of the twentieth century, more a symbol of the American future than its past, divorced from the rest of the South at the end of a railway line that was only built in the 1890s and was already on the wane by the 1920s. It is stuck out on the end of the finger of Florida, pointing towards the Latin south whence its later energies derived.

But since the South had this reputation for being stuck in the past, I thought it might be interesting to approach it from the future. In addition, Miami's notoriety as a violent place was a trait it did have in common with the 'real' South. Southerners were supposed to be habitually violent. These were the people who invented lynching after all. With the sock story fresh in my mind, I set out the next morning for the American Police Hall of Fame and Museum to get the law enforcers' angle on the issue. Since Miami doesn't run to very efficient public transportation, I had to telephone for a taxi to take me.

As soon as I climbed in behind him, the taxi driver asked, 'You don't live in there do you?' His voice was laced with a mixture of suspicion and incredulity.

'No, I'm staying with a friend.'

'No. I thought not, because these condos are all for old people. You're too young.'

The driver, whose identification badge announced his name to be Marvin, eased his vehicle forward along the drive and turned right past the line of expensive motor-yachts moored opposite.

'They're real discriminatory in these places,' he told me. 'Fifty-five minimum. They don't want any young people. They don't want the noise or the music.'

He gently took a traffic calming bump and pulled up beside a small pillbox, a barrier blocking our way. The young Hispanic guy inside the box stared at us for a moment before pressing the button that raised the barrier. 'What's he looking for?' breathed Marvin. 'Thinks I'm going to *steal* one of his old people?'

Marvin stepped on the accelerator and immediately hit the brake for another traffic calming bump and we both rose from our seats involuntarily. 'They built that one up from last time,' he said enthusiastically, 'to wake 'em up.' We turned onto the highway and gained speed.

'Yeah, if you're young they don't want you,' Marvin continued some moments later. 'They look at you funny in the elevator because they don't understand you: you stand too straight and you walk too fast; you're not stiff like they are, and you're not riding the bus with them to the doctor every day. They just don't want you there.'

I laughed, but Marvin was serious. His short dreadlocks were suddenly whipped away from my line of vision as he turned his head to look at me earnestly from beneath the visor of his white baseball cap. 'No, I'm not kidding you man, they don't want no young people there.

'It's a problem of longevity,' he announced, putting his eyes back on the concrete highway. 'They just won't die! They're all living too long and they want somewhere warm to play things out so they all come down here in droves and hide out in these condos.' He waved his hand at the window, towards the procession of highrises we were passing. 'Ghettos for old people, that's what they are.'

'I guess we'll be old too one day,' I ventured.

'No man, I don't wanna be old like these people. They got nothing to do but go to the doctor and worry about what's wrong with them. Popping pills and wondering whether they got to have this operation or that one. It's not right. It's not natural.'

We sped over a short bridge. 'It's a problem for the building manager because they've got fixed incomes and he can't hike the rent. They'd like to get rid of a few. You see that one over there? They got young people on the first five floors and old people on up. They had a fire in that building a few months back, and you know what? It started on the sixth floor and burned *up*. Now who ever heard of that?' He paused for a moment. 'They were trying to burn 'em out!'

'Did they manage it?' I asked.

'No. There was a night man whose job it was to get people out of situations like that, put them in the elevators and get them out of there. And he did it. He saved them all.' We pulled up outside a white concrete box of a building with a white police squad car stuck vertically to its side. In front of it was a line of flag poles.

7

'He did his job well then,' I said as I pulled a wad of dollars from my pocket and handed Marvin his fare.

'Not according to the building manager he didn't: he wanted to lose a few.'

The entrance to the American Police Hall of Fame and Museum was round the side of the building. The small car park you had to walk through to get to the door was full of curious-looking motor vehicles which reflected the type of law enforcement Miami's police force had to implement, if not on a daily basis, then frequently enough to have developed this interesting array of urban assault vehicles. It was not the sort of display that the average senior citizen would feel comfortable perusing. The 'cop tank' looked like someone had sawn off the back of a Cadillac and replaced it with the rear end of a tank: it had caterpillar tracks over the back wheels. Small missiles were mounted on its bonnet and a bespoke turret sat on the roof with a very long gun poking out of it. The whole thing was painted in camouflage green, which must have been utterly useless on the city streets. Metro Dade law enforcement officials obviously took this on board when they designed the more modern version. It was painted bright red and looked indestructible and menacing in a long and pointed way, like an attack pike. It was built of sheet metal, with machine guns in its snout and a satellite dish on the roof, perhaps so that the police could watch themselves in action on CNN.

Inside, the museum began with a picture gallery of famous Americans, none of whom are commonly associated with law enforcement. They included Bob Hope, Cheryl Ladd and Richard Gere. These were members of the Citizens Celebrity Advisory Board according to the explanatory plaque below the photographs. Did Bob Hope advise the police on how to deliver a good punchline? I wondered. Was Richard Gere consulted on what brand of sunglasses they ought to be wearing? No in both cases. The role of these people was to offer celebrity condolences to the families of dead policemen.

Much of the rest of the ground floor was taken up with a marble wall engraved with the names of police officers killed in the line of duty and a memorial chapel dedicated to Michael the Archangel, described as 'the first law enforcement officer sent by God to defend against the evil works of the fallen angel'. Upstairs, there were displays of children's art with captions such as 'Policemen are cool and their dogs rule' and 'Only dopes do dope'. Another display case showed how kids who miss out on the policemen's art classes apply their creative energies. It contained handmade 'teen war' firearms fashioned from all sorts of everyday objects including clothes pegs, paperclips and the spokes of a bicycle. Elsewhere, more grown-up weaponry included umbrella swordsticks and lipsticks that turned into daggers at the flick of a switch, but surprisingly enough none of the display cases contained socks. Nevertheless, a whole section was devoted to hidden firearms, most inside handbags. The concealed weaponry came with helpful fashion tips for law enforcement officers who carry handbags, on or off duty. Styles for men were also available, in a portfolio clutchbag and in denim.

Toy guns and X-ray letter bomb detectors gave way to displays of police helmets and handcuffs through the ages and a bullet fired from 'the most famous gun in the world', the Jack Ruby Colt Cobra .38 special. Over on the opposite side of the floor the exhibits were more interactive. A full-size replica of a gas chamber came complete with an entertaining voice-over from a hidden speaker. A not-too-serious commentator gave a short description of the methodology, involving secure strapping, cyanide pellets, deadly gases and lethal fumes. It ended with an invitation to the listener, 'Please feel free to sit in the gas chamber seat and have your photograph taken. Enjoy yourself!' and faded out with a snatch of jaunty music. It was a display designed to put the fun back into capital punishment.

The fun continued nearby with the approach 'affectionately referred to in Florida as "Old Sparky"'. The write-up made the electric chair sound like a very jolly little piece of equipment. Any sick bastard who happened to wander through the museum could snuggle down in the friendly seat for another quick photo-call, and to add to their amusement, the voice-over went through a mock final few minutes:

'Prisoner, before sentence is carried out, do you have any last words? No? Then let's begin. Guard, restrain the prisoner. Doctor, are you ready?

'Prisoner, under the laws of this state, you have been tried by a jury of your peers. You have been found guilty of a crime against society. You have been sentenced by the court to die in the state's electric chair. You have exhausted all available appeals, and, in a moment, the state will carry out the court's sentence of death. (Fade in more jaunty music.) In a moment, two thousand volts of electricity will surge through your body, killing you instantly. Begin the count.

'Five. Four. Three. Two. One.'

There was a noise like a gameshow buzzer being pressed.

'You may inform the governor that the sentence *has* been carried out.'

The accompanying explanation stated that the button is pressed by a volunteer. Only the Americans could turn state-sponsored execution into a themepark amusement ride.

As it happened, Old Sparky was in the news whilst I was in Florida. The future of the vintage oak electric chair was under examination at the Tallahassee Supreme Court. The debate focused on whether it represented a cruel and unusual punishment and thus violated Florida's constitution. It sounded like a pretty sterile debate to me, but it had been 'sparked' by unpleasant things happening to recent prisoners in Old Sparky. Final meals tended to exit bodies from the usual orifices and on some occasions flames were seen to leap from the victim's head. The museum mock-up of Old Sparky had omitted these details. Lethal injection is now favoured by most of the 32 states that retain the death penalty. Twenty states have abandoned the electric chair since 1935, leaving just seven. Most of these are in the South. Virginia has a good solution in keeping with the spirit of a free market and consumer choice. The state offers a choice of execution methods to its death row inmates.

A week or so later, in the north of Florida, I drove out to the State Prison where Old Sparky is kept. I was disappointed to find the atmosphere of the place not quite as endearing as the museum would have you believe. I passed three Baptist churches along a road lined by fir and pecan trees before a huge, bleak clearing in which sat the low-slung peppermint green complex of buildings run by the Department of Corrections. It had been necessary to stop in the nearest town to ask for directions. A woman selling watermelons and boiled peanuts didn't bat an eyelid when I asked her for the prison. She told me to drive on to the fifth set of red lights and take a left on the Raiford road for about nine miles. I saw most of the town before the turning. It had the usual fast food outlets, a welding shop and a wooden shack with an illuminated notice that welcomed sunbirds to step in and look at its memorabilia, curios and stuff. It was a dreary spot with an appropriate name. It was called Starke.

2

Northward Southbound

The American Police Museum's presentation of the electric chair as a sort of moral equivalent of the whoopee cushion was unfortunate. The proprietors seemed to have lost sight of the fact that Old Sparky should actually be a deterrent. Their approach may have had something to do with the fact that Dade County accounts for nearly a quarter of Florida's serious crime and also holds the unenviable record for the nation's worst crime statistics. I had such a good time with Old Sparky that I felt like going out on to the streets of Miami and murdering someone, just so that I could have a go on the real thing.

Instead I opted to walk from the Hall of Fame south towards downtown and Little Havana. This in itself seems like an innocuous little statement, but the fact that the stroll just stated covers a distance of two or three miles means that it's not one many North Americans would make. Walking in most American cities is an activity confined largely to the indoors. The average North American might 'walk' from the lounge to the bathroom, or from one counter to the next inside a shopping mall. Outside, this activity means the four steps from your front door to your car, or maybe the ten steps from your car to the shopping mall. These generalisations are fairly universal, but particularly they apply to Miami because it's very hot and humid, as well as being occasionally dangerous. If you're walking on the streets of Miami you must be poor, probably from an ethnic minority, full of illegal substances or just plain crazy. Alternatively, you might be English.

Whatever the reason, the experience was an eerie one. Biscayne Boulevard was pretty dreary on the stretch outside the American Police Museum and I took small comfort from a shop called Miami Spy, which offered night vision equipment, body armour and other personal defence gear. Walking, I felt like the last member of a near-extinct species. If I'd been a visitor from outer space I'd have quickly formed the impression that the people of Planet Miami had become enslaved to a superior race. A race that was more durable, moved faster and was better equipped for the streets of this city. The motor car had taken over and the people had all been reduced to being chauffeurs.

Cars cruised by looking menacing with their tinted glass windshields. Most of the buildings looked sinister too. They had blinds or darkened windows so you couldn't see in. Some didn't have windows at all. They were just plain concrete blocks that sat there looking ominous from the outside. The result was that everywhere looked closed down. Nothing was designed to be seen on foot.

I continued down Biscayne past the Christian Science Reading room, which offered dial-a-healing in English and Spanish, and sidewalk benches for the underclass all sponsored by the Royal Pawn Shop. As I neared downtown a large hoarding screamed in big, bold lettering that 'Drugs are unbelievably easy to get hold of in Miami'. I couldn't quite believe what I was reading, but as I got closer all became clear. The smallprint offered a helpline, but it still seemed strange to me that this part of the message was probably too small for most passing motorists to notice. By this time, after about two miles of walking, I had passed three fellow pedestrians. Two of them were hobos.

The highway now widened to four lanes in either direction and turned sharply beneath a flyover. As I rounded a concrete pillar I almost walked straight into a naked man crouched down in what looked like a concrete flowerbed. The man had his back turned to me and he was having a crap. I stopped. The naked character in the flowerbed hadn't noticed me. Cars whizzed by at some speed, also oblivious to my situation. Beyond the defecating figure I could see a disused plot of land that had once been a petrol station. The forecourt was decorated with old shopping trolleys and sheets of newspaper strewn around like tumbleweed. In amongst the rubbish I could see a number of dishevelled men in various states of disarray.

A little voice inside me suggested that it might not be a good idea to stroll blithely through this lot. I thought perhaps I might cross the road to avoid any unpleasantness, but I didn't fancy my chances on the eight-lane highway either. Trying not to look too cowardly, I turned and walked back the way I'd come until I found a crossing place.

On the opposite side of the road the landscape was just as derelict but without the down-and-outs. I was near Miami port and passing somewhere called the New World Center, an open grassy space that looked as if it had once been a park. Now it looked more like a Third World Center.

Two fenced off plots and the Greyhound station led me into a much more prosperous zone. Suddenly the smoky glass frontages of smart hotels and banks replaced the wire fences. The broken glass disappeared from the sidewalk, and the litter was gone. Parking meters were in working order and the fire hydrants looked like they'd just been polished. The palm trees in the central reservation were healthier and I was relieved to see that I was no longer the only person walking. This was not the sort of zone where people relieved themselves in the herbaceous borders.

I turned onto Flagler Street. Just as abruptly, corporate America ended and Latin America began. Flags of South American countries adorned a continuous strip of small shops, each with their doors open to emit inviting air-conditioned draughts laced with the sounds of merengue and salsa music. Here the street was positively bustling with shoppers perusing the shop fronts.

The driver of the taxi I caught back up to Sunny Isles was a Cuban. He told me he had arrived in Miami with his wife three years before. They came on a raft made of truck tyres and rope. After two days drifting, being circled by hungry-looking sharks in the Gulf of Mexico, they were picked up by the US coastguard. The driver's name was Enrique Castro and he said he had been a musician in Havana, but opportunities for musicians were limited in Miami. When I asked Enrique if Miami was a dangerous city he snorted and waved his hand in dismissal of the idea. He was probably comparing it to the sharks in the Gulf of Mexico.

Just as I was settling into my seat an announcement came over the loudspeakers. A voice gave us our itinerary, a string of stations between Miami and New York, and then issued an extraordinary statement, 'Remember the train is constantly moving . . .' I stopped rummaging through my bag and looked around at my fellow passengers as the voice followed this up by warning anyone who wanted to walk through the train to do so carefully. Did they think this reminder was out of the ordinary? Apparently not. I was perplexed. Unthinkingly, I had assumed that the train's constant motion was the precise reason that we were all on board, but perhaps not.

The woman across the aisle nodded sagely, as if she was now reconsidering the heart bypass operation she had been intending to carry out on the journey. The man behind me looked mildly shocked. The message had obviously stymied his plans to practise his headstands en route to Charleston. Had I missed something? Was I the only passenger who genuinely expected the train to arrive at its destination by moving? Did Amtrak usually transport passengers by thought transference?

I was still mildly perturbed that I had missed the point of this public information broadcast when I made my way to the restaurant car and bought a coffee. It came with a lid so that I wouldn't spill it on the way back to my seat, but when I got there I noticed another warning: 'Caution,' the lid was saying to me, 'contents hot.'

I am accustomed to warnings against the improper use of products by imbeciles, but this sort of advice was new to me. The pen I was using to make notes came with a prominent 'Caution!' written on the side: 'Keep pen cap out of mouth. It can obstruct breathing if swallowed.' I understood why this was there, despite the fact that as far as I'm concerned anyone fool enough to swallow a pen cap deserves to choke to death. But even this cautionary pen did not arrive with a warning that it would write.

Perhaps the next batch of biros will, because the USA is full of these constant reminders of the obvious which on first encounter give the visitor the impression that the country is populated entirely by morons. It's not of course. The US population does not include a higher than average proportion of educationally challenged individuals, and in fact it's not the morons that the companies worry about. The morons, like me, *want* the trains to move constantly; they *expect* their coffee to be hot. No, the real danger comes from people with too much of the wrong sort of education, and the thing that makes them dangerous is litigation.

Now I remembered reading about the person who took a fast food chain to court because their coffee was too hot. She won a large sum of money and now US coffee cups are printed with prominent warnings about the high temperature of their contents. What utter nonsense. How can you run a country like that? As an English-speaker, the USA had lulled me into a false sense of security. I had expected the place to be a bit whacko, but incidents like these suggested some deeper differences.

Fortunately for me I was heading for the South, home of traditional values and plain talking. Outside the train window, the country consisted of lots of swampy bits interspersed with pine trees and wide flat sandy areas, occasionally populated with a few cows. Grain silos and orange groves confirmed the agricultural nature of the scene. Every so often, strips of landscape came wreathed in creeping kudzu which smoothed telegraph poles and trees into aerodynamic bumps like a covering of heavy green snow. Only the spiky palm fronds poked out from these mini jungles.

Kudzu is one of the defining features of the South. It is a vine brought to North America from Japan in 1876 to form part of a garden exhibition to celebrate the USA's 100th birthday. The new immigrant was welcomed with open arms. American gardeners fell in love with its large leaves and fragrant blooms and kudzu thrived in the perfect growing conditions. In the 1930s, kudzu was promoted by the US Soil Conservation Service as an ideal way to protect soil from erosion. Kudzu not only thrived, it became rampant, growing up to sixty feet in a good year. In Georgia, children are warned to close their windows at night to keep the kudzu at bay; the poet James Dickey dubbed it a 'vegetable form of cancer'. The vine that ate the South is now considered to be Public Enemy No. 1.

If you plot the geographical distribution of kudzu on a map, the result looks like an attempt to delimit the South. It manages to grow in eastern Texas but spreads no further west because the rest of Texas is too dry. Its northward limit, a line through Virginia and central Kentucky, is where the winters become too severe. It thrives in central

Florida, but has been hesitant to venture further down the peninsula. It's probably worried about getting shot in Miami.

Mapping the distribution of kudzu is just one of many ways of charting the Southern states because there is no definitive version of where the South begins and ends. John Shelton Reed, a sociologist at the University of North Carolina, has tried it with states mentioned in country music songs and states where the most lynchings occurred back in the days when lynching was a popular leisure pursuit. There is a core that most people would agree upon: Louisiana, Mississippi, Alabama, Georgia, Tennessee and the Carolinas. Folk argue over Texas, which feels more like the West. Florida only half counts. Its southern parts are out on a limb and full of old people but no history.

History is the key ingredient in the make-up of the South, stretching back to where the plantations bloomed and the cotton thrived. Some assume that the South begins at the Mason-Dixon line, the border with Pennsylvania that set the northern limit for slavery, but that would include such states as Maryland and Delaware, and even Washington DC, and somehow that doesn't seem right. Others say the South is the Confederacy: the 11 states that seceded after Lincoln's election in 1860. They cover an area almost the size of the European Union but have a population slightly smaller than Germany's. But if the truth be told, the South is as much a state of mind as a physical entity, and it was this very particular state of mind that interested me.

I had opted to start my journey by train for a number of reasons. Miami had effectively come into being thanks to the extension of the rail line to south Florida so it seemed appropriate. Rail transport in the USA had all but lost out to the car and aeroplane and I wanted to see just what was left. Not a lot was the answer.

The demise of the train had been brought home to me back in England when I came to plan my route. I dug out a map of the USA that had come with the *National Geographic* magazine some years before. It was a good map, showing all the states with their borders outlined in different colours. It marked battlefields, monuments, historic parks, forts, ferries, volcanoes, airports and highways. But no railways. In the Blackwell's travel bookshop they had a good selection of US maps, but only one of them showed rail routes. It was huge, and took up most of the floor of my study at home. On it, I identified a line that stretched from Miami all the way up the east coast to Washington and New York. My initial travelling would follow this route, stopping off at selected spots on the way. My first destination was Palatka, a small dot on the St Johns River up at the neck of Florida, a spot where my research suggested that Florida became part of the South.

Travelling by train was also better than travelling by car because it would give me the opportunity to meet people, so I thought. However, the train was very wide and the space for each traveller was more than generous. If I sat with my bottom back in my seat and stretched out my legs, I could barely touch the seat in front of me with my feet. With all this space, you'd have to shout to be heard in the next seat. No doubt this is part of the reason why Americans talk so loudly.

Conversation was available, but only in an unexpected place: the smoking area, a transitory zone set aside for the pariahs still addicted to tobacco in a country apparently heading for a complete ban on this antisocial activity. Every three hours, smoking was permitted in half of the saloon car for half an hour. The rules were adhered to very strictly. At twenty-five past two I arrived to find a small group of smokers sitting around nervously fingering their cigarette packets and lighters waiting for the off. The black man behind the counter was giving them a countdown. 'Just five minutes to go folks,' he said cheerfully as he produced a stack of saucers covered in silver foil and placed them on his counter in readiness.

This announcement, coming as it did with the sight of the make-shift ashtrays, sent a wave of excited anticipation through the addicts in the half-saloon car. People checked their watches as I took a pew between an oversized middle-aged white woman in a sweat top and a lean black man who was minding his own business pretending to look at something interesting out of the window.

'Almost there,' the fat white woman in the sweat top told me as she flicked her lighter to make sure it was ready for the big event.

'It's like prisoners' exercise time,' the lean black man said to no one in particular, without turning his head.

'OK folks,' announced the man behind the counter, 'you got yourselves thirty minutes of smokin' time.' He came out from behind his counter and proceeded along the half-carriage to place the saucer ashtrays on the tables. In one smooth, coordinated action, like a team of performance artists, the entire assembly extracted cigarettes from packets, popped them into their mouths, and flicked lighters or matches to fire them up. In no time at all the atmosphere in the half-carriage was tinged with a grey-blue smog and people were chatting to each other with the sort of familiarity that comes from being fellow members of an endangered fraternity.

The lean black man turned away from the window to tell me that this was better than the train he had taken to come to Florida from Charleston, South Carolina. 'There was no smoking on that sucker whatsoever,' he informed me, flicking his ash on to the saucer at his arm. 'That was thirteen hours without a cigarette.' He turned back to gaze at the procession of pine trees and small lakes that still made up the view. 'Man, I was climbing the walls by the end of that journey.'

The woman in the sweat top had already finished her first cigarette and was lighting the next from the stub. The nicotine was starting to loosen her tongue and she asked me where I was heading. It turned out to be an excuse for her to tell me her life story.

'I'm going to Petersburg, Virginia,' she said, 'for my mother's seventieth birthday. It's where I was born and raised, but I've been living in Coral Gables, that's near Miami, for the last fifteen years.' She was a realtor, she said. I nodded, 'That's selling real estate is it?'

'Yep,' she said, 'that's right, and that's a British accent if I'm not mistaken.' I told her she wasn't and she took it as a cue to tell me about her visit to London back in 1979 which she had enjoyed immensely. I asked her what Petersburg, Virginia was like.

'There's nothing there,' she said, throwing her short arms up to emphasise the point, 'killed off by the war.' I raised my eyebrows, wondering which war she was referring to. She read my eyebrows. 'That's the Civil War, or the War Between the States as Southern folk like to call it. It was a thriving town before that little episode, but it never recovered. Today there's nothing there. It doesn't even have a mall.'

The one thing going for Petersburg, Virginia today was also a relic from the War Between the States, she told me. 'The site of the Battle of the Crater,' she announced, 'the first battle involving the use of dynamite. There's a story behind it. You want me to tell it to you?'

By the end of the thirty minutes of smoking time, the woman in the sweat top from Petersburg, Virginia had got through six cigarettes, despite talking virtually non-stop. I had decided against visiting Petersburg, Virginia since apparently all it could offer the visitor was an old hole in the ground. At three o'clock on the dot the man emerged again from behind his counter and collected the ashtrays and slowly the smoking fraternity retired from the half-carriage back to their seats.

Outside, central Florida was still flat and agricultural, like a subtropical version of the Netherlands only less well-organised. We passed places that had been named for agricultural reasons, like Frostproof and Winter Haven, and it was outside Winter Haven that I saw my first greenhouse. Further north, a crop that might have been small orange trees was being grown beneath black netting with a very close mesh. The black netting was propped up like a series of large tents that looked like wedding marquees for a tribe of Bedouin dwarfs. I knew I was getting close to the South because the kudzu was getting thicker and gas station signs began to indicate the acceptability of Dixie credit cards. The shadows were starting to lengthen as we pulled into Palatka, halting the traffic on the main road as we stopped across it for several minutes while I dismounted.

Palatka station had no platform, no staff, no snack bar and not a taxi in sight. It comprised a small wooden building and nothing else at all. Inside the wooden building the toilets were open, but the other door was shut. This didn't matter too much because the other door led into a railway museum. On the grass behind the station building four men had parked their pickup with a trailer behind it. Actually it wasn't a trailer at all, but a huge mobile barbecue that was alight and billowing with the smell of steaks. The men all held bottles of beer and were chatting animatedly in a language that was hard for me to understand. It was the languid drawl I'd been looking for. I had arrived in the South.

3

Gator Country

If I hadn't been expected, I'd probably still be in Palatka now. But fortunately my older sister, Cherry, was there to meet me and whisk me off to Gainesville. My occasional visits to the USA over the years have been punctuated by stopoffs to see Cherry, who used to live in Kentucky. She moved there with her husband in 1979 after he was unable to find a job in Britain. He is an academic. After a few years they moved from the Bluegrass State to the Sunshine State. Until now, 'Sunshine State' had always struck me as a misnomer because on my previous two visits it had poured with rain. This time the sun was shining and the lovebugs were out in force. I took it as a good sign.

After an hour of driving, we arrived at their house, a wooden affair in suburban Gainesville. It was located on a winding road in a new residential area or 'subdivision'. All of Gainesville's new subdivisions are built along winding roads because otherwise the town is laid out on a grid system: in a town of straight lines, curves are fashionable. The road itself was more than half a mile long and there can't have been more than twelve houses on it. Between the houses were trees and large open spaces. Behind them was forest as far as you could walk. It was an idyllic spot where a dozen American families lived in quiet isolation in an area the size of Berkshire.

The most recent national census demonstrated that, for the first time in US history, more Americans now live in suburbia than in cities or rural areas. Gainesville is a classic example of how this has come about. It is a town with 100,000 people and a severe case of suburbanitis. It is huge and sprawling, as if a giant had come along and stepped on it, squirting the place out in all directions. It's still squirting. Everywhere you go you pass signs for new subdivisions, little pieces of custom-built suburbia hacked out of the forest. Next to many of them are plots of condemned trees indicated by signs which read 'Let us build your dream home on this lot'. The pace of building is so fast you can never buy a decent map of Gainesville, they just can't keep up with the sprawl.

Most of these houses are built of wood, because bricks have to be imported from neighbouring Georgia. You go along and buy your plot and then hire someone to design your dream house for you. This is what my sister and her husband did. After that, as my brother-in-law put it, 'Some guys come in a truck with some wood and nails and bang, bang, bang: there it is. And you think, shit, I paid a hundred thousand dollars for that.'

Although I had been there twice before, I had never really felt properly orientated in Gainesville. Normally this is not a problem. In fact I often enjoy turning up in a new town or country with no idea of where anything is. I have a good sense of direction, and I usually find my bearings quickly. Doing so is all part of the adventure of visiting a new place for me. But this had never happened in Gaines-ville. It was all too spread out and nebulous. The roads were multi-laned, the houses huge, and the spaces between the houses like small game parks. I began to think that the only place Gainesville residents get to meet each other is at traffic lights.

My disorientation was not helped by the fact that virtually all of the town's streets are nameless. As in many US towns, they only have numbers. I always used to think of the Soviet Union as a faceless monolith of a country, but when it comes to street names the USA wins hands down. To further complicate matters, Gainesville has numerous thoroughfares with the *same* number: there is a 54th Avenue, but also a 54th Place, a 54th Road and a 54th Lane. I asked my sister whether any streets had names like they do in Britain.

'There's Main Street and Newberry Road, oh and University Avenue.' She paused for thought. 'I think that's it.' Cherry has lived in Gainesville for nine years and she still gets lost.

I consulted my brother-in-law on the matter. He said that once you got the hang of it, the system was understandable. 'Streets and places run north to south, whereas avenues and lanes run east–west. But an interesting phenomenon is the disappearance of either in a sudden and unexpected manner,' he added. 'This may occur because someone didn't want to sell their land, or due to the presence of a building in the middle of the road, because they didn't do the planning right.'

A couple of days into this visit the feeling of disorientation began to get me down. When I thought about it, I realised that an important part of the reason for this feeling was that I had never been to the centre. During a cumulative period of nearly three weeks of cruising the smooth highways in suburban Gainesville, I had never once passed a signpost to Downtown. One evening, as I was drifting off to sleep, I wondered why not. Were they trying to hide something? Then the terrible thought struck me that perhaps there wasn't one. Perhaps the Americans had developed a new sort of town that was made up entirely of suburbs, sustained by multiple service centres but no middle. Coming from Europe, I've been brought up to assume that all towns and cities have centres, and I wasn't quite sure how I was going to cope with a place that didn't. After a restless night, I broached the subject the next morning. 'Is there a downtown Gaines-ville?' I asked Cherry tentatively as we drove from the Publix super-market to the bank.

'Oh yes,' she replied, 'it's down that way. We can go and have a look if you like.' She was pointing along a highway that arrowed straight into the distance, slicing its way through a forest. It looked like it was going nowhere. Relieved, but somewhat suspicious that she was just having me on, I said, 'Yes, let's go.' Half an hour later, we arrived. It was cute, just like a proper town. The buildings were close together and there were pedestrian crossings. It even had a duck pond. For the rest of the day, I felt much better. But we never went back there and soon I was suffering from disorientation sickness again.

One way out of this predicament was for me to pretend I was in the country, which given all the trees was not hard to do. Very near my sister's house there was a nature reserve called the Devil's Millhop-per. 'What's that?' I asked as we drove past the entrance one day. 'It's a big hole in the ground,' came the reply. Having turned up my nose at the thought of going to a hole in the ground in Petersburg, Virginia I found myself visiting one in Gainesville instead.

The Devil's Millhopper is 120 feet deep and 500 feet across. Its name is derived from the hole's funnel shape. Back in the nineteenth century farmers in these parts used to grind grain in a mill that had a funnel shaped container on top called a hopper. The hopper held the grain as it fed into the mill. The devil bit came from the fact that this hopper points towards you-know-where and that fossilised bones and teeth have been found in the bottom. A local native American Indian legend invoked a Satanic explanation for its formation. The devil kidnapped a squaw and conjured up the hole for pursuing braves to fall in to. The devil then turned the braves into stone. Unable to climb out, the braves started crying and their tears formed the streams that trickle down the hole's rocky slopes.

If you want a more scientific explanation, the geologists have come up with one. The Devil's Millhopper is a collapsed cavern. It's made of limestone, which is prone to this sort of event. Most of Florida is underlain by limestone and one of the interesting properties of this rock is that it dissolves in acid. Since rainwater is slightly acidic, thanks to carbon dioxide in the atmosphere, limestone dissolves most of the time. The acidity is enhanced as rainwater seeps through dead plant material and down below the limestone dissolves even more. Occasionally, great underground caverns are formed and when they're bored of being caves they collapse.

Safely protected in a Florida Park Service reserve, where firearms and alcoholic beverages are prohibited, a sinkhole like the Devil's Millhopper is a scenic attraction, but elsewhere these things can be positively dangerous. Every now and again there is a story in one of the local newspapers about a new sinkhole opening up without warning. Parking lots can disappear while you're in the mall. People come out having finished their shopping and find a big hole where they left their car. 'What happened to the car Mom?' 'It fell down that hole. Looks like we'll have to buy another one.' Sometimes entire houses disappear down them. I asked my sister whether they had had their plot of real estate surveyed before they built their house. 'No,' she said, 'no one does it round here.' I hesitated for a moment and then changed the subject.

The heat was up and the humidity was high as we drove into the Devil's Millhopper reserve and bought our ticket to hang inside the windscreen. The track leading from the car park was littered with pine cones, a few acorns and hundreds of hickory nuts gnawed by the local squirrel population. It wound its way through noble trees draped with Spanish moss to a wooden staircase that led down into the hole. Ferns carpeted the steep slopes, while mosses and liverworts lent a soft veneer to rocks and slender tree trunks. The sound of crickets and running water filled the sticky air and bunches of elderberries were starting to fall from their branches. For a moment the scene was like parts of Devon with humidity, until an exotic butterfly floated past like an offcut of blue-black silk. Down at the bottom of the sinkhole, where the temperature rarely falls below freezing, the streams formed small pools and tiny needle palms that looked like pin cushions nestled beneath the sun-dappled rocks. It was a side of Florida that I hadn't been expecting, a world away from the sun and the beaches, the Miami metropolis and the Gainesville sprawl. It was also a relief to look up the luxuriant slopes and get a vertical perspective on one of the flattest states in the USA.

Gainesville was not just a contrast to Miami, it was the direct opposite according to several recent surveys in US publications. While Miami is often deemed the worst place in the country to bring up kids, Gainesville basks in its reputation as one of the best places to live in the USA. The town is safe and the air is clean, the medical care is top-notch both for the people and their pets, and you can watch television on the gas pump while you fill up your car.

Gainesville's raison d'être is the University of Florida, and its football team, the Gators, is one of the best in the country. The alligator is a popular symbol hereabouts. Every other car has a 'Go Gators' licence plate or bumper sticker, the University has invented a soft drink they call Gatorade, and companies call themselves Gator Fertilizers and Gator Pool Chemicals. In the past, the Floridians did their best to exterminate one of the world's largest living reptile species, but the alligator is now protected so they have a few real ones left. Most of them still live in the wild. They are a common sight, sunning themselves on the riverbanks or floating in the swamps and lakes. Being cold-blooded is their excuse for being one of nature's lazier creatures except when it comes to dinner. The advice you get on what to do should you stumble across an alligator during a stroll on the riverbank is don't feed it. I have to say that offering the beast a meal would not be my first reaction (it would come way down the list after things like scream and run). But apparently not all people think like this. There is a certain type of person who will offer the gator his cheeseburger. Where I come from, this type of person is known as a half-wit.

But they're out there, and not surprisingly their actions end up giving alligators a bad name. You see, the designers of the average cheeseburger do not intend their product to be eaten by a twelve foot carnivore, about half of which is mouth. Consequently, when the alligator is presented with a cheeseburger, it often takes a little piece of arm to go with it, sort of like a side order. This serves the half-wit right, but needless to say he blames the gator. The problem is compounded by the fact that the gator then develops a taste for cheeseburgers with arm, and the next time the gator spies a person he thinks it's dinner time again. Under normal circumstances, alligators are not dangerous to people, but offer one a cheeseburger and you get what you deserve.

Probably the safest place to see alligators in Florida is in an alligator farm, and down on the Atlantic coast, St Augustine has the world's oldest. Cherry and I drove down there to have a look. Out in rural north Florida, I got more of a sense of being on the borders of the South than I had in suburban Gainesville. I had been expecting Jesus to be a popular figure round here, but I hadn't realised just how ubiquitous he would turn out to be. (That's a stupid thing to say, of course, since it's one of his defining properties, but you'll see what I mean.) I wasn't surprised by his presence behind an endless string of real estate in a wide variety of flavours, from Baptist and Episcopal to Presbyterian and Seventh Day Adventist. But when he turned up on a large hoarding to welcome you to Hastings, with long hair and open arms, I began to wonder whether maybe he lived around here. Then I saw that he did lunch in Palatka (Jesus loves you today special: liver and gizzards). After that, he popped up everywhere I looked. Jesus appeared to sponsor recreational vehicle parks and boiled peanut stands, complete horse facilities and Adopt-a-Highway litter control programmes. There was no doubt that in this part of the world the man was a phenomenon.

Apart from the religious overtones, the landscape between Gaines-ville and St Augustine was flat, agricultural and unpretentious. It is home to the crackers: simple, white, rural people born and raised in northern Florida or southern Georgia. The term has been around since the 1800s and either came from the cracking sound of the pioneer cattleman's rawhide whip or the grinding ('cracking') of dried corn to make cornmeal. Being poor, white and Southern, this makes the cracker a cousin of the redneck, that mythically fearsome charac-ter who prowls the highways of the South in a mud-splattered pickup garnished with Confederate stickers and shotguns. But they say that one sure-fire way to identify a redneck is to find a man with a home that's mobile and five cars that aren't, and this certainly seemed to apply to the crackers of northern Florida. Every other house was a trailer and all of them were surrounded by dead motor vehicles.

The St Augustine Alligator Farm was on the edge of town. It was fronted by a whitewashed Spanish-style building where you stubbed out your cigarettes before entering in order to comply with the Florida clean air act. Inside the compound, approximately 1500 Crocodilians hung about in a selection of enclosures doing what Crocodilians do, which is not much. In the main pen, the alligators were laid out in a rather haphazard fashion around a long piece of water. They looked like a selection of display models that was about to be arranged into a more attractive pattern. There was a snack bar and wooden benches located right beside the main pen so I bought a Coke and sat down to watch. Nothing happened. None of the alligators moved a muscle. I don't mean that they didn't wander about or slip into the water. I mean they simply didn't move at all, not even an eyelid, not even an eye. They just lay there. I thought one of them was looking at me, with that impersonal stare that comes with being the closest nature has come to producing a ready-stuffed animal, but after a short while I realised I was wrong. The only indicator that I was viewing two dozen real amphibian descendants of the dinosaurs was the strong smell of alligator shit that pervaded the pen, and it rather put me off my Coca-Cola.

Nearby was a reptile theatre full of glass cages with snakes inside and several small families were huddled together pointing at speci-mens and telling their family snake stories. A very large man with a tattoo of a dolphin on his upper arm was holding court in front of a Sinaloan milksnake.

'There's a poem goes with this one,' he said to his son, ' "Red touches yellow kill a fellah, red touches black . . .' He frowned. '. . . Something,' he tailed off and the boy looked adequately impressed. His huge father raised his hand to play with the clip-on shades that he had swivelled up from his glasses.

'Cain't rightly remember,' he said finally, 'but red touches black is something. This one's right dangerous.'

My sister told me that her husband had once been startled by a snake falling out of a tree right beside him while he was mowing the lawn.

Back outside, more alligator inaction was taking place at the swamp, a simulated wetland wilderness with an appropriately fetid look about it. Here the gators were floating in the shallow water surrounded by small shoals of fish as dragonflies flicked back and forth in the hot sun above them and cicadas chattered away in the background. The alligators' pace of life was aptly illustrated by the fact that several of the specimens seemed to sport sizeable growths of swamp algae on their backs. I have to admit to being rather disappointed, but at the end of the wooden walkway that crossed over the swamp my need to see animate alligators was finally sated. I strolled over to a compound full of juvenile gators where juvenile humans were pushing quarters into a small slot machine to buy a handful of alligator biscuits. Down below, about a hundred shiny black, junior primeval monsters lazily writhed over each other to snap at the cascade of snacks. The children were awe-struck and so was I. The scene was like your worst alligator nightmare come true just four feet below where we were standing. Over the tannoy, an announcer told us that in half an hour we could see the grown-up gators being fed. I didn't think so somehow.

As my sister and I made our way out of the alligator farm, we passed a small pen containing two pocket sized albino gators. Cherry pointed. 'Look at those two,' she called, 'they look like they're made of white chocolate.' They did, but it didn't make them look much more attractive to me.

The St Augustine Alligator Farm is billed as the only place in the world where you can see all 23 species of Crocodilians on display in one location. Americans like this sort of statement and St Augustine was able to make more than its fair share of them. For a start, it was the nation's oldest city, or America's oldest continuous settlement, depending on which piece of promotional literature you read. It also boasted Florida's first lighthouse, the oldest wooden school house in the USA and North America's oldest masonry fort.

St Augustine was founded by the Spanish in 1565. That's 42 years before the English set up their colony at Jamestown in Virginia and 55 years in advance of the Pilgrims' landing at Plymouth Rock. The settlement was subsequently razed to the ground a few times by uninvited guests like Sir Frances Drake, but the Spaniards kept on rebuilding it and what's left is still pretty old. To keep it that way they've turned the downtown bit into a National Historic Landmark like virtually all the other nice old bits of US towns and cities that I was to visit. It was a pretty little place made of cobblestones and coquina, a sort of do-it-yourself cement full of seashells. The buildings that weren't preserved as museums were full of restaurants, craft shops and T-shirt outlets, so as one guidebook proudly put it, the town was like Europe by Disney without the admission fees.

The oldest wooden school house in the USA was built of cyprus and cedar over 200 years ago and has never been reconstructed. It looked very old and, well, wooden. It even had wooden tiles on the roof. Inside, the wooden theme continued with a Disneyfied teacher and seven authentically dressed student mannequins in a typical colonial classroom setting. The figures were animated and having a conversation, about chopping wood. Apparently, this was why little Johnny had not learned his six times multiplication table for his homework the night before. The professor had shown little mercy. Johnny, already wearing a dunce's cap, was being threatened with a stretch under the stairway, a little cubby hole the professor called the dungeon. Best place for him, I thought.

At the end of the pedestrianised road on which the school house was located sat the Castillo de San Marcos, North America's oldest masonry fort, overlooking Matanzas Bay. The Spanish started building the fort in 1672, after tiring of the effort involved in putting up new wooden ones to replace those burnt down by marauding Englishmen. They didn't mess about. The walls are 16 feet thick at the base and 30 feet high. It has never fallen to an attack but was handed back and forth between various opposition groups over the years.

Throughout the seventeenth century and the first half of the eighteenth century, St Augustine was at the front line between competing European superpowers intent on getting what they could out of the Americas. It was one of the last outposts of Spanish Florida before the English bit in the Carolinas. The Spanish never got the hang of slavery like the English did, and in an attempt to undermine the British plantation system, Spain offered freedom to fugitive slaves who had committed 'theft of self' from their plantations. Runaway slaves who turned up in Florida had to convert to Catholicism. When they did, the Spanish fixed them up with a place to live. It was called Fort Mosé.

Today Fort Mosé is just an archaeological site, but there was an exhibit about it in one of the cavernous rooms in the walls of Castillo de San Marcos. Because it was created by colonial decree, they can call it the first known free black settlement to legally exist in North America. It was established in 1738, which meant that Spanish Florida was way before its time when it came to race relations. Fort Mosé folded when the Spanish upped stakes and left in the 1760s, having swapped Florida for Cuba with the British. It was another 200 years before the official end of discrimination against slaves and their descendants in the 'Land of the Free'.

We played out the end of the day on St Augustine beach, a stretch of fine white sand with brown pelicans hovering out to sea and dive-bombing the waves to skewer their dinner. Gentle waves lapped at the beach and children built sandcastles. It was a beautiful spot. Except for one thing. It was covered in cars.

I couldn't believe it. We had parked in a dirt lot by some wooden steps that took you up to a walkway over the dunes. It was about a hundred yards to the beach, but too far for the small army of cretins who have to drive all the way. They cruise up and down the beach looking for somewhere to park, put out their towels and breathe sweet exhaust fumes. These are the people who drive to work and drive to the mall for their shopping. When they're hungry, they drive through a restaurant and pick up something to eat. When they want to go to the bank, they drive there. They don't even have to get out of their car, they just drive through and talk to a woman in a window who hands them their money. They drive through pharmacies and drive in to movies. As I now saw, they even drive on to the beach to sun themselves. It's great. They can do everything in their cars. I bet they even drive to the toilet. Then after a while they lose the use of their legs, but it doesn't matter because they don't need them any longer. I suspect that when these people have children, the kids are born without legs.

This is just the most recent chapter in the long American love affair with the motor vehicle. The USA is the car capital of the world. It has more cars per head than any other country on the planet and by far the longest road network to drive them on. While I was travelling through the South, the latest edition of the occasional Nationwide Personal Transportation Survey was published. It made startling reading. Since 1969, when the first survey was made, the vehicle population of the USA has grown six times faster than the human population and twice as fast as the number of drivers. All over the world experts drone on about the human population explosion, but in the USA they have to go one better. They have a vehicle population explosion instead. Drivers used to outnumber motor vehicles by 30 per cent, but not any more. Now the two are equal. My feeling of disquiet in Miami at the thought of cars taking over the country was accurate. It's happening. In 1969, 20 per cent of American households didn't own a vehicle. Today, that figure is just eight per cent, but they all want one and they'll get them soon enough.

Transportation experts suggested that the phenomenal growth in vehicle numbers was probably stabilising, and that once the number of vehicles equalled the number of drivers it didn't matter, because a driver can only drive one at a time. Well yes and no. It might not matter, but it's unlikely to stop there. Just because every US citizen with a driver's licence has a car doesn't mean he's not going to buy another one just for the hell of it. When every US household owned a TV set, they didn't stop buying them. They kept going until they had one in every room.

Perhaps the most alarming statistic in the Nationwide Personal

Transportation Survey was the fact that one in five US households already has three or more cars. Cars are becoming like shoes. Most people own dress shoes, sports shoes, summer shoes, winter shoes, and shoes to loaf around the house in. Those who can afford it will just keep buying motor vehicles in the same way. They'll get a vehicle for shopping and another for driving to church, a sporty number for posing in and an off-road vehicle for jaunts on to the beach. US citizens like consuming things. They aren't going to stop just because they have one each. That's only the start. And from what I'd observed of North Florida's cracker community, those that can't afford it are also in on the act. They just buy dead motor vehicles instead.

I will admit to having an ambivalent attitude towards motor vehicles. Although I learned to drive when I was 18, it wasn't until I was 32 that I first owned a car. The truth was that I really didn't need one and anyway cars are expensive and I couldn't afford it. In retrospect, I tell people that this was my contribution to saving the planet, which it was. Ha, ha, ha.

As I sat on St Augustine beach mulling over the automotive problems of the USA, a middle-aged woman carrying a metal detector hove into view. She was concentrating hard on her work, head down, sweeping the white sands in front of her with her gadget as she walked. I moved over to her and asked what she found.

'Trash mostly,' she answered without looking up, 'but I got a ring and a hearing aid today.' Her machine beeped and she knelt down to scrape sand by the handful into an old colander that she took from the canvas bag on her shoulder. She sieved methodically, found nothing and swept the area once more with the metal detector. It beeped again so she reloaded her colander with more handfuls of sand. As she shook the sieve, a blackened penny emerged. She rubbed the penny on her shorts and slipped it into her pocket.

I left the woman to it. She was fifty yards along the beach before she stopped again. I watched as she sieved four colanderfuls, a sizeable hole appearing before her in the beach. She dug some more, and appeared to find something. She widened her hole and tugged at something large. Finally it came out and she stood to rub the object on her shorts. It was a hub cap.

4

Billy Bob and the
Vitamin-Enriched Cardboard

I was back at Palatka Amtrak station. It was broiling hot and the air was so still and humid you could touch it. Across the open track and beyond a patch of wasteground a refrigeration plant sat shimmering in the haze like a mirage. Nasty-looking black flies that they call lovebugs were coupling everywhere: on the wooden rafters of the station building roof, on the wire fence that surrounded it, on my bag, on my trousers, in my hair. For a moment, the combination of heat, wasteground and insects made me think that North Florida came pretty close to being a developing country at times.

I had wanted to continue my rail journey from another station, but the only other option was Waldo and the sole departure going north from there left at half past midnight. Palatka had three northward departures a day, which made it a major terminus by comparison. There was a small group of people surrounded by bags waiting for the Silver Meteor Atlantic coast service bound for New York. Two white ladies who might have been mother and daughter sat motionless on the step, a middle-aged white couple stood on the concrete beside the track, and an elderly black guy stood alone minding his own business gazing through the wire fence at the refrigeration plant opposite. It was nearly 3 p.m. and the train was late.

'It's late,' I said to the black guy.

'Sure is,' he replied, 'one hell of a thing ainit?'

I asked him where he was heading. I think he said Charleston, but he pronounced it 'Chaastun'.

Everyone was looking off to the left, towards where the train should have been coming from. The woman on the concrete strip beside the track said, 'Maybe it's been cancelled.'

'They don't cancel trains just like that,' her husband immediately snapped back. There was a pause. Beside me, the man heading for Chaastun asked if I'd got change for the telephone. He wanted to ring his sister, he explained. I dug into my pockets.

'There might have been an accident,' the man said to his wife, in a more conciliatory tone this time. 'Amtrak are always having accidents.'

I found a quarter and handed it to the black man. He offered me a few pennies in return but I shook my head. He moved to the telephone, picked up the receiver and dialled.

Outside the fence, the man's wife suggested that maybe they should ring the Amtrak toll-free number scribbled in felt-tip on the telephone.

'What's the point of dialling the 800 number?' her husband said aggressively. 'What are they gonna tell you? That the train's late? You know that already. So what's the point?'

The black man got through. 'I'm still here at the station,' he announced. He shook his head as he listened to the reply. 'No, the train ain't arrived yet.' He listened some more and then replaced the receiver in its rest.

Everyone was quiet, staring up the track as more time ticked by. I brushed a couple of lovebugs off my trousers.

At a quarter past three I picked up the telephone myself and dialled the Amtrak 800 number. 'I'll see if they know anything,' I said to the two ladies sitting on the step. When I got through, a chirpy Amtrak employee asked how she could help me. I explained about our late train and she asked me to hold. When she came back on the line, she said that the Silver Meteor had last been seen leaving DeLand half an hour behind schedule.

'It was last seen leaving DeLand, half an hour late,' I said loudly so that everyone could hear.

'DeLand,' muttered the older of the two women on the step, 'it's got to cross two rivers yet,' as if she was willing the train to have an accident.

Out on the concrete strip, the husband was puzzled by the information. 'How do they know that?' he asked. 'If DeLand is a non-personalised station like this one, how do they know?'

'They got a computer probably,' offered his wife. 'They know everything by computer these days. They probably got a computer down there.'

'A computer,' the man said suspiciously, as if this was an ominous development. He looked up at the rafters. 'You think they've got one here too?'

Everyone followed his gaze to inspect the rafters for evidence of hidden computers. It didn't seem likely. All I saw was peeling paint. 'Probably,' said his wife with a minor note of glee in her voice, both because her suggestion was taken seriously and because it had obviously rattled her husband. 'I bet they communicate with it by e-mail,' she added.

'E-mail! Huh!' replied her husband, now thoroughly despondent and disadvantaged. He walked up the track a little way to distance himself from the unknown, turned and came back, a scowl on his face. 'How do they work anyway?' he demanded of his wife.

'What, computers or e-mail?' she said.

'Yeah, both.'

'Dunno.'

'We must be the last people in America who don't.' He turned again, to face away from the direction the train was expected. A little way up the track, a set of lights went on. A green one and a red one simultaneously.

'They've put the lights on,' observed the man. We all turned to look at the lights. 'That means something,' he added in a triumphant note. This was a technology he was familiar with. 'But it's a green *and* a red,' he said with a mixture of mild hysteria and major disappointment. 'That's ambiguous.' He shook his head, as if the incident confirmed his impression of Amtrak as an untrustworthy company, one that used secret computers but couldn't get their basic lighting signals right.

'A green and a red,' whispered the black man beside me. 'Yip, that sure is strange.'

Up the track, beyond the ambiguous lights, two black children had appeared and were walking away from us between the railway lines, oblivious to the danger of an approaching train.

'Those kids ought to be more careful,' the man said.

'They probably know it's not coming yet,' said his wife.

'How could they? It's a green *and* a red.'

'They live around here. They must know.'

The man shook his head again. It was all too much for him. I checked my watch. If the train was half an hour late leaving DeLand, it should be arriving at Palatka any moment. From way off, out of sight, the sound of a train's horn reverberated on the still air, as if to put our minds at rest.

Ten minutes later I was on board the Silver Meteor buying my ticket. I had made a reservation over the telephone and I read out my six digit reservation number to the conductor from my notebook. He nodded as he ran his finger down his computer printout.

'Protect code?'

I read out the other number I'd been given over the phone. 'What's the protect code for?' I asked him.

'That's in case someone else tries to use your reservation number,' he told me knowingly, as if stealing reservation numbers was a popular felony in this part of the world. I looked around the carriage. It was empty, the other passengers from Palatka having boarded another carriage. 'I see,' I said, which I didn't at all.

'How would you like to pay for your ticket today?' the conductor asked me, just as though I might choose a different method on different days of the week. I showed him my credit card.

'I'll need some ID with that,' he said, and I dug my passport out from my bag and handed it to him. He frowned as he took it, turning it over in his hand. My passport often causes such suspicious scrutiny because it looks like I made it myself after watching an episode of *Blue Peter*. It is an old style British passport, or more accurately two old style British passports stapled together. It must be the most unwieldly travel document in the world. It is also battered and dog-eared, and the name and number on the front are totally illegible thanks mainly to a misadventure with a Ugandan toilet some years ago.

'Young man, you've got two passports,' the conductor announced accusingly, like I might not have noticed before. I explained, as briefly and convincingly as possible, that this was due to an error on the part of the passport office in London. I had applied for a second passport some years ago, asking to keep the old one because it contained a still-valid visa. My application had been dealt with by a gentleman of Asian origin whose English hadn't been too hot. The result was this apparently DIY construction involving staples and a piece of green ribbon.

The conductor nodded as he took in this story, flicking through the pages of my passports. 'Boy! You been to all these places?' he asked as he turned the pages, apparently no longer interested in the double-passport conundrum. I confirmed that I had. 'Republic of Ghana,' he read aloud, 'where's that?'

'West Africa.'

He turned another page. 'Mongolian visa. They got a lot of sick people there?' he said seriously. I just sat with my mouth open.

The conductor closed my passports and looked at me. 'Tell me young man. This is a thing someone asked me over this Princess Diana business. How come Prince Philip isn't the king?' He had effortlessly switched subjects with the intellectual agility of a man fresh out of mental hospital. I explained the British monarchy to him as he filled in the credit card slip. When we had both finished, he frowned. 'They'd get in trouble over here, the Royal Family. We'd call that discrimination.'

I fell asleep after the conductor left and woke to a rainbow on a grey sky in Georgia. In my semi-slumber, I thought that sounded like a good title for a Country and Western song. Through the window, below the grey sky, tall pines combined to make a dense forest. Every once in a while, a clearing would pop up to give me a view of a low-slung wooden house or a trailer, to be replaced just as quickly by more tall forest. Then the trees became stunted as we passed through a swamp.

We pulled into a place called Jesup. 'Jesup,' piped up a voice of authority from behind me. 'Jesup, Georgia,' he said, to make sure there was no doubt about it, 'this is where the speed trap was invented. Right here in this town.'

I consulted my Amtrak timetable. I had slept through Jacksonville, which was where the authority on speed traps must have joined the train. I looked it up in my guidebook to see what I'd missed. Jacksonville was the largest city in the USA in terms of square miles. It also boasted the first graded road in Florida (Old King's Road, 1763) and the first building using skyscraper technology (1901). Still feeling a bit groggy, I turned to my Georgia handbook. There was no mention of speed traps, but the short entry for Jesup noted that it had the largest chemical cellulose-producing plant in the world. Shit, I thought to myself, it was impossible to keep up with all the superlatives in this country. Everywhere you go something is the largest, the fastest, the tallest in the world. It was no wonder the conductor thought Mongolia was an asylum and hadn't even heard of Ghana. What was the point of learning about other countries when the USA had the best of everything? These people ate more, drove further, talked louder and walked taller than anyone else, anywhere, ever. No wonder their country has never been invaded. No one would have the nerve to try.

Of course that was why the South was supposed to be different I thought to myself. While the USA had never been invaded, the South had. And by their own people to boot. But it was more than a hundred years ago. The extraordinary thing was that the South was still getting over it. Outside, the trees had suddenly disappeared. They had been replaced by wide flat areas of what looked like grass. A river was snaking through the marsh-like reeds. We were coming into Savannah, or at least the railway station of that name. The town itself appeared to be absent.

I grabbed my bag and climbed down the steep carriage steps on to a platform that was being reconstructed. As I walked towards the terminal building I noticed a few cars in the parking lot but none was obviously a taxi. Then a light blue Cadillac, circa 1970, rounded the bend and purred into a bay. On its side, the words Barry Cab Inc. were written. I quickened my pace.

The door with Barry Cab Inc. written on it opened and a large man emerged. His hair had slipped to leave a bald patch on the top of his head and a stringy ponytail down his back. He stretched to punch the air and turned to face the train. From the front, he looked decidedly ugly, largely due to the fact that several of his front teeth had gone missing. The absence of teeth was revealed when he smiled, which made him look friendly and welcoming in a retarded sort of way. I slowed my pace.

It was too late, he had seen me and was now waving. 'You lookin' for a cab friend?' he called. I was of course, so I nodded.

'Sit up front,' he said when I reached his car. 'Put your bag in back if you want.' Up close, he looked even more like the result of many generations of inbreeding than he had from a distance. I wasn't sure about sitting next to him, but I thought that if I refused his offer I might regret it even more. I opened the door and climbed in to the front passenger seat.

He jumped in himself and turned to face me. 'My name's Billy Bob by the way. How you doin' today?' He was holding out his hand. It was the first time a cab driver had ever introduced himself to me.

Billy Bob gunned his Cadillac into action and eased out of the parking lot. 'I should say that my other name's Romeo. Had it since I was five years old.'

'How come?' I asked him, unnerved at the sudden intimacy of our relationship.

'Oh, there was some talk you know,' he replied with an earnest look on his face. Romeo was about the last label I'd have attached to Billy Bob, but I couldn't really say that. As I considered an appropriate response, his walkie-talkie crackled and a voice came over the airwaves. 'Billy Bob, you there?' Billy Bob Romeo grabbed the mouth piece from his dash board. 'Reading you loud and clear Leroy.' Leroy broke the bad news that Billy Bob's number hadn't come up in the lottery draw.

We were approaching a built-up zone, a large building looming on our left. 'That there used to be the station,' Billy Bob informed me, 'before they moved it out of town. Now it's the visitors' centre. That's where you go if you wanna know anything about Savannah's history. It's all in there.'

From a wide highway, we turned right on to a much narrower road lined with leafy trees and terraced brick houses. The smooth tarmac of the highway had given way to that agreeably tactile sound of tyre on cobblestone. A few hundred yards along we entered a large square. 'This square's where I used to ride my bike as a kid. I was born right here in Savannah,' Billy Bob said with considerable pride. We rounded the centre of the square where huge oak trees draped in Spanish moss stood in a jungle of lush green foliage. In the middle was a monument of some kind. Billy Bob slowed his Cadillac and pointed across me along a road. 'See that blue door at the end there?' I did. 'That's where I was born.'

'Have you lived here all your life?'

'Yes sir.' He nodded definitely, his stringy ponytail riding up his back as he did so. 'Don't reckon I'll ever feel the need to leave. You know what they say: "East, west, home's best."' We drove on through another square, and another, and another, before we pulled up outside my bed and breakfast. Billy Bob wished me a pleasant stay in his town and I felt bad for thinking he looked inbred.

As I settled in to my room, I switched on the television set which looked strangely out of place in front of the bare red-brick walls, the highly polished sideboards and the four-poster bed. I channel hopped from 42 down until I hit a plastic man on Channel 7 sitting at a desk talking to me from a blaze of triumphalist muzak.

'. . . manager Bret Wilson ensures everything is just perfect,' the plastic man was announcing. 'Everything's homemade: you'll know that by the freshness and quality of every dish, the great fresh salads, the muffins and cornbread and the wonderful entrées.'

I pulled a couple of shirts out of my bag and laid them over the back of a chair in the vague hope that a few of the worst creases might disappear. 'Try the chicken and dumplings,' plastic man enthused, 'fried chicken, boiled chicken, chicken livers . . .' I grabbed my washbag and walked into the bathroom. '. . . teriyaki chicken breast, roast beef, corned beef, boiled fish, battered fried fish . . .' plastic man shouted after me, '. . . boiled liver and onions,' he added hopefully from the bedroom. 'It's all home-cooked and delicious.'

I emerged from the bathroom to see that the picture of the plastic man had been replaced on the TV screen by a panning shot over dishes of plastic-looking vegetables. Although plastic man was no longer on view, he was still waxing lyrical. '. . . succulent vegetables: black-eyed peas, string beans, squash, corn, macaroni cheese, mashed potatoes, fried rice . . .' If this was a commercial it was overlength and low budget, the shots of vegetables looked as if they'd been taken by a tourist with a cheap film that didn't reproduce colours very well. 'And don't forget to top up with the wonderful homemade pies. It's just like Mom's,' plastic man continued. It struck me that he'd been talking for several minutes and he hadn't yet paused for breath.

'For decades, Morrison's cafeteria has been cooking up delicious homemade food and mixing in top quality service and value,' he forged on. 'It's simply as good as it gets.' He was back on screen. 'We now have ten dollar certificates available for Morrison's for five dollars. Discovery Dining,' he said, as if he had just picked up a telephone (he hadn't).

'This is Jackie for Morrison's,' a woman's voice said.

'OK,' said plastic man, and he was on to another call. 'Discovery Dining, hello?'

'I'm Steve,' drawled another dismembered voice, 'is that Morrison's in Ogelthorpe Mall?'

'Sure is,' sung plastic man, 'Morrison's cafeteria where you just can't go wrong. We'll send your voucher right along. Keep the calls coming everybody.'

I zapped Discovery Dining and picked up a sheaf of leaflets I'd gathered in the foyer of my bed and breakfast. A booklet called the Simply Savannah Visitors Guide, without an apostrophe, had a section on restaurants and I looked up Morrison's. It was a short walk away. I checked my pocket for money and went out.

I was looking forward to getting stuck in to some proper home cooking because while most Americans don't appear to care less about what they eat, the South is proud of its culinary heritage. It's a cuisine with a few staples, a sort of frontier diet that stuck. Meals were originally designed to fuel the bellies of field labourers and were based on the three M's: meat, meal and molasses. There was lots of animal flesh, great hunks of cornbread, vats of fat, too much salt, and lashings of bacon. It was all washed down with strong coffee and hard liquor. The few vegetables that got a look in were rendered more or less useless by fat and long cooking, whilst fruit was a complete non-starter. The average Southern menu was a nutritionist's nightmare.

Some have blamed the early Southern settlers' eating habits on the English, who brought with them a great appetite for meat and the ability to distil spirits developed in the cold fogs of Britain. For more than 200 years, travellers in the South have reacted to the local diet with equal amounts of amazement and despair. In the mid nineteenth century indigestion cures were among the most widely advertised products in local newspapers, indicating that Southern stomachs were subject to great strains. Outsiders also reckoned the poor diet was responsible for the locals' lack of energy. Not eating properly sapped their ability to work. By the early part of this century, a disease linked to vitamin deficiency was widely reported. Pellagra resulted in cracked skin, dementia and ultimately death. It was almost entirely confined to the South.

Studies of pellagra, and the publicity and health campaigns that resulted, were deeply resented in the South. Many viewed the pellagra epidemic as another Yankee conspiracy to erode Southern culture. The government-required Nutrition Facts staring out from packets on supermarket shelves are still seen by some in the same light. Southerners have been slower than their northern neighbours to change their eating habits. Not many have thrown away their frying pans. The South's rebellious spirit lives on in their stomachs and arteries.

Morrison's was a self-service cafeteria done out in green and terracotta. The walls were adorned with a few framed prints of bunches of flowers, and wooden ceiling fans incorporated lighting in the form of four glass lampshades. The seats were made of brown plastic with tapestry backs that didn't go with any other part of the decor. When I reached the food counter I mentally withdrew my criticism of Discovery Dining's poor camerawork. The spread actually looked more plastic and less appetising than the TV pictures of it.

As it turned out, however, the grub wasn't plastic. If it had been it might at least have offered some interest. No, the problem with Morrison's food was worse. It was completely lacking in flavour of any description. I had already encountered tasteless American food several times on this trip. I had been disappointed by gator meat and memories still lingered of a hot ham and cheese baguette served up on the aeroplane to Miami. It had tasted like hot nothing. Indeed, there was a much stronger cheese flavour wafting up from the feet of the man sitting next to me. It must have taken a lot of ingenuity to remove all the flavour from the ingredients, but Morrison's appeared to have gone one better. Their philosophy seemed to be to remove the normal constituents altogether and replace them with a special ingredient that tasted of nothing at all.

Clearly this material was infinitely versatile because Morrison's had moulded it round pieces of chicken, crisped it up and named it southern fried. They had also managed to colour it canary yellow and inject it with a serum that made it crumble instantly to the touch. This they called cornbread. The secret substance featured again in the crust of a buttered coconut pie. By the end of my meal, I was pretty sure of its identity. It was cardboard.

As I strolled back to my bed and breakfast, the cardboard still lingering heavily in my stomach, I consoled myself with the thought that I had probably fallen victim to a shady, government-inspired plot to improve the Southern diet. This being the case, at least the cardboard was likely to have been vitamin-enriched.

5

Burning Issues

Next morning I was up bright and early to have a look around Savannah's historic district. The air had that cool fresh taste that comes after a night shower, but you could tell that nature was stoking up its furnaces in preparation for another torrid day. The previous evening the historic district had been a dark and sleepy place with unobtrusive street lighting that at first had seemed threatening. One or two joggers plodded the sidewalks but they had seemed at odds with an urban setting that looked like it was designed for top hats and flowing capes. At night, the Spanish moss on the oak trees was spooky, but in the crisp morning light it just looked like streamers from some forgotten party. The streets and squares had an organic feel to them, wreathed in thick vegetation with buildings peeping out of the trees and creepers. Unlike in St Augustine, most of this historic district appeared to be residential, but like St Augustine the architecture did not look American. There were redbrick Victorian terraces and Gothic mansions with oriel windows. Greek revivalist piles had porches supported by Doric columns, while ornate wrought ironwork hemmed in neat little balconies on houses I thought should have been in New Orleans. There were brick pavements and sometimes even brick roads. Little details gave the place a whimsical flavour: the ends of drainpipes were moulded into the shapes of dolphins and water fountains had been provided for dogs.

Savannah was founded in 1733 by an idealistic Englishman, James Oglethorpe, an Old Etonian and Oxford man who wanted to establish a new colony without slavery, religious persecution, alcohol or lawyers. The intention was to give debtors languishing in English prisons a fresh start in life. He had the backing of King George II, so he called the colony Georgia. Oglethorpe designed Savannah himself and it is his basic gridiron layout of streets and squares that survives today.

The modern authorities have furnished most of the squares with metal plaques telling you a little of their history. Several had statues in the middle. I sat down on a bench in Wright Square which the plaque informed me was also a burial ground. Somewhere beneath the foliage lay the remains of an American Indian named Tomo-Chi-Chi, chief of the Yamacraws, a tribe of the Creek nation. Tomo-Chi-Chi can justly lay claim to being the co-founder of Georgia, since Oglethorpe could not have realised the new colony without his co-operation. The two negotiated a treaty and became firm friends. Oglethorpe even took Tomo-Chi-Chi on a trip to England, where he met King George, and when Tomo-Chi-Chi died James Oglethorpe acted as one of his pallbearers.

I wandered south from Wright Square and found myself in Forsyth Park, a formal affair where the paths were lined with huge oaks. High in their branches, squirrels scampered back and forth with mischief in their tails while down below early morning joggers bounced along with grim looks on their faces. I passed a children's playground where a black lady stood watch over her three-year-old. The kid was more interested in demolishing his pushchair than pursuing the more formal leisure pursuits, but his mother was having none of it.

'Don't mess with that buggy,' she said with a venom that was surprising for so early in the morning, 'you want me to get my belt?' The kid stopped, his hand on the pushchair, caught like a criminal in the act. He looked at his mother. 'You want me to beat you?' she asked, making the question more transparent. The kid obviously knew this was not a rhetorical enquiry and let go of the buggy. He wobbled, bent down and picked up a stick. He proceeded to administer sharp whacks to a puddle on the ground instead.

Somewhere in the middle of the park I came across a Civil War monument. The monument to the Confederate dead was a bronze statue of a grey-coated soldier stood on the top of a pedestal almost as tall as the surrounding trees. The inscription was taken from the prophet Ezekiel: 'Come from the four winds, O breath, and breathe upon these slain that they may live.' The monument was erected by the Ladies' Memorial Association to honour the men and boys who gave their lives for the cause. The ladies were adamant that it stood for the spiritual victory of the South and decreed that the monument should have absolutely nothing to do with the North. A design was accepted from a Canadian sculptor and the whole thing was shipped to Savannah on strict instructions that it should not call in at any Yankee port on the way.

The sculpture that arrived is not what you see today. Two pieces were unloaded from the ship, a figure of silence for the top of the pedestal and a figure of judgement for one of its arches. When the monument was assembled, the figures were thought to be much too ornate for the plain tastes of the South, so they replaced them with the simple bronze soldier. Silence and Judgement were found perches in nearby graveyards instead.

Near the monument was a fountain surrounded by a ring of park benches. I sat down on one of the benches to gaze at the cascading water, my brain still only semi-operational. Out of the corner of my eye, a young black guy inspected a couple of benches before taking a place next door but one to mine.

'Good morning,' he said pleasantly.

'Morning,' I replied.

'You have to get the right bench,' he told me, 'this one's dry enough. Those over there are still wet. They get that green mould all over them and when you sit down it stains your pants.'

I nodded, not thinking he expected an answer.

'It'd be nice to have breakfast out here wouldn't it? You can get it in a restaurant but I'd like it here.'

'Yes, breakfast out here would be nice,' I said, not really feeling up to a full conversation. I'd only had one rather weak coffee for my breakfast because wads of Morrison's cardboard were still making their way through my intestines. It was a noisy process. It sounded like there was a man on a motorbike in my tummy, reversing up my alimentary canal. We both just sat there, transfixed by the falling water in the fountain. A squirrel skipped on to the path not three feet away from where I sat. It threw a glance in my direction and bounded across in front of the fountain and scampered up an oak tree.

'Normally I'd just be getting up right now and eating breakfast,' said the guy on the nearby bench. I nodded again, not wanting to be rude, but wishing that he would shut up because I didn't want to think about breakfast. I waited for ten seconds and then pulled my notebook from my top pocket and flicked through the pages hoping that the guy would get the message. He sighed loudly. I pretended to be engrossed in reading some notes I'd made in the foyer of my friend David's condominium in Miami. It was full of no smoking notices: 'No smoking allowed. Florida Clean Air Act F1. Statute 715.07' declared a plaque on the wall where you first walked in. Over on the carpeted area a free-standing notice rammed the point home: 'Positively no smoking on carpeted area. *No fumar.*'

'That's why I mentioned breakfast earlier,' the guy's voice came again. 'I haven't had it this morning because last week my house burnt down.'

This made me sit up more sharply than a decent dose of caffeine. There was no way the guy could have seen my notes, sitting as he was some ten yards away. The coincidence was uncanny. And now that I'd been presented with this piece of information, I couldn't really continue going through my notebook so I turned my head to look at the guy. His eyes were still fixed on the fountain, as if he knew I really wasn't interested in his plight, but he had to get it off his chest anyway.

'Some people say smoke makes you sleep better, but I don't agree. It woke me and my bedroom was full of it. Had to break my own window to get out of there.'

I didn't know what to say. What do you say to someone whose house has just burnt down? Fortunately he just kept talking. 'It was wooden you see, not like these brick houses round here. It was all built of wood. They burn easily those wooden houses.'

'How bad was the damage?'

'Pretty bad, it burnt right down to the ground. There's nothing left.' Again I could think of nothing appropriate to say. My stomach made a long, low rumble. In truth, the word 'scam' had flashed up somewhere in the back of my mind, but I struggled to keep my cynical side down and the cardboard noises in check. If it was a scam, the guy was being very measured in his approach.

'I need to use the bathroom,' he told me clutching the front of his jeans.

47

'Aren't there public ones?' I asked.

'Yeah, there's one over there,' he gestured beyond the trees, 'but they don't open it for another two hours.'

I looked around. 'I don't suppose you can even use the bushes, they're too low,' I said.

'No. They cut 'em down. Those bushes used to be eight feet high, but they cut 'em down 'cos people would come into the park at night and get mugged and stuff.' He paused again. It was a very drawn-out, Southern conversation.

'I'm hungry too,' he said after some moments. He told me he ate his meals some place, but not until 5 p.m., which was a long time away. Definitely a scam, I thought to myself, and he's about to deliver the punchline. My tummy rumbled in agreement.

He didn't. He asked me where I was from instead.

'England.'

'Oh yes, I thought I heard something in that accent. I thought either Australia or England.'

I asked him whether he had always lived in Savannah. 'No,' he said, 'I'm originally from South Carolina.'

We could have sat there all day, exchanging small talk, but somehow I just couldn't manage it. I got up to leave. I was about to say goodbye when my stomach made some more deep rumbling noises and I felt a pang of guilt at thinking the guy was trying it on with his house-burning story. I found a dollar and offered it to him. 'Have a coffee on me,' I told him, 'where there's coffee there'll be a bathroom.' The guy said thanks and pocketed the dollar. I moved on, past the monument to the Confederate dead, back towards my bed and breakfast.

Savannah's Civil War monument was the first of many I was to see during my journey through the South. Indeed, if the South has a physical symbol, then this is it: the statue of the Confederate soldier standing like a lonely sentinel from a past long gone but never dead. With knapsack and blanket roll on his back, he clutches his rifle, staring in stony silence out towards the invading Yankee army.

The military defeat of the Confederacy didn't destroy Southern identity, it sharpened it. The monuments to a defeated army, most erected fully two generations after the Southern surrender at Appomattox in 1865, became emblems of the Lost Cause, a romantic version of the antebellum South that still prevails. It is the Old South as portrayed in *Gone with the Wind*, a land of beautiful belles, chivalrous beaus and happy slaves, a land that was easy to imagine on the streets of Savannah. Southerners fought for what they thought was right: the pre-eminence of states' rights over federal authority, a theme that still runs strongly through American politics to this day. When faced with what was seen as the North's reinterpretation of the American Constitution, the Southern states had no choice but to secede. Then they were forced to defend this legal right. It was a matter of honour. What is remembered today is not the fact that the Confederacy lost the war but that they were willing to fight valiantly, against a stronger foe, for their principles. This cult of the Lost Cause is a means for coming to terms with defeat. The War Between the States is viewed as a holy war and the religion of the Lost Cause is this cult of the dead. You find these figures all over the South, often in county seats, usually in the courthouse square. They stand proud as one of the few distinguishing features of a landscape increasingly engulfed by the tide of neon and concrete sweeping across the South like a new invasion from the North. They remain as noble celebrities of failure, symbolic of a place apart.

Savannah still thrives on memories of the War Between the States because one of the city's many claims to fame is that it was too beautiful to be physically damaged by the unpleasantness. General William T Sherman, who liked burning things, balked at the idea when he arrived with his Union army in Savannah. Although Sherman burned his way across several southern states during the Civil War, it is the trail that he blazed through Georgia that most people have heard about. He torched Atlanta, warmed his hands on the flames, and kept on doing it until he reached the sea. Homesteads, hamlets, fields of crops, whole towns, you name it, Sherman burned it. But when he got to Savannah he stopped. It looked too good to incinerate, so he gave it to President Lincoln as a Christmas gift instead.

The walls of my bed and breakfast were covered in period engravings of General Sherman conducting his troops outside the city and holding court inside it. The house where he took up residence and celebrated Christmas 1864 stands on Madison Square and is open to the public. It's a Gothic masterpiece, owned at the time by a British cotton merchant, but which is now in the hands of the Episcopal church that stands next door. I was shown round with a small group of fellow sightseers by a tiny little old lady with long arms who wore a powder blue dress and a neat white scarf round her neck. Attached to her wizened head was an enormous pair of spectacles that made her look like an elderly mosquito. But although she seemed old enough to remember the Civil War, she wasn't going to tell us about it.

'I've had enough hearing about the War Between the States and General Sherman,' she told us, 'so I'm not going to talk about them.' She announced that she was only going to tell us about the furniture and fittings.

After a short while I tired of her descriptions of the expansive carpets and silver-plated keyhole escutcheons, the ornate Austrian mirrors and Carrara marble fireplaces, the hefty dark doors ('they're made of walnut, stained to look like mahogany') and the tapestry upholstery on the chairs. But there was no let up; this woman could have talked for Georgia and the small size of the group meant that it was impossible to slip away without being noticed. Occasionally, Miss Mosquito laced her boring descriptions with tales of her childhood which were of more interest. She was originally from Memphis, Tennessee, she told us, but came to Savannah with her mother in 1940 when there were only two Cadillac cars in the whole city. 'I should know because my mother owned one of them,' she informed us, 'but that didn't mean we were wealthy, she just had to have all the latest things, and you should have seen her with it. She knew just how it worked.'

The lady was also good at answering her own questions: '. . . now how do I remember that?' she'd ask rhetorically. 'Well I'll tell you . . .' and off she'd go into a detailed explanation of how good a competitor she'd be in a memory contest.

She floated through the heavily ornate rooms with a familiarity that made you think she owned the place. She'd grasp the back of a chair with a hand that was more gnarled than the branch of a tree and talk about the chair as if she'd been there when it was first delivered.

'Now look at this chest,' she commanded, 'the only way to see this chest properly is on your knees.' Everyone in the group hesitated, not quite sure whether this statement was a direct order or just a figure of speech. 'When there are children on the tour, that's what they do: they get down on their knees.' There was an audible sigh of relief at the realisation that since we weren't children we wouldn't have to prostrate ourselves. 'I said that to a group once and I turned around and back and there were two gentlemen on their knees,' she added delightedly. 'And do you know what they said? They said "You know you're right, you can see it better", and I said "I know".'

After we had toured the upstairs, my group returned down the spiral staircase and stood in a small gaggle to hear about the slate used on the terrace outside. It was brought to Savannah as high-class ballast in ships and there was still a quantity of it down in the cellar. 'Now let's go and have a look at that terrace,' she suggested, and as the group filed out through a back door I made my exit through the front and out into Madison Square. A few moments later, an elderly man who had also been part of my group emerged to feed the parking meter beside his car.

'Just fascinating,' he said to me. 'All that history huh?' Not wishing to be rude, I agreed with him, a comment that prompted an enquiry into my origins.

'From Oxford, England? I'd like my wife to meet you,' he said immediately. He held out his hand. 'My name's Dan Bruton, we're from Edgefield, South Carolina. We rent a condo out on the beach for a week every year and we come into town on the Thursday to see something in Savannah. We love it here,' he added with some feeling.

Mr Bruton asked what I was doing in this part of the world. I told him I was touring the South and he became visibly more friendly still. I mentioned a few of the places I planned to visit as the smile widened on his face.

'Well if you go to Athens, Georgia you must see the University garden,' he told me, 'it's the centre of the Garden Society of America. And Greenville, North Carolina? Well, there's a wonderful orthopaedic surgeon there called Diane something . . .' He paused, looking

51

down at the pavement to see whether it might remind him of Diane's surname, but apparently it didn't. 'So if you break your leg up there and you find yourself in emergency, ask for Diane, they all know her there.'

I smiled, nodded, and told him thank you. I was pleased to be armed with this useful information. It would certainly add to my peace of mind while I was in Greenville, North Carolina.

We both paused in our conversation as a loud jet passed out of sight overhead. It was a signal for Mr Bruton to change tack. 'We'd like to go to England,' he said, 'out in the countryside. We'd like to see where we're from.' I nodded some more. I had a feeling I could tell what was coming next.

'We met some English people in Greece some years back,' Mr Bruton told me. (I thought as much.) 'John . . . what was his name?' He looked to see whether the paving stones might give him a clue as to this man's surname. He was out of luck again, and I thought he could have used some memory lessons from Miss Mosquito. Mr Bruton was annoyed at himself because it was clear that he thought there was a good chance that I would know John from England. 'He was what we call a principal of a school there,' Mr Bruton added, as if this might be the vital missing piece to the jigsaw. He was looking at me expectantly. I pretended to be thinking, but after a moment I shook my head. I didn't like to tell Mr Bruton that there were probably up to a million men in England who were called John and that a fair number of them were teachers who had holidayed in Greece at some point.

I was saved by the arrival of Mrs Bruton, who emerged from the house somewhat annoyed that her husband had missed the tour of the terrace. But her mood changed abruptly when Mr Bruton introduced me as a gentleman from Oxford, England.

'He's touring round the South,' Mr Bruton informed his wife proudly, 'he'll be going to Greenville, North Carolina and I told him to go see Diane if he breaks his leg or anything.' Mrs Bruton nodded approvingly, as if her husband had done the right thing in this instance.

'You having any trouble driving here?' she asked me.

'I haven't actually done any driving yet,' I said, and immediately wished I'd lied because Mrs Bruton looked at me as if I'd said that I was in the USA to murder the president.

'He's only just arrived,' Mr Bruton cut in quickly. 'He doesn't need a car here in Savannah.'

'Yes,' I agreed, 'I'll be renting one to drive into South Carolina.'

Mrs Bruton regained her composure. 'When I went to Bermuda, someone gave me a good piece of advice,' she told me, 'always look the right way for traffic when you cross the road.'

I thanked her for passing on this tip and told the Brutons that I ought to be moving on. We all shook hands again and said how pleased we'd been to meet each other. I left them trying to remember the surname of Diane the orthopaedic surgeon from Greenville, North Carolina.

6

Colour Coding

One of the characteristics that supposedly defines Southerners is their friendliness and hospitality. Down below the Mason-Dixon Line life is supposed to be more leisurely and people have more time for the courtesies of life. I certainly found this to be an accurate description. Most people I came across were, like the Brutons, immediately open and amiable. Whenever I sat down on a bench in one of Savannah's leafy squares someone on a nearby bench would always turn to me and say 'How you doin'?' This amicability went beyond the standard 'have a nice day' mentality that you find throughout the United States, a recommendation that sometimes comes as a cheery salutation, and on other occasions as a more-or-less aggressive command.

'Have a nice day', or 'You have a good day now' always throws me when I first arrive in the USA, and this trip had been no exception. The first few times it came as such a surprise that all I could mumble in response was a somewhat stunned 'Thank you.' But this is the worst reply, because in the verbal equivalent of a boxer's one-two your assailant quickly follows up with the knock-out punch: 'You're welcome.' It's a polite finesse that leaves you feeling completely out-manoeuvred and utterly niced-out.

Somehow in the South this feeling wasn't so bad because people seemed to mean it, but another supposed facet of Southern culture is its tendency to be Janus-faced. Chivalry is said to be tempered by arrogance, honour with violence, and paternalism with racism. It had crossed my mind that the friendly welcome I received might be somewhat muted if my face was not white, but of course I would never know. And even if you're my colour, a Southerner is supposed to have this ability to be real polite right up to the point where he takes out his gun and kills you.

The first hint of a slightly less amiable side to the South came in an unexpected place in Savannah. After my unfortunate encounter with cardboard in Morrison's, I made a concerted effort to find an establishment that served more authentic Southern fare. All the literature I perused, and the people I asked, pointed to one place: Mrs Wilkes' Dining Room.

Mrs Wilkes' establishment was just a few blocks away from where I was staying in the historical district. It was only open for breakfast and lunch and I'd been told to get there early because there were always queues. I wandered along at 12.15 one day and was confronted with a line of about twenty people already snaking its way along the street. I wouldn't normally have waited forty minutes for lunch, but this place had been so highly recommended that I stuck it out. The queue consisted of a tour group and sundry other visitors to the city along with a small gathering of local office- and shop-workers on their lunch breaks, which I took to be a good sign. During the wait in the humid air beneath the trees, I also learned of a novel use for peanut butter from an overheard conversation in front of me. Apparently it is very good for getting chewing gum out of your hair. You rub it in, which dissolves the gum or so these people reckoned, but must still leave you with your hair full of peanut butter.

Inside, Mrs Wilkes' Dining Room was like somebody's front room with large tables and brick walls plastered with clippings of magazine and newspaper articles all saying what a good place this was to fill your face. Around each table about ten people sat down to eat from a wide selection of communal dishes in classic Southern style. There was Southern fried chicken, Brunswick stew (a gumbo-like mix of beef and chicken), okra, squash, beans, potato salad, rice and good corn bread. Pudding consisted of banana pie and fruit salad. It was all washed down with ice tea, the staple Southern beverage that I have to describe as an aquired taste because I haven't acquired it yet – it just never seems right to drink tea *served* cold. The food was good; the chicken tasted real and the vegetables fresh. It was not quite as exceptional as the propaganda had led me to expect, but it was still light years ahead of the cardboard fare I'd endured at Morrison's.

The unfortunate incident came right at the end of my version of Mrs Wilkes' dining experience. On finishing, customers were asked to carry their plates to the kitchen. I did this, and standing at the entrance to the steamy washing-up zone, I asked where exactly I should deposit my dishes. Four black ladies turned from their washing-up duties to face me and one motioned to a pile of other plates. As I turned to leave, the woman touched my arm.

'Where you from?' she asked gently.

'England,' I told her.

'I like your accent, sounds like . . . Elton John.'

'Thank you.'

'Yeah, real nice,' she told me, beaming.

As I smiled back, an old witch of a white woman in horn-rimmed spectacles, who had clearly overheard this little encounter, said waspishly, 'You hold your tongue.' She was glaring at the black washer-up with about as much charm and affability as you'd expect in a maximum security prison.

Stunned, I leapt to the defence of the black woman. 'She didn't mean any offence, and I didn't take it so,' I told the white woman as the black washer-up faded back into the kitchen scowling at her opponent.

'She's stupid. Doesn't know what she's saying,' the horn-rimmed spectacles explained.

As I made my way out of Mrs Wilkes' Dining Room, having paid, the black woman was clearing a table by the door.

'I don't like her accent,' I whispered in her ear.

'Yeah,' she whispered back, obviously still smarting from the incident, 'and they get all the tips. I don't get none.'

It was only a minor incident, and there could have been any number of explanations for the white woman's venom, but it was difficult not to interpret the event in a racial light. The old woman's staccato scolding seemed to be rooted deep in a mentality that equated black women with servants who should be seen and not heard. Whatever the cause, it spoiled my enjoyment of Mrs Wilkes' establishment and the incident bothered me for some time afterwards.

Relatively speaking, Savannah has not had a bad reputation when it comes to racial issues. James Oglethorpe's original plans for Georgia to be a colony without the evils of slavery did not last long, as economic pressures from slave-holding neighbours in South Carolina resulted in the repeal of the prohibition of slavery just sixteen years after the founding of the colony. But in 1964 Martin Luther King called Savannah 'the most integrated city south of the Mason-Dixon Line'.

Experts still debate the importance of slavery as a cause of the War Between the States, but with the beginning of postwar Reconstruction and the ratification of the Fifteenth Amendment to the US Constitution in 1870, black people were transformed from slaves to free citizens and given the right to vote. Within a few decades, however, this right was being eroded in the Southern states, and in the first half of the twentieth century a grand experiment in social Darwinism, where blacks were treated as 'separate but equal', took place all across the South. The official segregation only ended with the civil rights protests of the 1950s and 1960s, and some see the civil rights 'era', as it's now known, as a black adaptation of the Lost Cause tradition, preserving the Southern practice of attempting the impossible at great cost. The events of the era, its legacy of memorials and museums, are viewed as the African-American rendition of the Civil War.

Savannah has a Civil Rights museum and appropriately enough it is located on Martin Luther King Jr Boulevard. The street hems in the historic district on its western edge and was formerly known as Broad Street. Towns and cities all over the USA, not just in the South, have commemorated the civil rights leader by attaching his name to a thoroughfare. Every one I came across was a boulevard, I guess because streets and roads are not considered grand enough.

Being on the edge of the historic district, Savannah's Martin Luther King Jr Boulevard was a transition zone that didn't quite live up to its grand name. It was where the neat, clean streets of history gave way to the concrete and garbage of modern urban America. Entering the Civil Rights museum put me in a predominantly black environment for the first time on this trip. In the house where General Sherman had set up his headquarters, everyone had been white; in Mrs Wilkes' Dining Room there was one black couple among roughly forty customers, and the small concentration of blacks had been confined to the kitchen; here in the Civil Rights museum, mine was the only white face.

The museum, a small affair, kicked off with a short video about the history of racial segregation and the resultant civil rights movement, a largely non-violent series of events in Savannah. One of the display panels showed a map that depicted the quaint Southern custom of lynching as practised in Georgia between 1880 and 1930. It indicated that most lynchings occurred in the Cotton Belt and in southern Georgia. The victims of this ritual were not entirely black – twelve white men were strung up in these parts of the state during the fifty-year period – but a black man was executed this way more than once every other month on average. For those black people who weren't intimidated sufficiently by the lynch mobs or random racial attacks by the Ku Klux Klan, a range of ploys was implemented in Southern states to ensure that they didn't vote. These included poll taxes and literacy tests. In other cases, a jar full of marbles served the purpose. When a black voter turned up at the polls to cast a vote, he was asked to guess how many marbles there were in the jar. When the guess was wrong, the guy was told that this was bad luck because it meant he couldn't vote. He'd have to come back next year and try again. These methods, used all over the South, were pretty effective. In the state of Louisiana, 130,000 black people voted in the 1896 election. In 1900, just 5,000 exercised their legitimate democratic right.

With the virtual abolition of the black vote came the introduction of laws to implement racial segregation in public facilities. The museum authorities had collected a selection of public notices and old photographs depicting the white and coloured rest rooms, drinking fountains, and separate entrances to shops. Interestingly enough, no blacks were allowed in most Savannah parks. The 'separate but equal' philosophy obviously held that black people didn't need leisure facilities.

The preposterous nature of these Jim Crow laws, named after a song and dance routine performed by Thomas 'Daddy' Rice in pre-Civil War vaudeville, was really brought home to me in a mock-up of a department store lunch counter. It was designed to illustrate the process of non-violent sit-ins by Savannah's black community during the early 1960s. The mock-up of Levy's lunch counter, an all-white preserve, involved a dummy of a white woman behind the counter, a black man in front, and a white policeman approaching the scene. A cut-out window revealed a black woman working in the kitchen behind. By pressing one of two alternate buttons on the counter, you could hear contrasting exchanges between the woman serving and a white customer on the one hand and a black person on the other. While the white man received the full and friendly service, the black man's efforts to purchase some fried chicken eventually resulted in his arrest for trespass.

Following these sit-ins in March 1960, modelled on the landmark lunch counter protests at Greensboro, North Carolina a month before, Savannah's black community staged kneel-ins at all-white churches, wade-ins on all-white beaches and a fifteen-month boycott of white stores that practised segregationist shopping.

The civil rights protesters got what they wanted, and the fact that this museum was here at all was indication of the fact that the era itself has now passed into the annals of history. There is no doubt that opportunities for many black people in the South are more promising today than at any time in the past, but of course you can't simply sweep away 350 years of history with a voting rights act. Some days later I was talking to a black taxi driver named Bill, who had retired early from the US Air Force and returned home to live in Charleston, South Carolina. Bill remembered having to sit upstairs in the movie theatre and drinking from separate fountains. He said he was worried about young black kids today with their rap music. 'It's angry, but they don't know nothing,' he told me. I asked him whether race relations were better now and he replied with a categorical 'No.'

'Those preventions aren't there,' he said, 'but it's not that simple. It's still in people's heads and there are economic factors.'

When I got to Athens, Georgia I heard a story that encapsulated Bill's views on the matter. It was told by a middle-aged white woman named Bonnie who lived in an affluent Athens suburb where she employed a 70 year old black Baptist preacher to mow her lawn.

Bonnie came from a liberal Northern background and she found the situation peculiar, but the Reverend William Jennings, who had been recommended to Bonnie by her neighbour, seemed to need the casual work. But stranger things were still to come. One day, Bonnie's next-door neighbour overheard her talking to the preacher and noted that Bonnie called him Reverend Jennings. The neighbour asked Bonnie why, seeing as how everyone else in the neighbourhood called him William. 'What else could I call him?' Bonnie exclaimed to me. 'He's older than I am and he is a reverend. I've been brought up to respect my elders and the church, so he is Reverend Jennings to me, even if he does mow my lawn.' This was what Bonnie told her neighbour, who just looked at her and said simply, 'But he's black.' Following this interchange, the neighbour wouldn't talk to Bonnie for three months.

Despite the end of the Jim Crow laws and the progress towards proper integration that has been made in the South since the 1960s, more or less voluntary segregation still persists in many parts of the region. Churches were the obvious example: most whites and blacks still seemed to prefer their worship to be colour-coded. Some whole towns, too, were predominantly one colour or the other. Much later in my Southern sojourn, I passed through virtually all-white settlements in Alabama and a whole string of black rural ghettos in the Mississippi Delta where whites had been clearing out since the schools integrated. The residual black population, whose parents and grandparents had worked in the cotton fields, had been superseded by machines and had drifted from working the land to subsisting on welfare, or 'the system' as they know it.

There were less depressing examples of segregation however. I came across one not far from Savannah when I paid a visit to the village of Oyotunji, across the state line in South Carolina. Oyotunji was distinctive because it called itself a village, not a word that I heard very often in the South. Some of the smallest places I saw were still referred to as towns, but if they got any smaller, words like settlement or community were applied. Hence, to visit a village was in itself an unusual event. The reason for this made the place even more unusual. Oyotunji village wasn't in the USA. It was a little piece of Africa in America.

'You are now entering Yoruba kingdom,' declared a notice at the entrance flanked by square mud turrets. The dirt track that led between the turrets took me to a series of ramshackle wooden buildings round an internal courtyard. The place seemed deserted.

I had learned of Oyotunji's existence from a brief one-liner in a guidebook perused and otherwise rejected in my public library at home. All the book had said was that there was this African village near Sheldon, South Carolina, a few miles off Interstate 95. It was not well signposted. I had driven right past the place in my hire car, done a U-turn and had to backtrack. Then I saw a homemade signpost pointing along a dirt track that disappeared into some trees. It didn't look promising, but half a mile up the track another sign showed a painting of a woman in batik robes next to an announcement that said 'African village – seen on TV', as if the village's appearance on television somehow made it more real.

In front of the gateway, another sign told me to sound my horn on arrival. I did so, parked the car in the least muddy bit under some trees, and walked into the compound. It wasn't immediately clear to me whether Oyotunji was a real settlement where people lived and worked, or whether it was some kind of ethnic museum. After a few minutes' waiting, a woman ambled up from inside the compound. She wore a billowing purple tie-dyed cotton dress and dreadlocks and she had a series of small incision scars on her forehead just above her nose. She said she would show me round.

Oyotunji was based on the traditional religion, customs and art forms of the Yoruba people of West Africa, she told me. The village had been established by members of the Black Panther movement in New York City when they bought these ten acres for $500 in 1970. It was designed to disseminate knowledge about the origins and culture of the African-American population and to 'de-emphasise negative stereotypes concerning African traditions, customs and religions', she added.

The village seemed to consist primarily of a series of shrines to various gods, many with offerings at their bases. Some of the offerings were in fairly advanced states of decay.

'We hold festivals here every month,' my guide informed me, 'and students come to do dissertations. We have guest houses where they can stay.'

There was an ancestors' shrine, and a shrine to a warrior god where they carried out tribal markings, I was told. Here was one to the goddess Oya, who specialised in hurricanes and was known for having nine different personalities, and there was the shrine to the god of thunder and lightning. 'Electricity,' the woman interpreted for me.

Through a mud archway in one of the compounds, she pointed out the house where the king lived. It was difficult to tell from a distance, but the king's house looked like it was built in more contemporary materials than any other construction in Oyotunji. 'He is seventy years old, has four wives and twenty-three children,' the woman told me. (And a Jaguar motor car, I noted, parked in front of his house.) 'He was coronated in Nigeria in 1981.'

'Is he, was he, Nigerian?' I asked.

'No, he was born in Detroit.'

I was having trouble categorising the village of Oyotunji in my mind. Here were all these shrines (more than you'd find in most African villages) and the king's place, but there didn't appear to be much actually happening. There were no children running around, no mothers grinding grain with babies strapped on their backs, and no old people sitting in the shade like there would be in all the African villages I had been in. No one was tending animals or making anything. In fact, we hadn't, as yet, come across anyone else in the village at all.

'What's the population of Oyotunji?' I asked tentatively.

'It varies,' came the reply, 'it's pretty quiet now, but when we hold festivals lots of people come. About twenty to twenty-five people actually live here at the moment. There used to be several hundred in the nineteen-seventies and eighties.'

I wanted to ask what people actually did. The best I could come up with was, 'What about employment?'

'We run a school,' the woman told me, 'and there's a vegetable patch over there. But most people here have clients they do readings for. Sex, business, whatever they want to know.' So that's it, I thought to myself, a commune for African-American shrinks. 'We charge a hundred dollars for a roots reading,' she added, 'to trace the ancestry of African-Americans back to Africa.'

Before we made our way back to the entrance, I asked for a toilet, and the woman pointed to a low white-washed building beside what looked like a fenced in piece of wasteground, until I noticed a small white emu inside strutting towards me. 'For the children,' I was told. The toilet smelled as rich as any African one I've experienced.

Back at the compound inside the entrance I noticed another sign, that I hadn't seen on my arrival. It said that there was a five dollar entrance fee, a first as far as I was concerned for an African village. The woman hadn't mentioned it.

'Should I give you my five dollars?' I asked her, pointing to the sign.

'OK,' she said.

Three children appeared out of nowhere, dressed in blue smocks and trousers. 'It's their lunch break from school,' the woman told me. The kids seemed a bit embarrassed at seeing me, but one soon approached and asked whether I'd like to buy a ring from her. She had a small caseful of them that she had laid out on a picnic table. I really didn't want any of the rings, but I didn't like to disappoint the girl. She obviously sensed that I wasn't interested because she disappeared and came back with a small carved wooden figure that looked African and a black Barbie doll dressed in a wrap-around batik skirt.

'Is it African?' I asked, picking up the carved figure. The girl shrugged. 'It could be,' the woman said over my shoulder. 'Some of them are made here, others we buy from African traders.' The way she said it was as if African merchants regularly turned up at Oyotunji plying their wares. Somehow I couldn't imagine such a scene in twentieth-century South Carolina, but you never know. I bought the carved figure, bade the woman and children farewell, and drove back along the track, away from this strange piece of Africa in America and on to the highway that would take me to Beaufort.

7

Timeout in Beaufort

Beaufort was a quiet little place down towards the coast. Its approach road was lined with the usual proliferation of chain motels, fast food joints and franchised retail establishments, but all of a sudden these melted into the sultry afternoon air and a choice selection of wooden antebellum houses materialised to overlook the salt marshes of the Beaufort river estuary. During the War Between the States, Beaufort had decided that discretion was indeed the better part of valour and had opted for an early surrender rather than face demolition. So, as in Savannah, its old part had survived the conflict largely intact.

I checked into a hotel and ate a late lunch in a restaurant that had formerly been a bank. There was a large safe in the foyer and the waitress introduced herself with the words, 'Hi, I'm Karen and I'm your teller for today.' I find this easy familiarity in restaurants disturbing and I dread the day when a waitress will offer to take me into the kitchen after my meal and introduce me to the chef and the guy who washes the dishes. But Karen wasn't about to extend such an invitation, probably because it took all of her brain power to memorise the ten different salad dressings her customers had to choose from. I had blackened salmon with a chocolate chip and horseradish dressing, or at least that's what it tasted like. The coffee came with a straw, which was strange: like drinking a cold drink through a straw only hotter. The bill arrived in an envelope with 'Thank you for your deposit' written on it.

Out on the river front, there was a small marina and a walkway lined with swinging benches where I sat and watched a line of people trying to catch shrimp for their dinner. They were doing it with hand held nets about a yard across, fringed with small lead weights around their circumference. The nets were swung from a line attached to the centre and cast out to open in a flash, briefly resembling a flying antimacassar, before hitting the water with a gentle spattering sound. It was hard work. A single four inch grey shrimp was the most I saw anyone catch with one throw. One of the women said that prospects were better when the tide went out.

Aside from the standard issue strip development on its outskirts, Beaufort had a short shopping street that was largely comprised of up-market knick-knack shops and art galleries. It also had a small mall that had obviously never really taken off and looked as if it wished it wasn't a mall. It contained another art gallery and a Civil War shop, which meant it sold bad paintings of Confederate battle scenes and bottles of Rebel salad dressing. Overall, I sensed that not a lot had happened in Beaufort since the war, and judging by the public notices dotted throughout the waterfront park, this was just the way the local authorities wanted it to be. Along the walkway, strollers were informed that there was 'No swimming or diving from seawall'; in the park itself there was 'No bike-riding', while the notice at the park entrance read: 'No consumption or possession of beer, wine or alcoholic beverages in city parks without special permission of the city.' It was made clear that violators would be prosecuted and something about the city's submissive atmosphere made me feel that this threat was somehow more serious here in Beaufort than it was elsewhere.

Late in the afternoon I drove out to the series of small islands that lie between Beaufort and the Atlantic Ocean. The easternmost, Hunting Island, was a state park covered in a subtropical forest of slash pines and palmetto trees that ran right up to the beach. The tide was out by this time, revealing a fifty yard stretch of spotless white sand running as far as the eye could see in both directions. The Atlantic sweeps away large amounts of this sand from Hunting Island every year, and the rate of erosion was signified in the fallen pines and exposed tree stumps that littered the upper portions of the beach. The park authorities reckon that the northern tip of the island has been diminished by about two miles over the last 200 years.

Hunting Island is strategically located on the shipping lane between Savannah and Charleston to the north, and in 1859 a lighthouse was built to guide passing ships. Within a few years, it was abandoned as its foundations were washed away. They put up a new lighthouse in 1875, a quarter of a mile inland, this one constructed of cast iron plates that could be easily dismantled. Fourteen years later, the lighthouse keeper noted that the last 400 feet of land had disappeared during the previous winter and they had to take the whole thing down and move it again. The lighthouse hasn't functioned since 1933 and today it stands just a hundred feet from the beach.

Such high erosion rates affect all the so-called barrier islands that line much of the eastern seaboard of the USA. Since Hunting Island is a state park, they just leave nature to get on with it, but elsewhere the local authorities fight a constant battle against the forces of nature because Americans like their beaches and they want them to stay where they are. In this respect, American citizens aren't particularly different from many other nationalities, but the lengths they go to to protect their sand take some beating. Needless to say, this is because there is big money involved.

Down the coast, Miami Beach has six billion dollars' worth of condominiums and hotels planted along ten miles of imported beach sand and every time the wind blows some of the sand disappears. This is unfortunate because the presence of the stretch of sand is Miami Beach's main selling point. In fact you could say that Miami Beach wouldn't be Miami Beach if it wasn't for the beach. If a tourist turns up for a nice relaxing holiday at the seaside to find the beach is gone, he's liable to complain. If the President decides to stay a while and put up in the Sheraton, as he usually does on sorties to South Florida, he'll be disappointed if his morning beach jog is not possible due to the absence of sand.

Twenty years ago, they solved the problem of the disappearing beach by dredging a large quantity of sand from off-shore and dumping it beside the strip of hotels. Today, Miami Beach is running out of sand again, but a similar scheme to replace it with dredged material has become locked in a legal dispute with a wealthy town just up the coast whose residents want to leave the sand just where it is, two miles out on the seabed. Other plans have been investigated, including buying sand from nearby Caribbean islands. The Bahamas looked like a good bet, until a biologist pointed out that the sand there was a lighter colour to that used previously. This would mean a lower temperature, because it reflects more of the sun's rays. So what? you might think, the average tourist isn't going to notice, especially after a few tequilas. But the biologist wasn't thinking about the tourists, he was thinking about all the loggerhead turtles that use Miami Beach for breeding. Loggerheads are an endangered species, and the sex of their hatchings is closely dependent on temperature. Cooler beach sand would be likely to favour the hatching of boy turtles over girls. Importing sand from the Bahamas could effectively kill off the whole population, or at least turn them all into homosexuals.

The moral of the tale is don't mess with nature, but I don't think moralising would be received too kindly in Miami Beach. There's too much money involved.

As I drove back towards Beaufort, away from the fresh Atlantic breeze, I was disappointed to see that the moon in the evening sky was just a thin sickle. In Mrs Wilkes' Dining Room in Savannah I had shared my communal table with a group of locals on their lunch break. One of them, a young man who said he worked in retail management (I got the impression that in his case this meant he was a shop assistant), had told me an interesting story about his home town of Beaufort. It was a very superstitious place, he said, where everyone paints their front doors red to ward off evil spirits. It was also full of ghosts. There was one, who everyone in town had seen, that carried a light and only came out at full moon. He was supposed to be a Confederate soldier who had wandered out of camp one night with a lamp and got lost, never to be seen in the flesh again. There was also a more modern story that went with this ghost, he explained. Some said the man with the light was the ghost of a bus driver who had rolled his vehicle over while driving a football team back from a match. The driver had taken a torch and gone to get help and had never been seen again.

'I've seen it,' the retail manager told me. 'I've chased it and it's chased me. The ghost always takes the same route, down the road and up across a fellah's porch and then disappears.'

Since there wasn't a full moon, I didn't rate my chances of seeing Beaufort's ghost with the light. It wouldn't have surprised me if the local council had threatened him with prosecution if he violated the ban on haunting at other times.

So I watched TV in my hotel room instead. I only have the five terrestrial channels at home, so it was always good entertainment to flick through the plethora of possibilities presented in American hotel rooms. Here in Beaufort, channels 1 to 42 were operational and then there was a big gap until channels 71 to 73. I had no idea what had happened to channels 43 to 70, but I had more than enough to be going on with.

When I first switched on, I was faced with a home shopping channel. On it a disembodied voice was proclaiming the merits of the Dirt Devil, a cordless mop-vac that cleaned just about everything you could think of. This was quickly followed by another hygiene product. It was a bar of soap. But this was no ordinary bar of soap because this mysterious cleanser from China did more than just make you clean. It also made you thin. 'It washes away unwanted fat,' claimed the woman who now filled the screen, holding up the innocuous little grey object for all to see. 'Japanese researchers found that eighty per cent of people lost weight on washing regularly with it.' The camera zoomed in on the exotic soap bar.

Extraordinary, I thought. 'It's amazing,' she said.

It was all the rage in Asia, according to an information box that flashed up beneath the woman. It was aluminium-free and contained ten different seaweed extracts. 'Lose weight and stay clean,' explained the next caption. 'We want you to see how it's made,' the woman told me. So she showed me a video of ten different types of seaweed being collected by a gang of small Asian people all with wide grins on their faces. They were obviously enjoying the thought of how rich they were getting just by gathering seaweed for stupid fat people.

'It's factory processed,' the woman told me, no doubt to allay any fears I might have that the Asian people who collected the stuff were carriers of exotic skin diseases. The next shot featured a large, spotlessly clean machine that noiselessly sucked in the ten types of seaweed at one end and spat out the small bars of magic soap at the other. The machine was attended by more smiling Orientals who still couldn't believe their luck. The Japanese company that had built the machine had invested $30 million in it, the female voiceover told me. 'Thirty *million* dollars,' she added, just in case I hadn't been paying attention.

Then I realised what it was all about. This was a cunning way of marketing a new brand of soap that had turned out to be pretty ineffectual at actually getting the human body clean. You probably had to rub so hard that you lost weight while doing it. The Japanese company involved were trying to rake back their thirty million bucks as fast as possible, before any of their impressionable customers realised what was going on. The aluminium-free cleanser made from ten different seaweed extracts was a hundred dollars for eight bars.

I changed channels and got a women's billiards tournament from New York City. Next came a studio of talking heads. The shot switched to focus on one of the men who was deep in thought. There was no sound. Then the man opened his mouth and said, 'Vending can be a component in the overall retail environment . . .' I changed channels again before he could finish his sentence. This time I got recorded highlights of Miss Venezuela 1997. I met a man once who swore that Venezuela contained many of the most beautiful women on the planet, but judging by the contest, he was sorely mistaken. I flicked the remote again and on it went.

By the time I had got to channel 73, I had ascertained that there was nothing I actually wanted to watch, but channel-hopping is addictive, and when I got to channel 73 I wondered whether perhaps channel 1 was now showing something interesting. And so I forged on, grazing the channels like a televisual smorgasbord.

I was enjoying playing the great American consumer. The entertainment was instant and gratifying, not because of the substance but because of the speed of change. It was all rubbish but I didn't care, I was gobbling it up and spitting it out like a couch potato with bulimia. It was a brain-numbing maelstrom of visual fragments, mind candy for the intellectually impaired, TV's equivalent of junk mail.

I thought it appropriate that this was what the television offered in the land of fast food and drive-through banks. More wealth seemed to have become equated with more speed and more variety. I felt I was peering through a cultural periscope at a society in turmoil, and it was small wonder that so many US citizens had turned to personal psychiatrists for help.

Or, in the South's case, to God.

I stopped channel-hopping at INSB, the inspirational network. Pastor Rod Parsley was striding around a platform whipping up a vast crowd of worshippers. 'In the middle of that heart attack, you can't call timeout,' he screamed. 'In the middle of that stroke, you can't call timeout. In the middle of that car accident, you *cannot* call timeout.' Sweat was streaming down his brow, frenzied commitment surged from every pore of his body. 'In the middle of that plane crash, you can't call timeout,' he continued. 'There is no timeout in the game of life, the clock is always running.' Mass hysteria was breaking out all around him. The crowd was jumping, screaming, dancing and crying.

Behind Pastor Parsley was a vast jumbled pile of pieces of paper surrounded by a small group of people on their knees. The pastor turned and pointed at the pile, 'These are the prayers you have sent in.' It was difficult to tell whether the gang of kneelers was trying to sort through the mound of papers in a rather haphazard fashion, or simply laying their hands on them to absorb their spiritual messages. 'Shout, if you feel the power of the Lord,' commanded Pastor Parsley, and the crowd roared.

Down in front of the stage a ragged line of worshippers had formed and Pastor Parsley was headed there next. He started laying his hand on the foreheads of the committed. 'Foul Satan, I command you to come out,' he cried at the head of a woman whose eyes were closed. 'Satan, I take hold of you now and I command you to come out.' He whipped his hand away and threw any Satanic influences up towards the studio lights. The woman keeled over and fainted, to be caught by the throng behind her. Pastor Parsley had already moved to lay his hand on the next forehead. 'Cancer, I command you to come out,' and so it went on. Most of the diseases known to mankind were ordered out of the bodies in which they had taken up residence and all the former victims passed out with the relief.

Finally I managed to switch off the TV set. The silence was palpable. I brushed my teeth and climbed into bed. As I drifted off to sleep I kept wondering what had become of channels 43 to 70.

8

The Grandees and their Bagpipes

The first sight you get of the Boone Hall plantation, a handful of miles up the coast from Charleston, evokes all the historical romance of a civilisation gone with the wind. The long straight approach is flanked by ancient oak trees that lean over from their grass aprons to offer pockets of much needed shade from the relentless subtropical sun. Spanish moss hangs from their gnarled branches, lending a festive air to your trip into the image of the Lost Cause. Slowly, the plantation house emerges like a shimmering icon from this idyllic advance, welcoming you to your encounter with history, to the land of cavaliers and cotton fields called the Old South.

But then you go and spoil it all by doing something stupid like looking sideways. I did it and saw the slave cabins, a line of small brick boxes set back from the approach road like a string of toy houses. Not many of the surviving Southern plantations have managed to maintain their slave quarters, but at Boone Hall they have and it's a good thing. They put the place in perspective because none of the splendour and grace could have flourished without them.

South Carolina was first permanently settled by Europeans in 1670 when Charles Town (later Charleston) was founded and the coastal Low Country of flat plains, swampy floodplains, wide estuaries and sandy islands became the focus of plantation agriculture. The early English planters experimented with sugar cane, olives and grapes before a passing ship's captain gave them a bushel of rice seed from Madagascar, thus introducing the colony's first viable cash crop. A few decades later, indigo was successfully introduced from the West Indies and joined the ranks of South Carolina's agricultural produce. Since indigo grew on well drained uplands, it complemented rice production, which took place in riverine environments. The blue dye processed from the indigo plant was in great demand in the English textile industry throughout much of the eighteenth century, but when indigo's profitability began to wane after the Revolution, the planters turned to cotton instead. This was black seed, long staple cotton and it thrived on the islands like those I had driven across from Beaufort. Hence it became known as Sea Island cotton. This cotton was of very high quality, much finer than the green seed, short staple variety grown in the inner plains and piedmont of South Carolina and other southern states.

So it was that three crops – rice, indigo and cotton – formed the basis of Low Country economy and society for two centuries. The fruits of the earth produced fantastic riches, spawning a grandee class of haughty plantation owners and Charleston merchants, the type of character forever immortalised in Margaret Mitchell's *Gone with the Wind*. The linchpin of this lost civilisation, the Southern plantation, can be viewed from a number of standpoints. Some choose to don the rose-tinted spectacles of the Mitchell approach, to see the gallantry and gracious living of a land called the Old South. Others marvel at the profitability and efficiency of a system of large-scale farming that paid for it all. Still others concentrate on the cruel and exploitative system called slavery that underpinned the whole operation. Whichever view you take, the plantation is a quintessentially Southern symbol, and nowhere was it more so than during the colonial and antebellum periods in the coastal Low Country of South Carolina.

Often seen as the nurseries of the rebellion against the North, the great plantations certainly suffered after the defeat of the South. Most never recovered from the blow struck by the end of slavery. They just struggled into the twentieth century finally to be killed off in the Low Country by a succession of hurricanes and the ravages of the boll weevil. Now all that is left is their graceful architecture, preserved as a series of tourist meccas to the romantic imagery of an aristocratic way of life whose memory still lingers in the minds of so many twentieth-century Americans.

In this respect Boone Hall was a little different, however. Founded in 1676 and first owned by Major John Boone, one of the pioneer group of English settlers to arrive in South Carolina, its agricultural character had been partly preserved. After the upheaval of the War

Between the States and the fall of King Cotton, Boone Hall switched to growing pecans. In 1904, it boasted the world's largest pecan groves and a small part of the estate is still producing the nuts commercially today. The remainder is a monument to a lifestyle that is no more. To get me in the mood a young Southern belle named Heather dressed in period costume was there to show me around the house, but only after a thirty minute wait on the Greek revival porch with about a hundred other people.

Just as we were all on the verge of heat stroke, the front door was opened and we were ushered into an oasis of air-conditioning, a modern concession to the climate that Major Boone would have approved of. I have to say that I was disappointed by the size of the house. It was smaller than the mythology had led me to expect, but Heather did her best to make up for it. She glided around with her little snub nose and pearl earrings in a huge green satin dress that matched the dining room walls. The best thing about her was her spiel, not its content or tone, which sounded like she was reading from a prepared statement, but because of her accent. It sounded measured, self-conscious and decidedly affected. At times, I would have been hard pressed to say that the language she was using was English. When she talked about the pecan groves, she pronounced them 'pi-kaan', although later I discovered that this was how all Southerners said the word. She pronounced her 'o's as if she was mocking an upper class English accent, while she clearly wasn't, and I've never met anyone who would refer to a silver platter from Sheffield, England as a 'plattair'.

Heather's period get-up was a nice touch. It helped to crystallise the contents of the house and make them more realistic. Her hoop-skirted dress even enabled us to see how impossible it was for the ladies to get through the narrow doorway into the smoking room. This is always the trouble with country houses that have been turned into museums, they have all these interesting old things on display but the people walking about inside them ruin it. Sweat tops and baseball caps don't really go with hundred-year-old pianos and silver 'plattairs' from Sheffield, England. But the thing that really made me forget the modern-day company was found in a room filled with more utilitarian items than the old bookcases and sideboard displays. It came at the end of the tour when Heather had left us to mosey around at our own pace before exiting through a side door.

Framed and mounted on one of the room's walls was a grocery list dated 1848. Its contents included many articles you might imagine, like coffee and molasses and a small pot for cooking, all written out in copperplate longhand. In this respect, it was comforting to see that grocery lists haven't changed much in 150 years. For the most part, it was just the prices that gave it away as a piece of history (13½ lb coffee: $2; 1½ gallons molasses: $7). But there was one other give-away. It was the very first item, at the top of the list. It read '1 Negro girl'.

I suppose the shock I experienced on reading this is a good sign of the progress we have made since the times when a trip into town for provisions could include a stop-off at the market to purchase a small human being. Standing there looking at the grocery list, I could just imagine someone like Heather sitting in the parlour writing it, or dictating it to a minion, saying, 'The first thing we need is another slave girl to help in the kitchen.'

'Yes, Miss Heather.'

'With all these silver plattairs to polish, Mammy doesn't have enough time to clean the vegetables properly anymore.'

'No, Miss Heather.'

'And you can get some coffee and molasses while you're about it.'

'Yes, Miss Heather.'

The other aspect of this list that surprised me was the price of the Negro girl. It was $998. I had never before paused to consider how much people actually paid to buy a slave. I'd always been too busy thinking what an unpleasant business the whole idea was to stop and think about the economics of the matter. Going into this level of detail, even in one's thought processes, almost seemed like a form of endorsement. Asking how much a slave actually cost seemed tanta-mount to admitting that I was thinking of purchasing one myself. Nonsense, of course, but even in my research for a book I wrote some years ago on the southern African country of Mozambique, source of more than a million slaves during the nineteenth century, I don't recall even once coming across any mention of how much they were sold for.

I know that it's irrelevant, and that this is the whole point. You can't put a monetary value on owning another human being because the entire concept is fundamentally wrong. But I have to admit that I was still surprised at the price of a Negro girl in South Carolina in 1848. A thousand dollars is a lot of money even today. In the mid nineteenth century it must have been enough to buy . . . well, your very own human being I suppose.

As I exited the mansion and wandered out into the hot sun that beat down on to the gardens, some more basic economics were crossing my cerebral desk. I'd read that shortly after the establishment of the first rice plantations in South Carolina at the end of the seventeeth century, the black population was greater than the white. On the eve of the War Between the States, more than eighty per cent of the people living in the coastal Low Country were black. To the grandees, these people were walking assets. There must have been billions of dollars' worth of capital tied up in those guys. No wonder the grandees broke out in a cold sweat at the mere mention of an end to slavery. It really wasn't surprising that South Carolina was the first state to secede from the Union.

No doubt there had been good and bad slave-owners. Heather had told us, for example, that historical records showed that Boone Hall was one of the first plantations to provide education for its slaves. But this struck me as being like pissing in the sea. It was a small contribution but it didn't make any difference. In some cases, educating the black man actually had unfortunate repercussions. Up the coast in Virginia in the early nineteenth century, a slave who was taken in to the big house in Southampton County and taught to read by his master eventually bit the hand that fed him in a big way. The slave became so inspired by his interpretation of the Holy Scriptures that he led a rebellion in which his master and his entire family were murdered. Nat Turner, the educated slave, was eventually hunted down and executed for his crimes, along with all his followers. Every one was given a proper burial except Turner, whose body was turned over to a local surgeon. The surgeon skinned Turner's cadaver and used the hide to make tobacco and coin pouches. A fat lot of good education did for him.

Another question about slavery in North America that had always bothered me was why the grandees of South Carolina and elsewhere bothered to import their human cargoes from Africa, which is a long way from North America. Why didn't they enslave the local Indian population? Well they tried. Apparently, when the English settlers first turned up in South Carolina, they were greeted by smiling red men who had seen the French and Spanish try to make it and fail. According to one of the guidebooks I had with me, the Indians jumped up and down shouting 'Hiddy doddy comorado Angles' (English very good friends). Not long after setting up shop, the English suggested to their new Indian acquaintances that they might like to come and work for them on their plantations. The Indians didn't warm to the idea and rebelled, so the grandees began importing black people instead.

Similar scenes were played out elsewhere in the South. In some parts, an alternative supply of labour came from indentured servants, men and women from England who were willing to sell themselves into personal service in return for the price of a passage to the new land. But after a fixed period these people had worked out their obligation and turned overnight from cheap bound labour into expensive free labour. It wasn't long before Africans became the only sensible choice. Indians were too much hassle and were driven out, exterminated or simply killed off by exotic new diseases brought over by the white man. For a time in South Carolina, the grandees played both ends against the middle. When the Indians rebelled, they armed the blacks to fight them off, and when any blacks managed to escape, the grandees hired Indians to track them down. But as the eighteenth century progressed, South Carolina began to run out of Indians. In 1685, there were an estimated 10,000 red men in South Carolina east of the mountains; by 1790, their number was just 300. So the grandees introduced bloodhounds to track down runaway slaves instead. Using dogs in this way became so common, and such fun, that it evolved into a sport. When Mr Lincoln freed all the slaves, the grandees used racoons in place of the black people and so the coonhound was born, and with it a sport that today rivals football, stock car racing and chasing women as one of the most popular Southern leisure pursuits. Some think this is how the racist term 'coon' originated, but not so. Its roots stem from the stockades, or 'barracoons', built to cage the first slaves who were brought to North America.

The more I learned about the grandees and their *modus operandi*, the more the mystical romantic image of the Old South paled. These weren't nice people and they didn't operate a nice system. The fact that many tend to view this section of the Southern past in an idyllic light, as a land of moonlight and magnolias, is easy to interpret as a form of back-dated racism. It's a white man's perspective on a white man's world and if you weren't white it really wasn't a very pleasant place in which to live.

But I've disgressed. Before any of these issues started whizzing through my mind, I had to deal with the 26th annual Charleston Scottish Games. I'd happily motored through the outskirts of the city, taking appropriate note of a sign that said the speed limit was enforced by Charleston police aircraft, and was proceeding in a northerly direction with one eye out for the turning to the Boone Hall plantation. I had the radio on and was listening to a stimulating phone-in programme about how to fix your car. Jim and Dave, the two resident auto-advisers, were gallantly struggling through a query from Bill in Lexington who had a problem with his '88 Cherokee. At first, Jim and Dave thought that the source of Bill's difficulties lay in a fuse underneath his hood, which was an opportunity for them to offer plenty of helpful advice on fuses. But Bill swore blind, on several occasions, that if he'd checked them fuses once he'd checked them a hundred times, and that they were not the source of his problem.

I saw the sign for the Boone Hall plantation, and took a left off the freeway, switching off the air-conditioning and lowering the windows to get a draught of hot air for a change. As I drove slowly along the avenue of oaks, Jim and Dave had finally hit on the true reason for Bill's misery. Bill probably needed a new TPS, and I just caught the beginning of Jim's analysis of the vagaries of throttle positioning sensors before the incongruous strains of bagpipes started filtering through the window into my car.

I cut off Jim in his prime and tried to listen, frowning as I did so, a foolish habit presumably based on the mistaken premise that my facial expression somehow affects my hearing. I looked left, to see the line of brick slave quarters, but the bagpipe music was not coming from that direction. Straight ahead of me, the plantation house was beginning to emerge at the end of the procession of foliage. I concentrated hard and realised that the bagpipe music was coming from there.

Directly in front of the plantation house a small sign declared that visitors to the Scottish Games should turn right at this point, and as I swung the steering wheel, the bagpipe music getting louder all the time, I was faced with a line of about a dozen shiny motor cars belonging to members of the British Car Club. There were several MGs and a Rolls Royce, but most of the vehicles had been manufactured by Mercedes-Benz.

Rather bewildered by this time, I slowed to ask a policewoman who was directing traffic whether I was going in the right direction to visit the plantation and she told me that I would have to park along with all the visitors to the Scottish Games. At the end of the track she guided me towards, I emerged into a large field full of motor cars. I parked, locked up and retraced my steps, counting the lines of vehicles as I passed them because I knew that if I didn't I'd have to wait until nightfall before I saw my hire car again.

Over in the corner of the field, people were lining up at a table paying an entrance fee. Although the 26th annual Charleston Scottish Games had not been on my itinerary, I thought I ought to take a look, so I handed over my ten dollars and joined the steady stream of visitors drawn across a wooden footbridge by the mass whining of the bagpipes.

I've never seen so many people wearing kilts. A vast grassy area, the size of several football pitches behind the plantation house, was full of them. They had proper black kilt belts and sporrans, long woolly socks, white shirts and woollen tam-o'-shanters. Many were collected in small clan gaggles, blowing their bagpipes, unfurling tartan flags and generally getting ready for some kind of display. Others were wandering around the tables that surrounded the main parade area, each dedicated to a different clan. It was midday, and the temperature must have been nearing a hundred degrees, but these gallant descendants from the glens were toughing it out, perspiring freely beneath their tam-o'-shanters. The sunglasses worn by one or two looked peculiar, but this was nothing compared to the fact that they were all speaking with a Southern drawl.

It was a major event, with a line of portable toilets and stands selling food and drink. As I wandered round the stalls, a voice that sounded uncannily like Jack Nicholson made occasional announcements over a loud speaker system. 'I'd like to remind you that the Shaws will be marching with the MacNeils.'

Ethnic identity is not supposed to be terribly important to Southern whites, who have long contented themselves simply with being not black. Most white Southerners claim English descent if they claim any at all, but of course they have come from all sorts of backgrounds. I had seen a shrine in St Augustine dedicated to North America's first permanent Greek settlement, and later in my travels I visited a predominantly German town in northern Alabama. People originally from Scotland, who had arrived in the South via Ireland, were said to be the ancestors of the rednecks. They were yeoman farmers with necks permanently sunburned from a life working in the fields. But the participants at these games didn't look like rednecks, and I hadn't seen a single mud-spattered pickup in the field where I had left my hire car. I also couldn't really see the stereotypical redneck showing much interest in the clan tables that sold tartan ties, painted crests mounted on wood, and tea cloths with clan maps on them, these wares often surrounded by photographs of Scottish castles. Books were left open so that you could add your name and address to their clan mailing lists. At the McKenzie stall I paused to look and the woman asked me whether I'd been to Scotland. Yes I had, I told her. 'I never knew there was so much history in Scotland until I went there two years ago,' she exclaimed.

We were interrupted by Jack Nicholson announcing the national anthem. To my surprise, the loud speaker system relayed a rendition of 'God Save the Queen'. People around me kept respectfully quiet, but when this was followed by the 'Star-Spangled Banner' everyone stopped dead, turned to face the loudspeakers and stood to attention. Many removed their tam-'o-shanters and held them over their hearts, while others made do with their hands. A brief, still silence hung in the sticky air for a second or two at the end of the transmission and then everyone starting clapping.

I moved on towards a stand selling tartan skirts, strategically located beneath a spreading oak tree. In front of it was a display of bumper stickers and I stood for a while, enjoying the shade, reading things like 'Kiss my thistle' and 'What's "worn" under the kilt? Nothing, all parts work okey-dokey'. Next to this a British grocery stand was selling highland shortbread and packets of Fox's Glacier mints.

Over in the far corner of the field, clan groupings were assembling with their flags and instruments for the march. I wandered away from the crowd, down a sandy path. On both sides of the path, the land was inundated with water that sprouted marsh grasses and snow white ibises which stood motionless like statues in the reeds. Away from the bagpipes, I could hear the chatter of insects in the still air. Far from any chance of shade, the heat soon became broiling and I wished I had brought a hat. A long slim black snake that had been sunning itself on the track whipped back into the undergrowth and I returned towards the tartan action. Despite the heat, I was hungry. One of the food stands, calling itself the Olde London Baking Co Ltd, offered British foods, but all it consisted of was baked potatoes. More imagination had gone into another food stand nearby, but I still didn't fancy what was on offer. Most of their plates were labelled 'Scottish ploughman's lunch', each consisting of two baguette slices, a couple of mini-burgers and a hunk of brie that was suffering badly in the heat. In the end I plumped for a hotdog and a paper cup of homemade lemonade.

By the time I had finished my snack the marching had begun, but I had had enough of the sun and I made my way to the house to join the queue on the Greek revival terrace. When I'd been refreshed by the air-conditioned interior and Heather's entertaining accent, I ducked from one patch of shade to another along the oak tree avenue to look at the small slave houses. You could go inside one of them, but there was nothing to see. It was just a shell with a dirt floor and a stone fireplace, an unsurprising contrast to the plush plantation house. At the end of the row of slave quarters, I followed a sign that led me to the dock house. It was a large wooden affair on the

Wampancheone Creek where the cotton had been loaded for the trip down river to Charleston. A teenage youth and a younger girl, his sister as it transpired, were hanging out on the jetty playing a word game that involved itemising alphabetically the contents of an imaginary picnic.

'I went to the picnic and I bought asparagus, a bottle of water from the North Pole . . .' said the youth as I approached. 'Let's ask the stranger what he would bring.'

He gave me a brief outline of the rules and I added a crab to their picnic. The youth flicked some of his hair away from his glasses and studied me briefly. I could tell he had been expecting something a bit more imaginative than a simple crustacean, but he said, 'OK. Susie, your turn.'

His sister wasn't sure about her brother's brazen approach to a complete stranger, but after a brief moment she overcame her embarrassment. 'I went to the picnic and I brought asparagus, a bottle of water from the North Pole, a crab . . .' she hesitated, 'and a doorknob,' she added finally.

'. . . and a doorknob,' her brother repeated, again masking his disappointment, but I suspect thinking that this was really all he could expect from a girl. He put his hand to his chin, covering a dozen or so of his spots, pretending to think carefully about his next move. Mine was to sit on the edge of the jetty and gaze out across the still water at the trees on the far bank.

'You're not from around here, are you?' the youth asked me.

'No, I'm from England.'

'Are you here for the games?'

'No, I just happened to come today.'

'We're here for the games,' he said wearily, 'we come every year.'

'Are your parents' roots in Scotland?' I asked.

'They like to think so,' he said, neatly reversing the conventional roles, tired of letting his parents indulge in their fantasies. 'I can't hack it anymore. All these people faking it, pretending to be Scottish, and those bagpipes grate after a while.'

I asked him whether he lived nearby, not really expecting him to say yes because his accent didn't sound Southern. His family lived in Columbia, the state capital, he told me. 'I was born in the South and

I've lived down here most of my life,' he continued in his world weary tone. 'Except for two years in Massachusetts. I didn't like it there, too cold in the winter and the heat was dry. I used to get nose bleeds up there because the heat was so dry.'

It was time for me to move on. I said goodbye to the youth and his sister. The youth replied, 'Farewell stranger from England' and his sister hid her face. As I walked away up the jetty, I heard the youth resume the game. 'I went to the picnic and I brought asparagus, a bottle of water from the North Pole, a crab, a doorknob, and a Eurocentric view of world history. Your turn Susie.'

9

Southern, Military and
Politically Incorrect

It was time to move on because I had to get my hire car back by
7 p.m. or face another day's rental charge. I was planning to linger in
Charleston for a while but by all accounts the old part of the city was
small enough to see on foot. I found the car in the field and drove
out of Boone Hall plantation the back way, through the pecan groves,
initially with my shirtsleeves over my hands because the steering
wheel was so hot. I had the afternoon before I needed to hand over
the car and with what was left of the day, I thought I'd take a look at
Fort Moultrie, site of one of the first decisive home victories in the
American War of Independence, located at the entrance to Charleston's bay. From the plantation I drove down to the Isle of Palms
along a straight concrete highway that rose up to cross a perpendicu-
lar waterway, itself as wide as an Interstate and humming with
motorcruisers. If the Italian city of Venice ever graduated to auto-
stradas, this is what I imagine it would look like, a subtropical aquatic
artery through a wilderness of reeds and slime.

The Isle of Palms was a resort island with smart wooden holiday
homes lining a long stretch of sandy beach on the seaward side.
Although the holiday season was drawing to a close, a good number
of people were still enjoying the sunshine and I stopped to buy a
pecan butter ice cream cornet from a busy café. The guy serving was
a middle-aged body builder who looked as if he had spent much of
his life on the beach and might one day sue a chemical company for
destroying the ozone layer and giving him skin cancer. He latched on
to my accent straight away and told me he had been in South
Kensington back in '79, 'loved it there', and had studied a little
Shakespeare up in Stratford.

Across the bridge on neighbouring Sullivan's Island, the houses looked more ramshackle, as if they were lived in permanently. At the southern end of the island, the road led to Fort Moultrie and stopped a few hundred yards beyond the car park. The fort was made of solid looking brick, sculpted into the flat topography by smooth grassy earthworks, but the original had been rather more rudimentary, constructed largely of sand and logs from local palmetto trees. In June 1776, when still only half-built, it was attacked by a British fleet but withstood twelve hours of bombardment to record a significant victory against the old mother country. The incident is immortalised in the state seal and flag, which bear representations of the palmetto tree, and in South Carolina's nickname, 'the Palmetto State'.

Today's visitor to Fort Moultrie can peruse the battlements without the need for a tour guide on what curators all over North America are pleased to call self-guided tours. This was fine by me, but a large official notice at the entrance warned against any of the unauthorised activities that you might think were the side-benefits of showing yourself around. The notice began with the command that 'Visitors will . . .' and proceeded to list a number of orders, like remaining on designated walkways, ending with the instruction: 'Have a safe and enjoyable visit. By order of the Post Commander.' This vaguely Stalinesque approach to the tourist industry put me in mind of the notices I had seen the previous day in Beaufort. South Carolinian officialdom obviously enjoyed throwing its weight around and they successfuly managed to make me feel like a criminal when I had to stray from the designated walkway to cross the grass to have a look at the narrow beach.

Standing on the granite boulders put there to protect the coastline, the gentle Atlantic breeze sweetened with a whiff of wild honeysuckle, I could look across the waters towards Charleston. More than 60 years before the palmetto fort was built, this was where the notorious English pirate Blackbeard held the entire harbour to ransom for a fortnight, cleaning out all ships coming and going from the city. Just a mile away, on its own little islet, sat another fort, Fort Sumter, where the first shots were fired in the War Between the States on 12 April 1861.

With the sun preparing to set I returned to my car, cleaned the salt spray from my glasses, and drove back on to the mainland to join the Interstate that took me to Charleston airport. I had decided that whenever I hired a car on this trip I would drive from airport to airport, both because I thought there would always be car rental agencies at airports and also because I figured that airports would be well-signposted and therefore easy to find. It was a sort of personalised fly-drive without the fly. Having deposited my hire car, I used the illuminated board of hotel advertisements and free telephone by the luggage claim to find a place to stay that was significantly cheaper than the bed and breakfast I had booked for the following nights in downtown Charleston. This was a Super 8 Motel, where they wanted you to pay up front, located on a grotty piece of Interstate.

I ate dinner next door in a 24-hour Huddle House. An elderly man in a heavy check shirt sat sipping coffee and smoking a cigarette at one of the tables, exchanging small talk with a very large waitress named Sarah who waddled up and down behind the counter. She welcomed me with a broad smile and called me Honey. 'What can I get you Honey?' she said. I told her I was hungry as I took up my position on a stool in front of the counter, and she handed me a menu. 'There you go, Honey, have a look at that.'

As I was perusing the Huddle House selection another old-timer walked slowly in through the glass door.

'Sidney! How you doin'?' called the man in the heavy check shirt.

'Not so good,' replied Sidney as he slumped down into a seat opposite the check shirt man. 'I got this lung thing.' The waitress moved out from behind the counter, a glass coffee pot in one hand, a china cup in the other. She reached the table and poured Sidney some coffee then offered the man in the check shirt some more. 'You want a top-up Henry?' Henry said he did.

'So you going to the hospital, help you breathe or something?' Henry said to Sidney.

'Yeah,' replied Sidney, tearing open a sachet of sweetener and depositing its contents into his cup.

'They think you got cancer or something?'

'I reckon so, but they ain't told me yet.'

'Sidney, there's nothing wrong with your lungs. You just need to eat better. Have a steak.'

The waitress was back behind the counter now and I put in my order for a burger, having not had a burger for a while. She filled a large polystyrene cup with ice for me and trickled some Dr Pepper in to flavour it. Henry and Sidney were busy discussing doctors and whether or not they were any good. I looked around the diner and noted that it was unusual in that it had ashtrays on every table. When my burger arrived it wasn't very appetising on account of its decidedly synthetic taste, but I'd only eaten that hotdog for lunch and I was hungry, so I didn't care.

The waitress was over with Henry and Sidney again and she had produced a photograph of her eleven year old son, possibly as a deliberate diversion from the depressing talk of breathing ailments. The old-timers were declaring what a fine boy he looked. He was interested in football and he listened to a lot of music, his mother was telling them. Sidney said he used to enjoy football, but he only watched it on TV since he had developed his lung problem.

When I paid for my dinner, the waitress showed me the photograph of her son. The boy was blond like his mother and he had a stringy little ponytail. 'He's a good boy,' the waitress told me. As I tucked a dollar bill under the salt cellar for a tip, she came out with the inevitable enquiry into my origins. When I told her, she followed up by asking if I was in the military. Puzzled, I said no. 'Then what you doin' in North Charleston Honey?' she enquired, as if this was an unusual place for an Englishman to be in if he wasn't in the armed forces.

'I've come to look around,' I told her.

She nodded. 'In Charleston,' she said.

'That's right.'

Henry was brow-beating poor Sidney as I left. 'It's not smoking,' he told him. 'Look at me, I smoke sixty a day, but I don't inhale. All you do is you inhale before you take a puff, see . . .' and Henry demonstrated his approved method for smoking without the risk of lung cancer.

The distinction between Charleston and North Charleston is a significant one. They are in fact two separate cities. Charleston, at the bloated south end of a peninsula, is all about prosperity, aristocracy and tourism. It is the Charleston of graceful architecture and Southern charm most outsiders have heard of. North Charleston, at the wider northern neck of the peninsula, is a poor, blue-collar military-industrial complex. It is the Charleston you've probably heard about if you're in the military.

Charleston was heading downhill rapidly at the beginning of the century, degenerating along with the plantation life that had spawned it, when the navy came along and saved the day. This was the beginning of a process that was to turn the city into the biggest fortress in North America. Before President Clinton began his post Cold War cut-backs to the military, the Charleston peninsula had a naval base, an air force base, a naval shipyard, a Polaris missile maintenance centre, a ballistic missile submarine training centre, an army depot, a mine-warfare centre, a naval hospital, a naval supply centre and weapons station, a marine air station, a marine recruiting depot and training centre, a Coast Guard station, and the head-quarters of the Sixth Naval District. Most of these were in North Charleston.

It is no accident that most of the armed forces personnel you hear being interviewed on television whenever the USA sets forth on a military adventure have Southern accents. Southerners have a long tradition of joining the military and the federal government has built military bases all over the South to encourage them. High unemployment, a keen sense of duty, machismo and a predisposition to violence have all been put forward to explain why Southerners flock to fight for their country. Whatever the reason, a uniformed soldier walking the streets in the South is likely to be a figure of some respect, while his counterpart in the West and Northeast is more likely to attract a catcall.

Charleston actually led the way in establishing a military tradition by building a military college back in the 1840s, way before the arrival of the military-industrial complex to the north. The Citadel has long had a reputation for being Southern in a hard and cruel way. A president of the college who resigned in 1980 over its inhumane practices was quoted in a national magazine as saying it was 'locked in pre-Civil War concrete'. But like other bastions of strict Southern values, the Citadel has recently fallen foul of Yankee federal 'interference', as traditional hardliners see it. For 150 years, cadets could be seen scrubbing the Citadel's famous red and white chequerboard parade ground with toothbrushes, a time-honoured ritual that helps to turn them into men. Now that the toothbrushes can be wielded by female cadets, the aim of this rite must be somewhat confusing. This was just the sort of change that the South could do without, according to an Alabama college professor who made headline news in the *Post and Courier* on the day of my arrival in Charleston.

I had taken the Super 8 Motel shuttle bus into town, saying I wanted to go to the airport when I asked at the counter, but telling Bill the driver my real destination when I was safely aboard. Bill didn't mind, he'd take me anywhere he said.

We soared over the cityscape of North Charleston on the grimy Interstate which returned us to street level half-way down the peninsula. Bill told me that North Charleston was facing difficult times now that the military was being downsized. It was the major employer by a long way. He had been in the air force, and had taken early retirement. To me he didn't look fifty.

'It was a good life, they look after you, but I was glad to get out. I hated flying.' He had been a ground engineer, he told me. Going up in those planes always made him sick. Now that he was a civilian, driving the shuttle bus was an occasional job.

'Something to supplement your pension?'

'They don't pay me nothing,' he replied. 'It's tips only.'

Having successfully negotiated Charleston's one-way system, Bill dropped me at my bed and breakfast on the northern edge of downtown. I tipped him overgenerously and he told me to keep to the south of the bed and breakfast. 'Don't go that way,' he said pointing north. From what I'd seen, the only difference between the wooden antebellum houses in that direction and those around us was their need for a coat of paint and the presence of two or three mail boxes outside each, indicating multiple occupancy. But Bill was adamant in his advice. 'It's a black area,' he said.

Inside the bed and breakfast, the two middle-aged ladies who ran the place were expecting me. They showed me around the communal areas, explaining the house rules in an almost flirtatious tone. Breakfast was served on the piazza, and tea in the parlour. The large leather-bound books laid out on that table were for comments, one for accommodation, another for restaurants. There were lacy curtains at the windows and sherry decanters on the sideboard. Wall clocks were ticking at me from every direction and muted classical music was emanating from the fireplace. Carnations and roses sprouted from every available vase space. The wood floors were so highly polished you could see your shoes in them, which in my case made me regret my choice of suede desert boots became they were impossible to clean.

'Before I show you to your room, could you give us some assistance?' asked one of the ladies.

'We're sorry to put you to work as soon as you arrive, but we need a man,' her accomplice added with what looked like a twinkle in her eye. I followed the ladies into the kitchen and was thankful when all I had to do was reach for a heavy cast iron pan in one of the top cupboards.

It was at tea time that I got to look at the *Post and Courier*, the South's oldest daily newspaper so it said on the front. The front page headline read 'SMI: Southern, military and politically incorrect'. The story was about a professor from Alabama who intended to recapture the golden days of the Southern past, when Southerners revered their heritage and reared their young men in a Confederate military tradition. The guy was leader of an organisation called the League of the South which, according to the report, was a secessionist movement whose goal was the creation of a new Southern nation.

A significant step along this road would be the establishment of the SMI, a Southern Military Institute to turn out graduates programmed to aid the nation's recovery from a deadly slip into moral decay. I made myself a cup of Assam tea with a tea bag and hot water for a change, piled a few cakes on to a plate, and read on.

The call for the SMI was a direct response to the federal government order that the Citadel and the similarly traditional Virginia Military Institute open their doors to women. With these bastions going soft, there was an urgent need for a new institution based on the old values. The price tag, just $50m, was actively being sought, and the League of the South was on the look-out for a campus to spend it on.

The SMI could be operational by 1999, the report suggested. It would provide an education rooted in strong Christian values and the community traditions associated with the South. Graduates would be taught more about Confederate heroes like 'Stonewall' Jackson and General Robert E Lee than cadets at any current military college. They would be educated in the tradition of gentleman officers, incorporating formal military dances with girls wearing pretty dresses. These graduates would be proper Southern gentlemen, not wimps kowtowing to the feminists. Their training would provide them with inoculation for life against the virus of political correctness.

The report broadened to take in the Alabama professor's views on things Southern in general. It was a unique place, he thought, with traditions of community and family conversation and story-telling. 'We are a civilisation apart,' he was quoted as saying, 'and I think there are things down here that should be protected.' This was followed by some generally negative comments about Yankees and other groups who were bent on committing cultural genocide against the South. To emphasise these points, the report stressed that the League of the South drew its authority from God and a cultural epicentre that was European. It didn't pander to ethnic diversity apparently; its communities would be free to choose whether or not to integrate blacks. The organisation's soul was the Southern Confederacy.

What struck me most about the story was not so much the existence of groups such as the League of the South (I had been in the region long enough to have come to accept their presence as part of the Lost Cause myth), but that they were taken seriously enough to warrant a front-page story in a Charleston daily newspaper. The tone of the report was generally negative. It included a quote from the Southeast regional director of the Anti-Deformation League comparing the League of the South to the Ku Klux Klan. But at the same time, there appeared to be a distinct likelihood that the $50m would be raised and that the Southern Military Institute would come into being. The Lost Cause, it seemed, was alive and well and living in Alabama.

It was also alive and kicking on the Internet. On my return home, I looked up the League of the South. My first dozen or so hits con-

cerned baseball, before I found an announcement that the League of
the South was the organisation's new name. It had originally been
called the Southern League, but this had been changed after the
Southern League of Professional Baseball clubs had threatened a
lawsuit. Antebellum politics and minor-league baseball were not a
happy mix. When I finally hit on the League of the South's web site,
I found myself at the heart of something called Dixienet, a web of
Confederate-leaning information, opinions and campaigns. There
were articles about palaeo-federalists and the Southern conservative
tradition, announcements of Confederate art exhibitions and advertisements by pro-Southern businesses, along with disclaimers about
alliances with white supremacist groups. A page of controversial issues
included a campaign urging all patriotic Southerners to boycott
Holiday Inns. 'There was a war,' the piece began. 'The South was
invaded. Homes were burned, property destroyed, people killed . . .'
and so it went on. The crux of the matter was that the current owners
of this originally Southern motel chain, a British company as it
happened, had started to remove state flags that included Confederate
symbols from its properties. The company had its headquarters in
Atlanta and the Georgian state flag included the Confederate battle
standard. Here was a foreign company, deriving revenue from Southerners while defying their traditions and insulting the memory of
their honoured dead. The League of the South steadfastly refused to
embrace the politically correct anti-Southern bigotry that sought to
define their national colours as a symbol of oppression or racial
hatred. Don't patronise Holiday Inns was the message, drive all night
or sleep in the car if need be. Supporters of the League of the South's
boycott would 'demonstrate true Southern grit by eating peanut
butter sandwiches, if necessary, rather than partaking of Holiday Inn's
Sunday buffet'.

Although I laughed when I read this, I shouldn't have done. The
League of the South's web site opened with a quotation from Jefferson
Davis, the first and only president of the Confederate States of
America. The quotation read, 'A question settled by violence, or in
disregard of law, must remain unsettled for ever.' These guys were
deadly serious.

10

Gullah Gates and Chickens

I spent a pleasant few days nosing around Charleston on a bicycle lent to me by the ladies who ran my bed and breakfast. The bike had a single gear and a braking system that was engaged by pedalling backwards. This meant that I could not cycle very fast, but the leisurely pace was appropriate in such an unhurried city. Charleston was packed full of wooden houses painted in pastel colours, all turned sideways to the street, so riding slowly enabled me to look at them properly. Some were so-called single houses, one room wide and two rooms deep, with an extended porch overlooking the garden or yard (or I should say an extended piazza since that's what they like to call them in Charleston). Other houses were more mansion-sized, but still with what appeared to be just two or three long rooms downstairs. Significant portions of the day must have been taken up just moving about inside these larger properties. You'd have had to leave the kitchen around eight in the morning to arrive in the dining room by lunchtime.

The majesty of the antebellum architecture reached its zenith along the Battery, a seafront street at the very tip of the peninsula that looked out towards Forts Sumter and Moultrie. Apparently, when the shelling of Fort Sumter began in April 1861, the grandees of Charleston lined the Battery seawall to watch the 40-hour fireworks display. The day I was there a few fishermen were dredging the murky waters for shrimp using small hand-held nets like those I had seen at Beaufort. Small cannon still lined the park that separated one stretch of houses from the water and today the cannon provide durable climbing frames for children to clamber over. Every now and then a horse and buggy would clip-clop along the road and stop while its driver explained the historic significance of the view to his passengers. At the apex of the Battery, in one corner of the park, stood a monument to the Confederate soldiers who defended Fort Sumter throughout the Civil War. It was unusual for such memorials in that it consisted of a woman in a long robe watching over a warrior with a shield on his arm and a fig leaf on his dignity. The inscription around the red granite pedestal read, 'Count them happy who for their faith and their courage endured a great fight.'

Just inland from the Battery was a house where George Washington once stayed and next door to this was Cabbage Row, inspiration for Catfish Row in the novel and eventual opera *Porgy and Bess*. I passed churches galore before I found the old slave market that had once been a museum but was now shut up. On the arch above the blue entrance doors, peeling letters said 'Old Slave Mart Museum' which struck me as peculiar because I had thought that mart was a modern word. To me it conjured up visions of Southern belles pushing supermarket trolleys down neon-lit alleys in their hoop-skirted dresses, pausing to choose a new servant from piles of Negroes stacked up on the shelves.

I spent an afternoon in the Charleston Museum, the oldest such establishment in North America they claimed, and only on the third day did I venture into the Charleston Visitors Center. Like all the other visitors' centres I had entered, none of which appeared to have heard about apostrophes, this one was huge and newly appointed. It offered banks of brochures and designer nooks and crannies containing helpful interactive video screens. A small army of pleasant employees was positioned behind chest-high counters, eager to answer your queries, offer you a map or book you a motel. They too had video screens at their fingertips to aid them in their task. The raison d'être of the place was to tell you how to visit Charleston. I had been getting along quite happily on my own, but there was one museum I had read about in a short newspaper column back home in England that I thought might make for an unusual diversion.

The newspaper story had been an ironic one, concerning the loss to Europe at auction of a bronze medal, The Blood-sucker on the Rhine. The medal was a work of political satire, made in 1923 to lampoon Germany's reparation terms at Versailles. It had been bought by the Charleston Museum of Leeching and Blood Letting. As a spokesman for the auction house had explained to the newspaper reporter, the Americans had probably taken the title a little too literally.

I joined the queue for the information counter.

'Good morning Sir, and how are you today?' came the salutation from behind the counter when my turn came. I was unfazed by this type of greeting by now and replied that I was fine and immediately followed this announcement with an enquiry after the young woman's well-being. She replied that she too was in a robust state of health that morning, so with the preliminaries safely out of the way, I asked her where I might find the Museum of Leeching and Blood Letting.

Her immediate reaction was to ask me to repeat the museum name. When I did so she calmly put her hand under the counter and I thought she was reaching for one of those panic buttons like they have in banks. Just as I braced myself for shrill alarm bells and the arrival on the scene of heavily armed representatives of the Charleston security services, her hand returned holding a large book like a telephone directory. It turned out to be the master list of Charleston attractions. It was peculiar, I thought, that she still used such an ancient piece of technology when she was surrounded on all sides by video screens. She opened the book at the back and ran her finger down the B column of the index. 'It's not an attraction I'm familiar with,' she said as she did so. She turned to the L column. There was nothing there either. She asked one of her colleagues, but she too denied all knowledge of the Museum of Leeching and Blood Letting.

'I'm sorry Sir,' she said, 'perhaps I can interest you in one of our tours of the city instead?' She was such a consummate professional that I asked what was on offer. Needless to say, there was a bewildering array. There were carriage tours and motor tours, walking tours and barrier island eco-tours, charter tours and boat tours. I could see Civil War Charleston, pioneer settlers' Charleston, black Charleston, or 'Doin' the Charleston' Charleston. I could tour historic houses, historic forts, historic ships, historic plantations, gardens and parks. In fact I could tour just about anything except the Museum of Leeching and Blood Letting.

I stood there with my mouth open, rooted to the spot. I should have known this would happen. You have to limit your encounters with these places to specific requests otherwise you'll find yourself spending your entire vacation wandering around the Visitors Center marvelling at all the possibilities but never actually seeing anything real. I caught sight of a brochure in a small cardboard stand on the counter beside the young woman. It said 'Gullah Tours – Afro-American sites and history'. I picked it up. 'What's this one?' I asked. Beneath the words 'sites and history' it said 'Uh gwoi onrabble muh mout' bout dees tings.' It was the first brochure I'd seen in this country that wasn't in English, and it wasn't immediately obvious to me what language it was in.

'Gullah, it's a local black American language,' the young woman told me. I booked the tour.

And so it was that I found myself on a Gullah tour of Charleston. In fact, Gullah hadn't been a complete surprise to me, because the woman who had shown me round the African village of Oyotunji had mentioned it. The language, a pidgin blend of English and various African tongues, evolved among the slaves brought over to work the plantations. It enabled Africans of different nationalities to communicate with each other and with the plantation owners. Gullah was preserved after the end of slavery by the inhabitants of the South Carolina Sea Islands, since they were largely isolated from the dominant white culture on the mainland. Today it is still spoken by African Americans living in coastal South Carolina, but for how much longer remains to be seen. With increasing resort development and the harmonising influence of modern telecommunications, the future of this black Southern cultural quirk is unlikely to be rosy.

One way of preserving Gullah in some form is through the tourist industry, and Alphonso Brown was doing his best to make a go of it. He had a small tour bus that about half a dozen sightseers had booked to ride that afternoon. Alphonso gave us a few Gullah words and phrases to warm up with but then appeared to forget the linguistic angle to most of what he showed us. His tour focused on the black side of Charleston, with bus-window views of the slave mart, a couple of black cemeteries, and a visit to Cabbage Row accompanied by the lowdown on Porgy. (The real-life character on whom he was based was a small-time businessman who worked the streets on a wheeled soapbox pulled by a smelly goat. He was also a scoundrel who killed three or four people, apparently, and eventually died while under the influence of witchcraft.) But the real thread that ran throughout the tour was a local black craftsman named Simmons who specialised in wrought-iron gates.

Mr Simmons appeared to have made the gates to most of the houses in Charleston, and wherever we went Alphonso Brown would point out another one on passing, all the while slowly adding a bit more bibliographic information concerning Mr Simmons. All this gate stuff became a bit tedious after a while, but I sat up with a start when we passed a large house on the east side of town, gated by one of Mr Simmons' creations, which Alphonso Brown declared was now a leech museum. I strained to see the name of the street and quickly scribbled it down in my notebook with a view to revisiting the spot later.

The Gullah tour ended with a visit to none other than the home of Mr Simmons. It was in a mildly derelict black part of town, near America Street, which Alphonso Brown informed us was the only America Street in America. Mr Simmons was an endearing old gentleman who seemed not unnaturally bewildered by the sudden arrival of eight complete strangers in his small front room. His walls were lined with certificates he had won for his ironwork and photographs of him receiving them from various artistic dignitaries. Among the certificates and photographs was a small piece of paper with a motto on. It was an appropriate maxim for Mr Simmons' life: 'If you want your prayers answered get off your knees and hustle.'

The following day, I got on my bike and found the house containing the leech museum. It was shut and there was no indication as to when it might open. I returned a couple more times during my stay in Charleston, but never managed to cross its threshold.

I enjoyed Charleston. It was relaxed and its traffic was gentlemanly, but I didn't take to the city quite as much as I had to Savannah. Visually, it was the foliage that gave Georgia's first coastal city the edge in my book: all that Spanish moss draped over the tree branches, like debris deposited by a storm of fibre glass wool. Charleston also seemed to me to be a bit haughty, while Savannah was more of a party animal. Other than my brush with Mr Simmons' contemporary wrought-ironwork on the Gullah tour, Charleston's offerings dwelt heavily on her historic past. Savannah had its historic attractions too, of course, but the city was not above cashing in on its more contemporary fame as well. The park bench used in the Hollywood blockbuster *Forrest Gump* had pride of place in the city museum, and every other Savannah shop window advertised some form of association with what was known locally simply as 'the Book' (*Midnight in the Garden of Good and Evil*, a contemporary, slightly wild story set in the city).

Everywhere in Charleston, by contrast, seemed to be a bit uptight and backward-looking. It was the sort of place where the law decreed that bars only sold spirits in miniature bottles, and where a municipally produced handbook suggested that short shorts and tank tops, while suitable attire for the beach, were not appropriate for in-town shopping and dining. All in all, it wasn't surprising that my bed and breakfast offered free sherry and decorative pillow shams. (I admit to not actually knowing what the word meant when I first encountered it in Charleston, but I understood when a small notice in my bedroom asked me not to sleep on them. My real pillows were in the cupboard.)

However, I did encounter a more down-to-earth side of the city, the day before I left, when I visited a barber to get my hair cut. The salon was located in the northern fringes of Charleston, in the area that Bill, the driver of the Super 8 Motel shuttle bus, had advised me against visiting. Inside, there were two chairs, positioned behind a counter, but just one barber. He was an ancient man, with a crewcut and glasses, who looked like he might remember the War Between the States personally. His skin was dotted with liver spots and had a translucent quality that made me think if you looked closely enough you'd be able to see his bones through it. His clothes were too big for him, as if his body had shrunk significantly since he had put them on that morning. His neck looked like he had borrowed it from a tortoise. Not surprisingly, he was also very hard of hearing.

'What can I do for you today Sir?' he asked when I had settled down in the chair. I told him I'd like a trim. 'Come in on a whim? Well that's as good a reason as any. How would you like your hair cut?'

'Just a little off all over,' I shouted.

He picked up an electric trimmer, and for one awful moment I thought that he was simply going to shave my head, but then he produced a comb from his top pocket and proceeded gently to skim the ends of my hair that he raised from above my ear with his comb.

'Cooler today,' he said to get the conversation going.

'Yes,' I replied, regaining my composure.

In my experience there are two basic types of barber, both of whom will talk at you non-stop while they snip away. Type one is opinionated and controversial at times, but type two specialises in noncommittal small-talk. Innumerable years of chatting to Charleston customers had taught this barber to keep any strong opinions he might have to himself. I had thought I might quiz him on some of the impressions I'd gained in and around the city, but his hearing impediment made this difficult. It also wasn't helped by the fact that there was a television set on a far ledge with its volume turned up very loud. Nevertheless, I tried. After he had completed his report on the local weather conditions, I turned the conversation to the South. I asked him whether he was a Southerner.

'My hometown's in New England,' he told me, 'bin here since '47, too late to go home now.'

'You like it here?'

'I go back occasionally, but I guess I'm here for good now.'

'So you must like it here?' I asked a bit louder.

'Wouldn't say I liked it; wouldn't say I disliked it. It's just where I live.' He shuffled around to tackle the hair over my right ear.

'What about Southern hospitality? Aren't people supposed to be more friendly down here?' I asked.

'What's that you say?' He craned his tortoise neck down towards me and I repeated the question.

'Hospitality, yeah that's what they say.' He obviously wasn't going to pass judgement on that one either, but he had cottoned on to the topic. 'Would you believe there are still some ol'timers here still sore at the Civil War?' The question came with a little throat gurgle that passed as a chuckle. 'Hell, there's bin lots of wars since then.' He flicked his comb to jettison the hair that had built up on it. 'I don't take much notice of that stuff.' He gurgled again. 'If you did, it'd be a long day.'

'It certainly would.'

'What surprises me is they got nothing better to think about.'

'Some people have long memories,' I said.

'No,' he said emphatically, and for an instant I thought he was going to become animated on the subject. But he had gone off on a tangent. 'I saw one in Charleston once,' he continued. 'He'd have to be a hundred years old if he was alive today.'

He had lost me. 'You saw one what once?' I called.

'An Indian,' he replied, 'he was walking down Broad Street.'

'I see.'

'Plenty of 'em out West though. They run casinos now. Guess they weren't as dumb as we thought they were. They catch on quick.'

'I guess so.'

'They have their own language, you know. But nobody cares much except the white folks.'

'I guess not.'

'Wouldn't work, though, if they tried to run their casinos in their own language.'

'No.'

'No one'd understand 'em. Except other Indians. And they got no money.'

'No, I suppose not.' He was round the back of my head now, still working without scissors. I asked him what Charleston people thought of the Citadel admitting women. He caught the question on the second time of asking.

'The Citadel? It's a military college, up there on Fishburne. You a military man?'

'No, no, I just read about it. I understand they're admitting women now,' I shouted.

'You know it's a funny thing,' he said, 'but they're fixin' to admit women to that place. Got along for a hundred fifty years without women, why they think they need 'em now?'

'I bet it's upset the traditionalists?'

'Yes, I guess so. You know a lot of ol'timers are pretty sore 'bout that.' He shuffled back to admire his work, then moved forward to deal with the top of my head.

'I don't take much notice of that stuff,' he went on, 'but they done got all them fancy weapons and tanks and stuff, smart missles and such like, what they want women for?' Another chuckle gurgled up. 'You seen them smart missles? I ain't seen 'em myself, but I seen pictures on the TV. They're somethin'. Fly up a street, take a left at the stop sign, knock on the door and go right on in. Blow the place sky-high.'

'There seem to be lots of military bases in the South,' I hollered, 'do Southerners like fighting?' He paused, slowly cocking his head to think. 'You know I never thought of it like that before.' He returned to his trimming, still pondering what I had said, and then proceeded to talk about chickens.

He paused to admire his handiwork again. 'Don't suppose no chicken ever cared who ate him, dumber than a box o' rocks your average chicken.' He fulminated about the historical lack of poultry at some length before effortlessly turning to the topic of homosexuality, a subject on which his opinions were more definite.

'*Gay* they call 'em. Hell, I can be gay without being no homosexual.' He pronounced the word in a long, drawn out fashion, getting maximum leverage out of its five syllables: 'ho-mo-sex-you-al'. 'I don't know why they do it, something wrong with them I guess.'

'You think they might be genetically deformed?' I called.

'No, they don't wear no uniform. Hell, that's the ugly part of it. Most of 'em dress like normal folks.'

I was just pondering whether or not to enlighten the man about the common association made in my country between homosexuals and members of his profession, when we were interrupted by a loud howling noise that emanated from the television set. The set was positioned out of my line of vision, so I couldn't see what was going on.

'What's that?' I shouted when the shriek had subsided.

'Them's hog-callers.'

'What's a hog-caller?' I asked.

'Yes, I guess so.'

I asked him again, and he still didn't catch the question, but he leaned down towards me, catching it on its third time of asking. 'What's a hog-caller?' I bellowed.

'Oh! What's a hog-caller? Someone who calls hogs.'

I had asked for that.

'Well that's you all done,' he said.

As I paid the man, another similarly ancient barber appeared from the rear of the premises. On reaching the door, I noticed my shoelace was undone and I knelt to retie it. As I did so, I overheard my barber say to his colleague, 'Interesting fellah; military man, I reckon. Probably in the catering corps. Talked a lot about chickens.'

11

Tobacco Country

It wasn't until I reached North Carolina that I got a more satisfactory answer to my question about hog-callers. I was back to using the train which meant catching a taxi to the railway station very early in the morning, before it was light. I was glad to be leaving Charleston, not because I disliked the place but because I had been forced to move to another bed and breakfast for my final night, and the woman who ran the new place turned out to be dangerous to my health. She was a nice woman in all respects except one: her voice. It sounded like a hacksaw blade making heavy weather of cutting through a metal pipe. She also insisted on calling me Nickelis, which annoyed me. I was convinced that she would damage my hearing if I stayed any longer.

I don't think it can have been just me who found her voice unbearable because she had learned to communicate largely via sticky labels. My bedroom was plastered with them. They covered every eventuality, from using the telephone to descriptions of the interesting objects that hung on the wall. But I got my come-uppance for being so intolerant of the poor woman when I opened my door to leave at 5.30 the next morning and found a plastic bag containing a packed breakfast beside the lintel. All the contents were summarised in great detail for me on sticky labels.

Suitably chastened, I climbed into the taxi that sped away down the narrow Charleston backstreets before joining the freeway to the station. We passed an appropriate precursor of my next destination, a big tobacco-growing state, in the form of an advertising hoarding for Virginia Slims cigarettes. It showed a picture of a glamorous woman looking sexy behind a wisp of smoke beside a slogan that read 'It's a woman's thing', and I wondered whether they had developed a filter that was lipstick resistant.

I bought my ticket and joined the train, along with a motley collection of other travellers, at 'boarding zone nine'. The sun was beginning to rise as the Silver Palm Atlantic Coast Service pulled out of Charleston and the steward came on over the tannoy with the by now familiar warning about the train's constant movement. He followed this with an announcement concerning the availability of breakfast. It was made with those curiously placed emphases beloved of public announcers: 'We *are* making our second call for breakfast in the dining car. Once again, we *will* be serving breakfast at this time in the dining car.'

What is it about these announcers? Why do they always put the emphasis on the wrong words? And where did the phrase 'at this time' come from? What's wrong with 'now'? I can only assume that Amtrak sends its employees on special training courses to learn how to speak like this. Such courses are probably run by the public relations equivalent of management consultants, and are no doubt designed to rethink Amtrak's information distribution strategy and implementation processes.

Maybe it was because it was so early in the morning, but even at the best of times this kind of thing really annoys me. Many of these forms of embellishment to the English language have found their way across the Atlantic, having originated in the US of A. Their roots are unlikely to be found in the South, however, and traditional Southerners tend to get as het up about them as I do. It was all part of the cultural homogenisation of the country driven by people from places like New York and California. Indeed, it was one of the eye-opening aspects of this trip for me to find Southerners talking about Yankees committing cultural genocide against their own people. Before this saunter through the South, I had only thought of such things happening outside the USA.

Of course there are some linguistic conventions and code-words that are just as common in the South as elsewhere in the country, and I was reminded of one of them after finishing my sticky-labelled breakfast. I made my way to the end of my carriage, pushed open the toilet door, and walked straight in on a middle-aged lady midway through her own morning ablutions. I'm not sure which of us was the more surprised but I shut the door immediately and suggested she lock it. Later, it occurred to me that leaving the door unsecured while sitting on the toilet may have been a Silver Palm Atlantic Coast ritual, because to my absolute horror, it happened again a few hours later. Thankfully, it was a different woman. If it'd been the same one she would probably have had me thrown in jail on a charge of gross indecency.

Assuming, of course, she could have brought herself to explain the situation to the Silver Palm staff. Such an explanation would have been severely hindered by the average American's reluctance to call a toilet a toilet. They employ a phenomenal rage of euphemisms for this convenience instead. These include way station, washroom, bathroom, restroom, powder room, little girls' (or boys') room, facility, commode and john. My own favourite is comfort station. And of course they can't bring themselves to speak of toilet paper either, hence bathroom tissue. One woman I spoke to in North Carolina suggested that the whole toilet thing started among the gentry of the antebellum South. These characters couldn't refer to such things directly because it was just too indelicate a subject for a society in which women weren't supposed to have any orifices below the neck.

The plethora of terms available can be confusing even for Americans. Someone told me a legendary story about a Southern lady who wanted to know whether there was a comfort station at the campsite where she was proposing to spend her vacation. She decided to write to the management to find out. After much deliberation, she settled on the abbreviation BC, which in her mind stood for bathroom commode. Unfortunately for her, the manager didn't see her euphemism in quite the same light. After some thought, he decided that the object of the lady's enquiry was a Baptist church, and he wrote back saying that the nearest BC was located ten miles down the road. It had seating for 150 people, he told her, and very good acoustics. He himself hadn't been for some years, but he would be happy to accompany her when she made her visit.

By the time I had calmed down from my own unexpected BC incident, the train was approaching Florence. We passed through a few distinctly grotty parts of town, that couldn't have looked less like its Italian counterpart, before pulling up at Florence Amtrak station. As with many of the other Amtrak stations I had come across on this trip, this one looked like it was midway between the outskirts of town and the outskirts of nowhere at all. In fact, if we hadn't just passed through what I assumed were bits of Florence, I'd have said that it was closer to nowhere at all. It was desolate-looking, with weeds on the platform and great swathes of kudzu enveloping everything else, which wasn't much other than a stretch of fence and a few telegraph poles. As we pulled out of the station, I saw a black man hoeing a field by hand.

A few miles further on, I caught sight of my first field of cotton near a place called Dillon, and then we left South Carolina and entered its northern namesake. Large portions were occupied by swamp, in some places decorated with white water lilies floating round tree stumps. Such areas were reminders of the sort of terrain that the first settlers from Europe had encountered. Wetlands had dominated this part of the South, and not for the first time did I marvel at the sheer pigheadedness of these people in staying put and setting up their plantations and farms. Not only were these swamps distinctly inconvenient when it came to farming (unless it was for rice), but they were also ideal breeding grounds for malaria. Until the recognition of mosquitoes as transmitters of the disease, malaria was thought to be quite literally caused by bad air, and the poisonous vapours, or miasmas, came from the swamps. Swamp air was particularly bad after dark and most dangerous during the summer, hence no one slept near the fields at night if they could help it and rich plantation-owners retired to the cities and towns during the summer months. Most of the fine old houses in Beaufort had been built as summer retreats from the miasmas, their porches facing the cooling sea breeze that was thought to disperse the deadly odours.

When the railroads were laid in this part of the South in the nineteenth century, passengers who gazed over the scene I now surveyed were struck with extreme anxiety at the thought that the train might break down and leave them exposed to the nocturnal miasmas. The necessary role of the *Anopheles* mosquito was only identified at the end of the nineteenth century, and it was not until after World War II that malaria was finally eradicated from the Carolina Coastal Plains, as more wetlands were drained and DDT became available.

After some more swamp and a few patches of kudzu clinging to the ubiquitous pine trees, fields of small brown maize plants were punctuated by the occasional patch of former forest. These looked like violent crime scenes, where nature had been raped with heavy, caterpillar-tracked machinery. The fruits of these endeavours were stacked at nearby lumber yards, where huge piles of logs were being sprayed with water to keep them cool in the smouldering heat. The small towns we passed through became signposted by their huge water towers, rounded metal containers with the town's name written on them, supported on stilts like flying saucers hovering above their prey. It was as if the swamps that had been drained had been packaged in shiny aluminium and hoisted up on to pylons to get them out of the way.

The swamps made way for tobacco, fields of which had also started to flick by, their knee-high plants marching across the landscape with their big leaves hanging in the still air. Sometimes an old wooden barn would be sat among the green rows looking derelict and outdated next to the new metal bulk barns that have taken over from the traditional curing process. North Carolina is the tobacco capital of the USA. More is produced here than anywhere else and it is the state's leading agricultural product. Tobacco is also the only agricultural crop in the USA to be sold by auction, and the day after I arrived at my destination, a small city called Greenville not far from the coast, I found myself attending one.

The guy I was staying with, an old friend named Michael, had suggested it as something that might be interesting to me. He had lived for several years in Greenville, where he taught at the university, and he had always thought it would be worth a look, but had never quite made it before. We found one thanks to a lucky encounter. We drove to a Waffle House for breakfast and ate our waffles at the counter. As luck would have it, the man sitting next to us was in the business and he told us where to try. He said he was originally from Rhodesia. 'It's nice to talk to people who know where that is,' he told us. 'When I first arrived here, people would ask me if I came by Greyhound.'

The cavernous warehouse was full of cured tobacco leaves piled in mounds and arranged in lines that looked like knee-high plough furrows. The piles of yellow leaves resembled thick heaps of shammy-leathers that had been swept on to a piece of sacking and labelled with a dollar price. Strung up above the tobacco heaps was a large red banner with the words 'DO NOT LITTER! Keep tobacco clean' written in bold white lettering. A vaguely sweet smell pervaded the entire place.

In the far corner, a couple of men were making their way along the tobacco rows, grabbing handfuls of leaves and dropping them back, scribbling on pieces of card and flinging them on to the heaps. These were government inspectors I learned later. They checked each pile and gave it a guideline price-tag that hovered around $1.80 per pound. This would be the starting point for the cigarette company bidders when the auction started. A few other people were milling about not looking terribly busy. No one seemed to mind that we had just walked in off the street and started looking.

Over on one side of the warehouse, a round man with a red face was leaning against the wall flicking through the pages of *Farm Chronicle*. He was smoking a short fat cigar. Behind him, on the wall, was a laminated poster about tobacco taxes. 'Enough is enough' it declared. 'Tobacco produced for domestic use generates $20.50 per pound in excise taxes. Today, the tobacco sold at this warehouse will generate $2,244,032.00 in excise taxes.' The numerals had been written on in black felt-tip pen.

I asked the man if an auction was due to take place here today.

'Yeah, right soon,' he drawled. He flicked through the last few pages in the magazine and threw it on to the plastic chair beside him. 'Two sets of buyers in town right now,' he said slowly as he shifted his weight from the wall to stand on his two feet.

I pointed to the poster behind him. 'If that's the tax revenue, how much will this lot be sold for?' I asked him.

'About hundred fifty thousand.' I whistled. 'Acre of tobacco generates sixty-eight thousand tax dollars. A farmer's income from that acre is thirty-four to thirty-five hundred dollars.'

'What sort of tobacco is it?' asked Michael.

'Flue-cured.'

There was a short silence as the man looked us over and chewed a bit on his cigar. 'Are you a buyer?' I asked him.

'No. I'm a farmer.'

Below the 'Enough is enough' poster behind the farmer was another request to keep tobacco clean. It was a painting of a white man in a field bending down to pick a tobacco leaf by hand to add to the bundle stuffed beneath his other arm. It was a period piece. The man wore an open-necked shirt and brown fedora hat. In the background of the picture was a wooden curing barn like the derelict ones I had seen from the train window.

'I don't suppose you pick it like that any more?' I suggested to the farmer.

'No,' he said. 'We do a lot more with mechanical means than we did used to. When I first started, when I was a young boy, when my father he had about sixty acres tobacco and we used . . . we probably had forty head for his sixty acres. Now, we got the thing cut down to about five, and we usually got eighty acres, you know what I'm sayin'? We've got it cut right down.' His accent was broad and he was drawling one word into another. I could just about follow what he said, so I nodded.

Tobacco was one of the last field crops to be mechanised. Developing a machine for harvesting was especially difficult since identifying a ripe leaf required human judgement. Mechanical harvesters did not reach the market until the late 1960s. The tobacco plant ripens from the ground up so the machine comprises a blade that can be set to cut every leaf at a particular height. It will cut some leaves that are already overripe and others that are still green, but the saving on labour is worth it.

The farmer had turned to talk about seedlings. 'Everything's grown in greenhouses now, so that everything grown in the greenhouse allows you to plant more uniformly,' he told us. 'And quality, quality is probably still the same.' He paused. 'I mean, used to be, when I was a young boy, everything was in bundles. Used to hand-tie them bundles to tobacco sticks to cure 'em in the barn.' He gazed out beyond us as if somewhere in the warehouse was a vision of the old days, when he was a young boy. I wanted to think that he was sorry about the passing of those old days, that somehow much of the romance of tobacco had disappeared with the arrival of the machines and the bulk curing barns.

I asked him how many crops he produced a year. 'One,' he said.

'And what do you grow in the land after the tobacco crop?'

'Nothing. You use a rotate. We'd probably come back with wheat one year, corn next year. Whether it's corn, beans or what, you need a rotation.'

'So you grow tobacco on a plot every what, three years, four years?'

'Some farmers grow it every year,' he said, keeping us on our toes by appearing to contradict what he had just stated. 'How much tobacco you got, you're tryin' to utilise to a particular farm, you know what I'm saying?' I didn't really think either Michael or I had much idea about what he was saying, but we both nodded some more.

'But they got chemicals to offset, like I say, but some farmers don't use those chemicals if they got enough land. They'll rotate. Farmers that don't probably spend hundred fifty dollars more per acre put chemicals in it.'

'And labour?' Michael chipped in. 'You use a lot of migrant labour?'

'Yep,' he said, barely audibly.

'And where do they come from?' I asked after a short pause. He was looking over our shoulders, into the warehouse. 'Mexico,' he replied.

He brought his eyes back to look at us and I thought he wouldn't be saying a whole lot more on this topic. But he may just have been thinking, because he continued. 'Aaah . . . I'll say eighty per cent use migrant labour . . .' He was looking behind us again, then he broke off and started to move. 'We getting ready for sale now.'

I had envisaged the auction as being like a fine-art auction, with a man behind a pedestal, hammer in hand, who takes bids from the buyers on the floor. But a tobacco auction isn't like that. Our farmer lumbered over towards a group of men who had gathered in one of the aisles between the tobacco heaps. They were just ordinary-looking guys, middle-aged most of them, all of them white. The farmer stood in the aisle opposite them with some other guys, also pretty ordinary looking in their polo shirts. Some of them wore baseball caps with the names of agricultural companies above the rims. There were five men in each group. It became clear that one group was the farmers and the group in the aisle opposite them was the buyers.

Several of the men in both groups lit cigarettes and without any other apparent preamble, the oldest man in the farmers' group started a low-pitched rhythmic chant. It was fast, almost like a children's tongue-twister, and to me completely unintelligible. This was the auctioneer.

Slowly the two groups made their way down the aisles, the auctioneer chanting continuously. The buyers used subtle hand signals to make their bids, with fists and fingers, sometimes shouting a single number: 'Five' or 'Four.' Every now and again, one of the buyers picked up a handful of leaves from the top of a heap, or lifted a wodge of leaves to inspect the centre of the pile, remaining totally poker-faced throughout. I had absolutely no idea who had bought each pile, but the groups continued moving to the singsong chant, to be followed up at a respectable distance by a third group whose job it appeared to be to tag the purchased piles. There was a tagger for each buyer. They were all young women, some of them black, whose job it was to scribble a tag with their tobacco company logo on it (Camel, Winston, Philip Morris etc.) coloured according to grade.

Tobacco has been a key Southern crop since early English settlers caught the habit of smoking it from local Indians. But while the Indians smoked only for religious and medicinal purposes, the English became addicted. Although today government programmes impose strict controls on planted acreage, this just helps to maintain tobacco's value as an extremely profitable crop for farmers lucky enough to own an acreage 'allotment'. Michael told me that the size of a farm's tobacco allotment is the main determinant of its market value if a farmer decides to sell his property. With its limited scale and its long historical roots, the crop is symbolic of many things Southern, of the defining obsession of owning land and the self-sufficiency and fierce independence that came from it. While to Northerners, the word plant has long meant factory, in the South it still evokes the smell of the soil. The agrarian ideal was a Southern phenomenon even before there was a self-conscious South. It was Thomas Jefferson, from neighbouring Virginia, who declared that 'Those people who labor in the earth are the chosen people of God.' It's a sentiment echoed in one of the most popular versions of that quintessentially American blend of homage to the motor car and adoration of the soundbite: the bumper sticker that reads 'American by birth, Southern by the grace of God.'

But like other defining traits, the Southern link to the soil has been diluted in the modern era as machines have divorced so many from the earthly plant. With the lawyers squeezing large compensation settlements out of tobacco companies, and the federal government now bent on treating everyone involved in tobacco sales as a peddler of legal drugs, the future of this Southern staple looks increasingly precarious. As our farmer friend had made clear, many things had changed since he had been a young boy. It was easy to see the whole process as the slow erosion of another characteristic linchpin of the South.

12

Hog Heaven

There is another Southern speciality that is traditionally associated with the tobacco crop. Back when the curing took place in the small wooden barns, a process that involved someone staying up all night to tend the fire and ensure constant temperature and humidity, the last night of the final cure was always celebrated by roasting a pig over coals from the furnace. Families across the North Carolina Lowlands still enjoy these 'pig-pickin's', although now they'll eat them at any time of the year. Pig-pickin's also continue to live on for a much wider audience in the distinctive North Carolinian style of barbecue.

Barbecue, like tobacco, was probably picked up from the local American Indian population. It is arguably the most Southern dish of all, but it is an awful lot more than just that. Barbecue is also a cultural minefield, a deeply contentious issue over which tempers can be lost and friendships severed. Before I came to the South, a Southern acquaintance in Britain gave me a rundown on things I might look out for. He told me I had to try barbecue in several different locations because it varied. 'Ask around for the best places to get it,' he said, 'but try to ask individuals. Don't ask a group of people, because you might start something.'

I got an idea of what he was talking about from numerous different individuals, all of whom had strong opinions on the subject. Someone in Georgia told me that the word itself could be used as a verb or a noun. Another expert, in Tennessee, informed me in grave tones that I should never say 'Let's go for a barbecue' or 'Let's barbecue tonight' since this was Yankee talk. 'Southerners don't *have* barbecues,' he said, 'they *eat* barbecue.' One aspect of the subject that all seemed to agree upon was that barbecue was pork. Then when I arrived in East Texas it wasn't pork at all. It was beef, and not just any old beef. It had to be brisket. Further confusion arose when I started reading on the subject. Barbecue wasn't pork *or* beef in Owensboro, Kentucky. It was mutton, and Owensboro was supposed to know because it called itself the World Barbecue Capital. But then so did Memphis, Tennessee, where barbecue was ribs.

Apart from differences of opinion over the meat, there was also a range of views on how it should be cooked and what type of sauce it should be served with. There was wet barbecue and dry barbecue; diced, shredded and sliced barbecue. I soon learned to remain totally passive whenever the subject was raised. I would just stand and nod, looking really interested with an idiot look on my face, wary that if I took a stand the conversation might end in bloodshed.

Michael took me for lunch to the best place in Greenville to eat barbecue. It was called B's Barbecue and it was located on B's Barbecue Road. It was on the edge of town and they had to call the road after B's because the barbecue joint was seemingly the only reason for having the road at all. The temperature had taken a significant downturn and it was raining hard when we arrived at B's, a light-blue brick affair with a blue and white awning outside. Over to one side, aromatic black smoke was billowing out of a lean-to into the rain. This was where the pigs were cooked. We ducked inside to have a quick look at what resembled a medieval scene with a lone black guy shovelling coals into huge encrusted braziers. It was unlikely that the cookhouse would win any awards for hygiene and the only light inside the place seemed to be coming from the gaps beneath the roof through which the smoke escaped. The guy in charge, who didn't quite know what to make of our lightning visit, told us he cooked ten to fourteen hogs every day. They were put over the coals at 10 p.m. and were ready to eat by nine the next morning. 'But we don't open 'till eleven,' the man told us. 'And what time do you close?' I asked him. 'When we run out o' food,' he replied. 'Don't matter what time it is.'

We dashed out of the shack into the rain. 'And you can't ring up to find out whether they have any food left,' Michael shouted as we splashed through the puddles. 'They got no phone.'

Inside, B's looked like a cross between someone's trailer home front room and a British transport caff. There were baseball trophies and a few plastic flowers, and the wet clothes of a fair sprinkling of customers had got a good fug going. The customers themselves represented a complete cross-section of Greenville's population. Business suits and ties were mixed in with guys who looked like farmworkers, dressed in grubby overalls and baseball caps. The love of barbecue was spread across all social classes. Neon strip lights lit the scene, although one of the fittings had lost its elongate bulb, and there was Formica everywhere. It may even have been on the walls, but I didn't get the chance to look too closely because Michael was briefing me on what to order. It was simple really, all they had was barbecue and luckily for us there was still plenty of it.

It was proper eastern North Carolina barbecue, shredded pork dressed in a vinegar-based sauce, and very good it tasted too. The meat was juicy, not too vinegary and I detected what I thought was a hint of apple. It was served unceremoniously on a paper plate and eaten with a plastic fork. The accompaniments were also standard, Michael informed me. They were called 'fixin's'. It was coleslaw and cornbread. Apart from the cornbread, which tasted of nothing as usual, it was the best meal I'd eaten since my arrival in the South.

'It's different in the west of the state. Up in the hills they put tomato in the sauce,' Michael told me as we shovelled down the succulent shreds of meat, 'while down in South Carolina the sauce is sweeter and mustard based. But you ask anyone here and they'll tell you that this is the only way to eat barbecue.'

Were we eating pig or hog? I wanted to know. Hog seemed to be a more common term from what I'd heard, but pig still turned up every now and again. Michael wasn't sure. I made a mental note to add this to my list of standard Southern questions.

Pigs, hogs, or whatever you want to call them, have inhabited North Carolina for longer than anyone can remember. From the earliest times, European settlers all over the South found feral hogs hanging around in the forests when they first arrived. These wild swine were probably escapees from the expedition of the Spanish explorer Hernando de Soto, who travelled far and wide throughout the South between 1538 and 1542. A long-standing relationship developed between simple backwoodsmen and the hogs that lived in the forests when, in the winter of 1611, feed became desperately short for the Jamestown colonists up in Virginia. So they turned their domesticated cattle and pigs loose to fend for themselves. The colonists assumed the livestock would die of starvation or exposure in the forest, but they found most of them again the following spring fat and healthy, having foraged off the mast of oaks, hickory and other hardwood trees. So was born a tradition of using the forests and woodlands of the South as an open range, of releasing hogs to fend for themselves and hunting them down with dogs once or twice a year, for earmarking, branding and subsequent re-release, while keeping some for butchering and barbecues.

It was a practice that was very widespread. The remaining woodland that I had seen from the train windows dominated the Southern landscape for centuries. Although scholars of the antebellum South have tended to focus on the plantations and the yeoman farmers who aspired to be plantation-owners, ignoring the stockmen of the backwoods or dismissing them as white trash and hillbillies, it was these subsistence families who were the more numerous in most parts. One estimate suggests that less than 10 per cent of the South had been 'improved' by 1850. Most of the rest was primal forest, and it was full of hogs.

The diet of most Southerners is more diversified today than in times past, but pigmeat in its various forms is still as popular as it has ever been. There was a bumper sticker that I saw on several cars in North Carolina. It read 'Welcome to North Carolina. Hell for humans, heaven for hogs.' So it might have been once, but not anymore. Like the tobacco industry, hogs have been modernised in the last few decades. Few feral hogs roam the backwoods today, and even the more recent tradition of small independent pig farms is being superseded by specialised pork operations that produce hundreds of hogs each week, of virtually identical size, shape and quality. Back in 1950, North Carolina had 1.3 million hogs on about 200,000 farms. By 1994, the number of hogs passed six million and the number of farms fell below 7,000. Most of the hogs are on the coastal plain, but you don't see any of them because they're all inside, victims of the industrialisation of the Southern countryside.

I saw one or two of these hog factories during my stay in the North Carolina Lowlands. They were all built of cinderblocks with metal roofs, with batteries of grain bins lined up beside them. These facilities tended to be far from towns and smaller communities because they smell. If you get downwind of a modern hog operation you know all about it, and North Carolina has a special Swine Odor Task Force to deal with the problem. The fragrant odours emanate from the open-air lagoons that are created to deal with pigs' waste. These lagoons tend to be large because the average hog produces a lot of waste; four times as much as the average person in fact. A 1000-sow, 20,000-head hog operation produces as much solid waste as a city of 80,000 people. Needless to say, the new industrial scale operations have raised fears about pollution, not only of the atmosphere, but also because of the possibility of leakage from the lagoons into the groundwater.

Some days after my lunch at B's, I was at a dinner party and asked whether the modern hog operations also came under attack from animal rights activists, like they would if they were in England. My fellow diners just looked at me as if I was stupid. I had already made a fool of myself by asking the largely female assembly whether they thought it would be interesting for me to visit a hog parlour. My question was met by a quite unexpected gale of laughter. The idea had been suggested to me by one of Michael's colleagues at the university. He had made it with a totally straight face, so I could only conclude that the apparent double entendre had not been known to him. One of the women explained to me that 'hog parlour' was a popular euphemism for brothel. 'So I guess you would find it interesting,' she said as she collapsed again into a fit of giggles.

My question about hog parlours had certainly helped to break the ice. But the looks I received when I asked about animal rights activists added to the feeling I had of being in a really foreign country, somewhere where my ignorance could spark misunderstandings, despite a common language. It wasn't a feeling I had expected to encounter in the USA, least of all when among academics. But one of the advantages of being in such company, and of people knowing that I am writing a book about their country, is that I can ask straightforward questions and weather the occasional gales of laughter that they engender. When the laughs had subsided I continued with my quest for hog information and enquired into the difference between hogs and pigs.

Tammie, from Louisiana, said that her father and his hunting buds always called domesticated oinkers pigs and wild ones hogs. 'I've heard those terms used in that context often in various places across the South, deep or otherwise,' she told me.

One of the other of Michael's postgrads present, a woman named Gina who had grown up just down the road on the North Carolina coast, gave me a more localised view. She said that her grandfather raised oinkers. 'Pigs are for breeding,' she said, 'and hogs are for slaughtering.'

I was reminded suddenly of my haircut in Charleston, and of the hog-callers on the television. 'And what's a hog-caller?' I asked.

My question was met with some more giggles. Almost inevitably, I suppose, one of the women replied, 'Someone who calls hogs.' Gina explained that there were hog-calling contests. Hog-callers shouted 'Sueeeeeee' and the one who held the call the longest was the winner.

The talk of hogs had been sparked by a discussion of Southern food. Much of the list that the women gave me was comprised of pork. Apart from barbecue, they had mentioned numerous strange parts of pigs. These included chitterlings – or 'chitlins' as they called them: boiled, battered and fried intestines; pickled ears and feet; hog's head cheese, and brains and eggs. Brain and eggs were mixed together and scrambled, I was told. 'Southerners eat everything but the squeal,' Gina said.

Other typical Southern delicacies included chicken and dumplings and collard greens. Deonna had provided some collards to go with the chicken we ate for dinner so that I could sample this traditional dish. The green leaves were boiled for at least an hour and a half, she told me, with small pieces of ham. I have to say now that I didn't think collards would ever rate as one of my all-time favourites, but at the time I played the polite guest and said it tasted good. I'm glad I did, because a little later I realised just how kind Deonna had been in preparing this dish. We were talking about religion, and the fact that Greenville seemed to have a phenomenal number of churches. Michael and I had passed a fair number, often with names that to me were rather unusual (I particularly liked an unpretentious little building in the downtown area that was called the Fire, Baptism and Truth Church Number Four). It transpired that Deonna was a Moslem. I asked her whether there were many Moslems in these parts and she replied, rather defensively, that there were two regular mosques in Greenville as well as a Nation of Islam mosque. I thought it interesting that she mentioned the Louis Farakhan establishment as a separate entity. She wasn't very forthcoming on the subject, and I didn't want to press her, but I was touched that she had prepared the collards despite their containing pork. This really was genuine Southern hospitality.

'Ayden has a collards festival,' one of the others piped up.

'What's in the collards festival?' I asked, and immediately wished I had phrased my question differently.

'Collards,' they all said in unison.

'It's all to honour the collard,' Gina explained, 'they crown a collard queen.'

The wine had been flowing and I had been treading a fine line between remaining on duty and trying to gather information on the South, and simply relaxing. It was a problem that arose every now and again when researching a book like this one, and not one that was easily solved. I have found from experience that it is not always the most obvious occasions that, when I come to write the book, turn out to be the most interesting. And of course conscientiously scribbling notes, let alone pulling out a tape recorder, often acts as a deterrent for people to say what they want to. The other side of the equation is that when I'm trying hard to gather material I sometimes miss the most obvious things. I had pocketed my notebook and almost turned off my memory bank when one of the most obvious aspects of this enjoyable evening struck me. It was simply that other than Michael my company was made up entirely of female postgraduates (they were also all white, but that didn't strike me as being unusual).

I asked whether this situation was indeed out of the ordinary in a place where women tended to be characterised as husband appendages and also-rans. All agreed that it was unusual and Emily, the fourth woman there, launched into an account of how she had been forced along the whole Southern belle track by her parents, a process in which she was trained in the social niceties and introduced to society. It had all been particularly inappropriate in her case, she observed. Emily was the eldest of the group, and she had passed up the chance of joining polite society and joined the navy instead. She had left after eleven years, just prior to Operation Desert Storm in the Gulf, or 'Desert Breeze' as she preferred to call it. She had always known that she wasn't cut out to be a belle. Her favourite hobby was deep-sea fishing for goodness' sake, but her parents had laboured under the delusion that she would grow out of it.

'They used to dress me up in Sunday dresses with voluminous petticoats with bells on,' she said, 'sent me to ballet lessons and made me practise walkin' with books on my head so that I'd do it straight.' In a moment that they could never have reproduced if they'd rehearsed it a dozen times, the other three women in the room unanimously claimed that they had also been put through the same book-walking routine. All said that their desires to further their education had been discouraged by one, other, or both of their parents.

The parental wish for their daughters to grow up as Southern belles had also been tempered by more pragmatic Southern virtues however. Tammie said her father had offered to buy her a handgun for her twenty-first birthday present. This comment led to a mildly drunken conversation about firearms, ending with an argument over the name of the local gun store in Ayden. Most of the women were convinced it was called Guns 'R' Us, but Deonna wasn't quite so sure.

Greenville and the surrounding countryside appeared to be riddled with these contrasts between old and new, between traditional Southern values and modern American influences. The city itself supported along with B's Barbecue a record number of more contemporary fast food establishments. Several people told me that Greenville had more fast food outlets per head of population than any other city in the USA. There were six McDonald's and six Burger Kings, four Subway sandwich outlets, and three Domino's Pizza. Three Kentucky Fried Chickens vied with three Taco Bells, two Wendys and a couple of Omar Expresses, and so it went on. And all these for a population of just 45,000 people. Michael said he thought it was because Greenville's demography made it ideal for the fast food giants to test their nationwide marketing strategies, but it made the place seem as though it was populated by a new breed of superconsumer.

An even greater range of choice was available to cater to the religious tastes of the Greenville superconsumers. The city had more than 200 churches. I didn't believe Michael when he first told me this, but he suggested I look in the Yellow Pages. I did so. There were eight pages of churches, between chiropractors and cigars. This did look like a lot to me, but for comparison I looked up churches in the Oxford Yellow Pages when I got home. For a start, the only entry under churches in the Oxford book, also between chiropractors and cigars as it happened, referred me to Places of Worship. No such sensitivities had been shown in Greenville, North Carolina, where the two mosques and the Hindu temple were churches as far as they were concerned. When I found the Oxford list, it barely covered half a page. This for a city more than twice the size of Greenville.

The Greenville Christian churches came in a bewildering variety of flavours. There were categories for the Church of God, the Church of Christ and the Church of the Nazarene; for the Full Gospel and the Foursquare Gospel, Presbyterian-PCA and Presbyterian-USA. You could worship Interdenominationally and Non-denominationally, at Deliverance Churches and Holiness Churches. I had no idea there were so many forms of Baptism: Southern Baptists, of course, but also Conservative Baptists and Free-Will Baptists, Independent Baptists and Missionary Baptists. You were fine too if you were a Methodist or a Pentecostalist, a Seventh-Day Adventist or a member of the Assemblies of God. And if none of these took your fancy, there was always the Fire, Baptism and Truth Church Number Four.

Michael took me on a drive out of town one afternoon, down towards the coast, through places that were a million miles from the Greenville superconsumers. Grimesland didn't live up to its name, it was full of low-slung wooden houses and was so small it didn't even have a set of traffic lights. I didn't see a single fast food joint either. Chocowinity was surrounded by derelict tobacco barns, and Whichards Beach was a trailer park with more than its fair share of

Confederate battle flags. As Michael put it, it was not the place to break down with a Bill Clinton sticker on your bumper. Washington looked like a potentially pretty little place on the Pamlico river, but it was almost deserted on this Thursday afternoon. Several shops were boarded up and not all of those that weren't were open. The most numerous inhabitants seemed to be a large flock of pigeons. On the way back to Greenville, along a hurricane evacuation route, we passed several green signs that recorded the city's seat belt use: Last month 92%; Record 93%.

Back at Michael's place, we ate large juicy steaks for dinner, cooked over a grill (I shan't call it a barbecue) on the balcony. Michael and his wife Jan lived in a new housing development that overlooked a small artificial lake. One of their neighbours had bought a few ducks that waddled back and forth along the lakeside. Jan told me about some voluntary work she had done the previous year at a local community centre. It had been eye-opening, she said. Many of her charges were young, barely literate black people from rural areas. Some of them didn't even know how to use a can-opener. The young mothers among them had some interesting names for their small children. 'Courageous was a common one for boys,' she told me, 'and Fimalé for girls.' I thought Courageous was a great name, but Fimalé was more unusual.

'The girls see their babies in the incubator with a label on,' she said, 'and think their kid has already been named. It's spelled F-E-M-A-L-E.'

The story put me in mind of an interview I read once with Floyd Patterson, one of a distinguished line of Southern black world heavy-weight boxing champions, who was born in North Carolina. Patterson spoke cogently in the interview and the journalist asked if he'd had a good education. No, came the reply, he had left school at 15. Did he read a lot then? Patterson was asked. 'I don't like to read books,' he answered, 'because my manager, he reads books, and my sparring partner, he reads books and to me it seemed a sort of disease. They used to read until they fell asleep, and then wake up and read again. If reading makes you that way, I'm not interested.'

13

A Long Way to Roanoke

I shouldn't have complained because I'd actually been very lucky with the weather. The rain in Greenville was the first I'd encountered since my arrival in Florida, but it still dampened my enthusiasm somewhat. Nevertheless, my despondency was largely offset by Michael's reaction to the elements. For him, the atmospheric conditions were a source of great excitement. This was because he was a physical geographer and he was particularly interested in rivers. Rain helps the rivers flow and Michael had got all sorts of equipment set up to monitor them. The few days I spent with him were punctuated by regular checks of the national and local weather channels on the television. When he couldn't get to a TV set, he would ring up Jan and ask her to tune in and tell him when the next weather front was forecast to arrive over Greenville. He was measuring water that ran off some tobacco fields outside the city to discover how much soil was carried with it. His turbidity equipment needed regular checks to make sure he collected a consecutive run of samples.

One evening after I had given a talk at the university, we retired to a bar to drink tequila, and by 10 p.m. we were decidedly half-cut. But instead of driving home to sleep it off, Michael wanted to go out into the field. Oblivious to the dangers of drinking and driving we jumped into his shiny black Ford Explorer and sped away towards his site, stopping only to pick up several bags of ice from an all-night store to pack his water samples in. The samples had to be kept at a low temperature until they were analysed because otherwise they would go off. When we reached the site, Michael booted up his laptop computer and then booted up himself, forging down the riverbank in his Wellingtons with a large stick to beat the grass as a warning to local snakes that he was coming. Physical geography fieldwork is like this, a curious combination of high-tech gadgetry and downright basic adventurousness. As it turned out, it was the high-tech gadgetry that let him down. The linkup from the turbidity meter to his computer didn't work and for the next forty minutes Michael stood in the river calling out numbers as I wrote them down on a very damp piece of paper with rain trickling down my neck. The whole process was an impressive display of dedication to his work. This is what good geographers are like, always ready to go out into the field and get their hands dirty. Michael loved it. He had even purchased a personalised licence plate for his vehicle to prove it. But his choice was unfortunate. The plate said 'DIRT DR', which to the uninitiated made him sound like a pornographer.

It amazed me, when I first watched it, that they could have a whole channel devoted to the weather on US TV. It was great for Michael, but let's face it, there aren't many like him in the United States of America. As with all the wall-to-wall topic based television stations, the Weather Channel became awfully tedious after a few minutes. They couldn't really help it because there is only so much you can say about the weather. The coverage of North America was pretty comprehensive and spiced up with sexy graphics and colourful satellite imagery, but even so it quickly became repetitive. They had tried their best to reduce the tedium with thematic forecasts, but these were just the same as the generic forecasts only with slightly different emphases. Hence, the conventional weather forecast was followed, after the commercial break, by the Travel Weather forecast. In the conventional version the plastic woman would wave her hand at the map and tell you that it was raining in Texas, for example. When the Travel Weather came on she'd tell you to be careful driving in Texas because it was raining.

The most entertaining bits on the Weather Channel, I thought, were the overseas forecasts. Every hour or so, they'd do the whole world's weather, continent by continent. The presenter would flick through the maps saying things like, 'Looks like they could have some rain down there in Australia, it's going to be cold in Poland, and hot in Africa.' Sometimes they would miss out Africa altogether, as if they weren't having any weather that day.

Of course the average American isn't very interested in what's going on in the rest of the world because he doesn't know where it is.

Americans are legendary as being the world's worst geographers, hence comments like the one the Rhodesian tobacco man had made to Michael and me at the Waffle House. I experienced a similar naivety of things foreign myself when I bought a ticket out of Greenville at the bus station. The guy behind the counter was very friendly, and as he took my money he looked at me with an amiable frown on his face.

'You from Italy?' he asked suddenly.

'No, England.'

'Yeah, I thought you were from one o' the two. Italian accent, English accent: more o' less the same.'

The nation's paltry understanding of where places are has prompted the National Geographic Society to sponsor a Geography Awareness Week, but as I settled into my seat and took out my map of the South, what I saw put this reputation into some perspective. Try telling an American that Jordan is a Middle Eastern country and he'll point out that it happens to be a lake in Alabama. Angola a state in Africa? No, a swamp in North Carolina. And Egypt is in Georgia while Lebanon is in Tennessee. Large parts of what I think of as Europe (Denmark, Norway and La France) turned out to be in South Carolina, while several of the continent's capitals lay in neighbouring Georgia (Amsterdam, Athens, Dublin, Rome and Vienna). The more I looked, the more it went on: Geneva was a town in Alabama, Panama City a resort in Florida. You could visit Delhi in Louisiana, Moscow in Tennessee and Warsaw in Virginia. Americans didn't need to travel the world because it was all there on the doorstep. Down in Florida you could even get to Jupiter and Venus.

Geographically speaking, I'd come up against problems of my own in trying to leave Greenville. My next stop was a place called Roanoke, near the home of another friend in neighbouring Virginia. Roanoke was considerably further inland than Greenville and a long way off the Miami–New York rail route that I'd been following more or less continuously. Although my map indicated that there were rail lines running inland to Roanoke from coastal Virginia, Amtrak didn't seem to have heard of them. Or at least, they weren't running any trains on them. If I wanted to take a train to Roanoke, I'd have had to go via New York, which seemed a little out of my way. So Amtrak was out of the question. I had looked into renting a car, but no one wanted to let me drop it off at Roanoke. I began to wonder what was wrong with the place.

That left the bus. Michael called up a Greyhound route map via the Internet on his laptop computer. Greenville to Roanoke was 183 miles as the crow flies. Great, I thought to myself, it can't take much more than three hours. Yes it could because I wasn't going by crow. We tapped in my departure point and destination and the Greyhound Routeplanner said the bus would take ten hours. We did it again. Yes, it was ten hours. I knew the pace was supposed to be slow in the South, but until then I hadn't fully realised just how slow.

Having convinced the man behind the counter at the bus station that I wasn't Italian, I settled down for my ten-hour bus journey to Roanoke. Outside Greenville we passed fields of tobacco, most of them now reduced to just a few stalks, while the cotton plants were green and sprouting their little white bobbles. The porches of the wooden houses were decorated with bright orange pumpkins in readiness for Halloween, and model geese and ducks were frozen in pecking poses on their patchy front lawns. In no time at all, we were approaching Rocky Mount, past a hoarding beside a church that asked, 'Troubled? Try Prayer. The family that prays together stays together.' The bus driver told us we had a layover of twenty minutes here.

Rocky Mount bus station was directly across the railroad tracks from the Amtrak station, where I had waited an hour for a connection on my way to meet Michael the previous week. On that occasion, I'd taken up position on a rusty trolley and watched as a middle-aged black man had walked towards me across the wasteground adjoining the weedy platform. It had taken him a good three minutes to cross the distance, nearly tripping over a couple of times on the rocks. As he came nearer, I could make out the saggy pockets in his jacket and the holes in his shoes. He walked straight up to me, thrust out a callused hand and said, 'Gimme a cigarette.'

'No,' I said.

He shrugged, turned around, and walked all the way back across the wasteground and disappeared behind some trees.

At the bus station, I bought a can of cold drink from a machine inside the terminal and wandered back outside. Opposite where the bus was parked, the wall was painted with a quotation from the Bible: 'Jesus said, "Come unto me all ye that labor and are heavy laden, and I will give you rest." Matthew 11:28.' A selection of my fellow passengers were standing around resting in the shade, some smoking cigarettes, some just standing. A young Chinese man dressed in a suit and tie looked nervous and out of place as he waited to join our bus. A plastic bag with Chinese writing on it was on the ground beside him.

At the edge of the terminal building stood a very tall black man, only now beginning to stoop with his advanced years, who had already been on the bus. His jacket was threadbare in a few places and the pockets sagged. His shirt, buttoned to the neck, had a fraying collar and no tie. He was staring over towards the railway line as a long goods train was rumbling through. Slowly he shook his head as he watched.

I thought I ought to stretch my legs so I moved over to stand beside him, thinking perhaps he had seen something interesting. He turned to me and shook his head some more.

'Now how does one engine pull all that?' he asked, revealing a distinct lack of front teeth as he did so. 'I'm sixty-nine years old and I ain't never worked it out yet.'

We both looked at the boxcars as they continued to trundle past. The company name on the side was from Louisiana. 'They're a long way from home,' I said.

'Yeah, a mighty long way, and it's just one engine gonna pull them all that way. I bin standing here for ten minutes and it's not done yet. Look at that thing. How do they do it? I ain't never worked it out.'

Slowly, he started counting. 'One. Two. Three. Four . . .' He stopped when he got to six. 'Look at those. I saw the engine at the front but I don't think we're ever goin' to see the end.' He raised his forearms as if he was about to start clapping, but he just gestured at the passing goods wagons, smiling now but still shaking his head in disbelief. 'I just don't geddit. I'm standing here looking at it, but I still don't geddit.'

The wagons passing now were open, loaded with tree trunks.

126

'Wood, ore, all kinds of stuff, but only one engine pulling.' We both just stood watching, mesmerised by what seemed like the longest goods train in the world. 'We ain't never goin' to see the end,' he chuckled, 'it's just not gonna happen.'

I couldn't think of anything to say, so I just took a long pull on my drink and watched. The next set of wagons contained kaolin, and were headed for Mobile, Alabama. A taxi pulled up in front of us and its driver opened his door to step out of the cab. He saw us transfixed and asked what was up. The old man pointed towards the passing train. 'We just looking at that there train. I done saw the front of that sucker but I don't think it's got an end.'

The taxi driver half turned to take in the locomotive. 'Yep, there's an end all right,' he said assuredly.

'Well I wanna see it, 'cos I don't believe it.'

I turned to check that our bus was still there. I wanted to visit the bathroom before it left, but somehow I couldn't pull myself away from a train that possibly didn't have an end. The old man started counting again. 'One. Two. Three. Four. Five. Six. They full of ore.' It was scrap metal, but who cared, the train was still going. The taxi driver walked towards the terminal building, leaving his cab door wide open.

'One engine,' the old man said again, 'just one engine. How they do that?'

I drained my drinks can and strained my eyes to see whether the end of the line of wagons was in sight. It wasn't, so I left the old man to it and made for the toilet.

When I emerged from the terminal building, the train had gone and the old man was reboarding the bus. 'So there was an end,' I said, relieved in a way.

'Yeah, I saw it,' the old man said, 'there's an end on it. Lord God Almighty, how do they do that?'

When I mentioned to people at home that I would be travelling part of the way through the South on Greyhound buses, each to a man laughed obnoxiously and said it had been nice knowing me. Greyhound has this reputation as being transport for the proles: cheap, dangerous, and not recommended for normal people. A couple of times later on in my journey, I enquired at travel agents about the various ways of moving from A to B. They were happy to give me the options available by aeroplane, less so for the railways, but whenever I suggested the bus, the travel agent just looked at me as if I had asked for directions to the nearest lunatic asylum. 'You'd have to call Greyhound about that,' they'd say curtly as they suddenly remembered an urgent appointment and asked me to excuse them.

Greyhound stations did tend to be in the less salubrious part of town, and the average Greyhound passenger was blacker than your average airline customer. Some of them looked like they might be on the run from the FBI, but on the whole they were just ordinary people travelling from one place to another by the cheapest method. As far as I could see, the only characteristic common to all of them was their poor dress sense. The fear many had of travelling on the bus appeared, therefore, to be based on no more substantial a premise than that people dressed in a certain kind of clothing are always dangerous. Nonetheless, the negative reactions I received from virtually everyone I spoke to about the bus did mean that I had started my journey with a mild feeling of paranoia. When I reboarded the bus at Rocky Mount, the seat I had been occupying since Greenville had been taken. My ticket didn't have a seat number on, so I just looked for somewhere else to sit. The bus was nearly full, so I picked a place next to one that looked as if it was occupied by a child. I worked this out from the presence of a hand-held computer game on the seat. It was a mistake.

As the remaining passengers climbed back on to the vehicle, I looked to see who I might have picked to sit beside. A small black kid of about ten years old seemed likely, but he walked on past me to the rear of the bus. He was followed by a gaunt white man who looked my sort of age going on seventy. He had long straggly hair and a distinctly sallow complexion. As he approached where I was sitting, I was struck by his unusually protruding Adam's apple. I silently congratulated myself on my seating strategy. This was just the type of character that all those knowing laughs had been about. The guy looked like his hobbies would include robbing convenience stores. He stopped beside me and grunted. He wanted to sit on the seat next to mine.

I needn't have worried. The guy remained totally absorbed in his hand-held computer game (which turned out to be poker) all the way to our next stop at Weldon, where he got off. At Weldon I talked briefly to a man from Ohio. He told me it was his first time on the bus, and it wasn't as bad as they say. 'Certainly a whole lot cheaper,' he declared. 'I'm going to Denver and it's costing me ninety-nine dollars. I called the airline and they said it'd cost me eight hundred bucks to fly. I don't think so, I said.'

He was obviously very pleased, both with his financial saving and with the fact that he hadn't been murdered yet on the bus. But there was still something bothering him.

'I drove down from Ohio through West Virginia and Virginia to North Carolina,' he told me. 'Shit, man, there were so many trees. I ain't never seen so many trees. What's it like on the east side of North Carolina?'

'There aren't as many trees,' I told him, 'it's more agricultural.'

'Not as bad, huh?' he said. The thought restored his good humour for a moment, but then he started thinking about those trees again. 'Just one solid forest,' he lamented. 'D'you think people go in there?'

After Weldon we entered Virginia. You can tell exactly where the state line is on most US roads because they put up notices to tell you. These notices don't tend to be very welcoming, they're more informational, but in a commanding sort of way. One sign just says 'Leave North Carolina', as if they don't want you there any more, and the next orders you to 'Enter Virginia', just like it's an instruction. We were on Interstate 95, and I had some sympathy with the man from Ohio, because the highway was hemmed in by thick forest all the way to Petersburg. It was only after we'd left Petersburg that I remembered the woman on the train out of Miami and her story about the Battle of the Crater, so it was too late for me to look out for the big hole in the ground. On reflection, I thought it unlikely that I'd have seen it, what with all the trees.

It was just a short hop to Richmond where I had to change buses. The bus terminal here was fairly new and quite smart, but the guy cleaning the toilets still tried to sell me a camera. 'It's a hundred dollar camera,' he said surreptitiously as I stood at the urinal. 'I've got a camera,' I told him, and I turned back to concentrate on the matter in hand. The red plastic anti-splash device I was peeing on to had the words 'Say no to drugs' printed on it, which wasn't a lot of help in the current circumstances. What's the advice on cameras? I wanted to know.

'I got to sell quick to buy a ticket to New York,' he said. 'It's yours for just twenty.' It seemed like a good deal, but I couldn't envisage me using two cameras. 'No thanks,' I told him.

'OK,' he said, 'can you give me a dollar for a sandwich?'

A dollar wouldn't have bought him a sandwich at the terminal cafeteria. The cheapest was ninety-nine cents, but they always add sales tax in the US. After standing for what seemed like ages in the long line, I bought a more expensive one. As it turned out, it was large enough to give me indigestion for the next three hours.

The trees continued outside Richmond. It was like driving at the bottom of a tree canyon. They were non-stop, which was more than could be said for my bus journey.

I fell asleep as we sped through the trees and awoke to find us approaching Charlottesville. I saw a hill out of the window which surprised me. I couldn't work out why for a moment, until I realised that it was the first hill I'd seen since my arrival in the States. Then we were driving down one, into town, past a hoarding advertising snuff. There were fewer passengers in this bus and I had two seats to myself. Behind me were a couple of young guys from the armed forces, and judging from the tone of their conversation they had been travelling for days, whereas in my case that was just what it seemed like.

'I don't trust Taco Bell outside of Texas,' one of them was saying. 'Down in southern Texas you get some real Mexican food, but Taco Bell in West Virginia? There's something missing.'

Having made just a five minute stop in Charlottesville, we were now passing through rolling hills, still with lots of trees. The scene was very rural and very green. There were bales of hay in some fields. I consulted my map. The route that we were taking, which would eventually land me in Roanoke, was about the most circuitous one possible. It was as if we were stopping at every other lamppost in Virginia before we got there. The guys behind didn't even want to stop at my destination. 'Why do we have to stop at Roanoke?' one of them asked, as if he had heard me thinking. 'I mean it's only a hole in the wall.' This was just what I wanted to hear.

The occasional house we passed in the countryside was still wooden, usually with a verandah like all the other houses I'd seen so far in the South, but they came with tell-tale signs that something here was a bit different. We passed some sheep in a little valley, and then a dry stone wall. The guys behind me had moved on to talk about guns and how much fun it was to shoot them. The trees had thinned out, but specks of reds and browns had started to appear in their foliage, indicating that summer was giving way to fall up here. We were in rolling green pastures, with grass that looked like it grew properly, not in patches like it had done further south. There were cows in some of the fields too. I could almost have been in England. As we drove on, the guys behind covered a range of other military topics, like stopping tanks (which was difficult), sweeping stairs (a bummer) and penalties (pointless). The discussion of penalties led to a long debate about what ranks they were expected to salute. They'd make good soldiers.

The houses now came with piles of logs neatly stacked beside them in preparation for the winter and a few of the trees had begun dropping their leaves. As the light began to fade, I saw a slope where the trees were all enveloped in kudzu. They looked like furniture does when you drape sheets over it. I didn't note what time it was when we finally arrived in Roanoke, but it was late. It was a surprisingly large city with what looked like a cathedral on a hill and an office block that resembled a stunted Saturn rocket plonked down in the middle of town.

14

Southern Heroes

After all that, I wasn't actually going to Roanoke at all. My ultimate destination was a place called Blacksburg, but the trouble I'd experienced in coming this far indicated that getting to Blacksburg would have been totally impossible. Roanoke was where I had arranged to meet the next link in the long chain of friends and acquaintances I had lined up as purveyors of spare rooms and floor spaces. Tyler Jo was originally from Oklahoma and had been in Blacksburg for only a couple of months, but this had been long enough to form a definitive opinion of the city. 'It's Bumblefuck, Virginia,' she told me over dinner. This I interpreted to mean that she hadn't really taken to the place.

I didn't like to say so, but I had been disappointed by Blacksburg long before I'd even arrived. Tyler Jo had scribbled her address down on a piece of paper and the name of the city looked to me like Blackberry. I'd been quite taken with the name, and had spent some time at home scouring maps and gazeteers in search of it. It was only when I looked up the city's university, Virginia Tech, that I realised I'd read her scribble wrong. But I didn't think it looked that bad the following morning when Tyler Jo drove me round for a quick perusal. OK, it seemed a bit soulless, but no more so than some of the other places I'd visited on this trip, like Greenville, North Carolina and Gainesville, Florida. There was a recognisable downtown area, with bookshops, a cinema and several tattoo parlours, and Virginia Tech was housed in some noble grey stone buildings. They were all very solid-looking, with steep slate roofs, giving the campus a vaguely medieval feel, but this impression was soon dissipated when I saw the huge acreage given over to the prairie-style car parks surrounding them.

It was a Saturday, and although still early, Blacksburg was already filling up with fans coming to watch the Virginia Tech American football team. Cars cruised by streaming purple and orange flags and pennants out of their windows. Like the university in Gainesville, the team had seconded a local animal for its nickname. The countryside in this part of Virginia is well known to be full of wild turkeys, but since turkey is a term more commonly used in a derogatory sense in North America, Virginia Tech plumped for Hokie instead. I asked several people about the word, and while all agreed that it meant turkey, there was some disagreement as to whether or not said bird had to be castrated to qualify. Either way, the local stadium said it was the Home of the Fighting Gobblers.

While Tyler Jo ran a few errands, she left me to mosey round what she called the university mall. It was a small affair as North American shopping malls go, with a limited selection of stores, a coffee shop, a Vietnamese restaurant and a couple of fountains. There was also a gym, with glass walls through which I could see lines of people on their exercise machines, most of them hooked up to Walkmans. I drank a coffee in the coffee shop and noted the irony in the fact that although everyone arrived at the gym in their athletic gear, they all came by car. I also had a look in the university bookstore. True to its name, it sold books, but only really as an afterthought. Most of the floorspace was taken up with Hokie equipment, like sweat shirts and baseball caps, flags and pennants. It was odd in this modern shopping context to see that the bookstore's plastic bags had 'Hokie Poke' written on them. It was the first time I'd ever seen the old English word used other than in that rather dated phrase involving pigs.

I shouldn't have been surprised to find a fragment of Middle English alive and well and living in Virginia because the state has deep English roots. This is where the South really began, in 1607, with the arrival on the coast of the first permanent English speaking colonists. They turned up in three little ships, managed to sail half-way up a river, and stopped to establish their colony, which eventually became known as Jamestown. It would be another thirteen years before the *Mayflower* landed at Plymouth Rock, but it's still the Pilgrims who get most of the glory as the USA's founding fathers. More anti-Southern Yankee propaganda, I suppose. Ask a Virginian, and he'll tell you that contrary to popular belief, even the first

American Thanksgiving was celebrated in his state, just down the road from Jamestown at a place called Berkeley.

The Jamestown colonists weren't the first Europeans to arrive in North America, of course. Not by a long way. That credit usually goes to the Vikings around 1000 AD, but reasonable claims can also be made for the Irish, Welsh and Bretons. And as I'd seen in northern Florida, St Augustine was North America's oldest continuously occupied European settlement, having been established by the Spanish nearly half a century before Jamestown took root. But none of these groups has had much of a lasting influence on the South. Neither, for that matter, have the people who were here when the first Europeans arrived. The local natives, the 'Indians', have been pretty comprehensively dispossessed.

The Jamestown immigrants weren't even the first English speakers to try to set up shop in the New World. Sir Humphrey Gilbert tried but never quite made it, his ship going down with all hands in an Atlantic storm in 1583. Gilbert's half-brother, Sir Walter Raleigh, managed to land a hundred-odd settlers at Roanoke (a different one, in present day North Carolina) in 1587. This was actually his second attempt at colonisation. The first team of settlers, who were landed three years previously, hated it so much they all went home to England. Wise men. Raleigh's 1587 effort never took off either. When supply ships reached Roanoke two years later, they found the place deserted. The colony's fate has never been satisfactorily explained.

So it was from Jamestown that English speaking settlers spread along the rivers and estuaries and eventually north on to Virginia's eastern shore and to Maryland. In its early days, Jamestown itself wasn't very successful and neither was Virginia. A couple of years after its first establishment, the Virginia Company dispatched a troubleshooter, Sir Thomas Gates, to be the new governor. He found a town in tatters. The church was ruined, gates had been torn from their hinges and empty houses pulled down for firewood, while just a stone's throw away was a forest full of trees. The dispirited settlers were too scared to venture into the woods for fear of attack by Indians; they preferred to sit at home in their crumbling settlement to die of hunger or disease instead. The Jamestown crowd, and other colonists who arrived after them, were encouraged to make more of an effort. Unfortunately, much of this effort went into burying their compatriots. Between 1607 and early 1625, 7,289 immigrants arrived in Virginia, and 6,040 of them died. Going to Virginia was like committing suicide. It was just a bit slower than more conventional methods.

Virginia's place as the fountainhead of Southern civilisation can be traced back to some essential differences between the Jamestown enterprise and the later Pilgrim effort up in Massachusetts. Jamestown was essentially a commercial venture, Plymouth a religious one. While the Pilgrims set out for a New World to escape the Old World's vices, Virginia was set up by entrepreneurs intent on transplanting the institutions and lifestyle of old England to the soils of a fresh wilderness. These initial differences soon diverged further. After its shaky start, Virginia took off when the colonists discovered tobacco. The streets of Jamestown were ploughed up and turned into green avenues of the weed. The crop did so well that five years after taking over the colony in 1624, the Crown imposed a poll tax payable in tobacco. This came a decade after the first shipment of Negroes was offloaded by a passing Dutch captain a few miles downriver from Jamestown. The scene was set for a fundamentally different version of the American dream.

Virginia can also lay claim to a central role in the later history of the territory that became the United States of America. George Washington, the man who was more instrumental than most in making it an independent country, was from Virginia. In fact, four of the first five US presidents were Virginians, and since each of them served two full terms, 32 of the country's first 36 years were presided over by this Virginian dynasty. After I had killed an hour in the university mall, Tyler Jo drove us to see the house built by president number three, Thomas Jefferson.

One of the first things I noticed on the roads in Virginia was that locally registered vehicles had licence plates (or tags as they call them) on both front and back bumpers. Vehicles in all the other states I'd passed through so far only had them on the back. The front space was used either for advertising or for a plate supporting the local football team, or simply left blank. I commented on this to Tyler Jo as we joined the Interstate near Christiansburg and was met with a barrage of abuse concerning the strange bureaucratic practices of Virginia.

'I had to register my car in the state *and* in Blacksburg,' she told me. 'I've never come across that before.' She had also been required to produce her social security card as proof of identity to get her Virginia driver's licence, whereas every other state she knew of was happy with just the number. 'I said this to a guy in Christiansburg and he agreed that bureaucracy here was terrible. "We don't call it Christiansburg," he told me, "we call it Communistburg."'

The road we were on sliced through rocky outcrops and forested hilltops. Huge articulated trucks rumbled through the scenic landscape, eagerly followed by mammoth motor homes with only slightly less mammoth cars in tow behind them. It took me a few moments before I realised why these mini vehicle convoys didn't look quite right to me. It was because the order of procession tends to be the other way around in Britain. It's the cars that pull the caravans. I've always thought that dragging an entire building along on vacation is a very curious thing to do, but I couldn't decide whether driving the building and pulling the car was more ridiculous, or less. My pondering of this conundrum was interrupted by the first of what turned out to be numerous signposts indicating that, as in the Carolinas, this state had only recently introduced legislation to enforce the wearing of seatbelts. 'Buckle up Virginia!' the spirited signs shouted, 'It's a law we can live with' suggesting that not everyone had been totally in favour of the idea.

It's taken a long time for the Virginians to get round to the notion of seatbelts. On this stretch of Interstate 81 we were following the trail of the Great Philadelphia Wagon Road, a rough track that served as a conduit for waves of settlers into the Southern interior east of the Blue Ridge mountains. Originally an Indian warriors' path, it had become a major highway for Scotch-Irish (Ulster Protestants of Scottish descent) and German settlers by the mid eighteenth century. It was difficult to imagine that Roanoke, at the southern end of the Shenandoah Valley down which the wagons had rolled, had been just a muddy pitstop on the trail to a new land only 250 years before.

We turned off the trail of the Great Philadelphia Wagon Road and headed for Charlottesville, but before we reached Thomas Jefferson's house at Monticello, to the south of the city, we stopped at the Historic Michie Tavern for lunch. It was a white wooden colonial building with black shutters and wooden 'slates' on the roof covered with lots of moss. The place was located in a nicely landscaped garden on a hillside above a big car park. We made our way up some steps to be welcomed by a woman in a flower print dress who was standing outside with a frilly duster on her head to welcome visitors and make sure they got some leaflets.

We perused the leaflets as we waited in line for a short while before being admitted to the Tavern's dining room, the 'Ordinary', which seemed like an odd name for a dining room. According to one of the brochures, the tavern had been established in 1784 by a Scotsman named William Michie. It had been moved 17 miles to its present location in 1927, but nowhere was it explained why. Perhaps more importantly, the brochure also informed me that it wasn't simply lunch we were waiting for, but a whole 'dining experience'. It was easy to imagine the sort of reaction William Michie would have received if he'd tried that one on with travellers arriving in their wagons in the late eighteenth century.

This dining experience featured hearty midday fare in a rustic tavern setting and was offered by servers in period attire. The recipes used dated back to the 1700s, apparently, and richly symbolised Southern culture and hospitality. They included Colonial fried chicken, black-eyed peas, coleslaw, green bean salad, potato salad, cornbread and biscuits. It wasn't until this trip to the South that I had properly realised why Americans prefer the term 'cookie' for something that I know as a biscuit. Here the biscuit is more akin to what I would call a scone, only Southerners eat them with meat, not jam.

William Michie's tavern was pretty well preserved inside, with wooden floors and plaster-and-plank walls, only it was probably rather cleaner than when Mr Michie ran the place. The modern proprietors had further sanitised history by putting up cute little No Smoking notices everywhere in the silhouette of a broken clay pipe. Nevertheless, they provided pewter plates to eat off and cups to drink from, which helped to make the experience seem more authentic.

After collecting our fare from the self-service canteen, we sat down on benches at a solid wooden table and proceeded to tuck in. You have to be on the ball all the time in this travel writing game. If you're not, you can miss things very easily. I was skewering my first piece of Colonial fried chicken when a youth dressed in white shirt and breeches moved over to our table and said, 'Hello, my name's Roger. I'm your servant for today. If there's anything you need just ask me.' I should have immediately picked up on his status. But I didn't and it was only a few moments later that I realised what he had said.

'Did Roger introduce himself as our "servant" or our "server"?' I asked Tyler Jo. She hadn't picked up on it either. 'I think he said server, but it may have been servant. Why don't you ask him?' I looked at Roger, who was now skulking over by the wall, and gestured for him to come over to us once more.

'Roger, two things,' I said to him when he arrived. 'Firstly, could you bring me a glass of water?'

'Yes.'

'And second, did you say that you were a servant or a server?'

'I'm a waiter,' Roger replied sincerely.

'But you introduced yourself as a servant.'

'No Sir, I said waiter.' (He didn't.)

'I'm pretty sure you said something beginning with S,' I said. Roger looked a bit crest-fallen. 'Maybe I got confused,' he said apologetically. 'I say it so many times.' And he turned to go in search of a jug of water.

I looked at Tyler Jo and we both laughed, but I felt a bit mean. I'd only meant it as a joke, but I think Roger had taken my question rather seriously.

Monticello was a bit further up the hillside from the Historic Michie Tavern. We parked the car and made our way to the entrance to part with our money. Amongst the change was a two-dollar note, the first I'd seen. 'It's got Thomas Jefferson on,' Tyler Jo pointed out. 'They must keep a stock of them.' On the back of the note was an engraving of lots of men dressed in breeches like Roger's. They were sitting round tables signing the Declaration of Independence on the 4th of

July, 1776. This is one of the scenes for which Jefferson is remembered, because he drafted the Declaration.

As we waited for a shuttle bus to take us up the hill to the Monticello house, Tyler Jo declared that Jefferson enjoyed the unusual distinction of his achievements being commemorated on two pieces of US currency. The house that we were about to see also featured on the nickel. I found one of the silver coins in my pocket and brought it out for inspection and in doing so was reminded of an embarrassing incident that occurred earlier on in my travels with its sister the dime. The dime was unusual in my experience of foreign currency in that it did not bear any indication of how much it was worth. It just said it was a dime, which if you didn't know meant it was worth ten cents left you rather vulnerable. I was buying a light breakfast in a roadside place in rural South Carolina. It cost a dollar eighty-one and I pulled out a handful of change to try and make up the eighty-one. 'How much is this worth?' I asked the young woman behind the counter, offering her the offending coin.

'Ten cents,' she said warily.

'Thanks,' I replied, and then, because she was still looking at me as if I might be dangerous, I added, 'It doesn't say so on it.' The woman took the coin, turned it over, and then shrieked with laughter. 'No, it doesn't say ten cents,' she exclaimed, as if this truly was a revelation. 'Where you from?' she asked, suddenly very friendly. 'England,' I told her. She paid me the usual compliment about my accent and then asked, 'You have different money over there?'

The shuttle bus arrived and Tyler Jo and I jumped on board to be taken up the hill on a journey that was much shorter than either of us had expected. It would have been easily walkable. At the other end we were handed a couple of coloured coupons and told that we had a 45-minute wait before our tour of the house. We whiled away the time wandering down the neat rows of vegetables and herbs that lined Mulberry Row, a short avenue that had been flanked by storehouses, workshops and slave dwellings in Jefferson's day. While most of these buildings had long since disappeared, the vegetable garden was still a thriving concern. There were waist high basil plants, strawberries, peppers, peanuts, and huge okra nestling in the bright red clay soil. Purple beans climbed a trellis where the hill dropped away to give a spectacular view over the rolling Virginia countryside bathed in brilliant sunshine. The asparagus had been allowed to flower, which I hadn't seen before, giving the stalks a feathery appearance rather like fennel.

Thomas Jefferson himself designed the house at Monticello, the only US structure on the World Heritage List, and it took him forty years to build. It was full of odd shaped rooms and all of them appeared to come with either an American first or some far-sighted Jeffersonian invention, and often both. The parlour had the first parquet floor in America (made of cherry and beech), over there was Jefferson's specially designed dumbwaiter, and out of sight were the nation's first waffle-maker and spaghetti-maker, both brought back from Europe by the great man. Most of the numerous clocks we saw had been designed by Jefferson too, a man who invented one of the very first copying machines and who slept sitting up. In the library, we learned that Jefferson could read in seven languages and that his immortal line in the independence document, 'all men are created equal', had changed the course of history both here and all around the world. I wanted to say that it had been nearly two hundred years before the line had materialised for black Americans, but I didn't.

Somebody else in the group brought up the subject of black people. We had just been told about Jefferson's essay entitled *A Southerner on Slavery*, in which he had condemned the whole business. 'But he still kept slaves,' piped up the voice from the crowd, and our guide launched into a brief account of the unresolved issue. Speaking out against slavery had been a courageous enough act in itself in those days, he told us, but then Jefferson hadn't lived up to his conviction by granting liberty to his slaves in his will. Part of the problem was that Jefferson was up to his eyeballs in debt when he died. Something we hadn't been told on the tour was that Jefferson had been forced to sell ten thousand of his books at one stage, a sale that had given birth to the Library of Congress.

Jefferson's involvement with slavery has come back to haunt him in recent times, along with a few other aspects of his life and works. He has been accused of plagiarism, bending the law and consorting with black females and he is not the only member of the country's most elevated dead white male fraternity to have come under attack. Even his fellow Virginian George Washington, the country's first president whose portrait appears on the one-dollar bill, has fallen from grace in some quarters because he owned slaves. While I was in Virginia, the New Orleans school board quietly changed the name of the city's George Washington elementary school, renaming it after Charles Drew, a pioneering black doctor. It was just the latest in a string of school name changes in the city, designed to shift away from the traditional emphasis on white heroes, many of whom also happened to be slave-owners.

No matter how much new wisdom can be generated with the aid of hindsight, Thomas Jefferson must always be guaranteed a place in US posterity. A notable architect, inventor, philosopher and scientist, as well as a great statesman, his list of achievements is arguably unrivalled. His Declaration of Independence and position as president are just two. He was also instrumental in giving the USA its Constitution and its Bill of Rights; as a member of Congress in 1783 he secured the adoption of the decimal system of coinage, and in 1803 he doubled the size of the country overnight by purchasing Louisiana from the French. He did prohibit the slave import trade and he also founded the University of Virginia. Although he left a long list of debts when he eventually shuffled off his mortal coil, he even managed to time this to perfection. He died on the fiftieth anniversary of the Declaration of Independence.

Jefferson was also unquestionably a Southerner. In 1785, he jotted down a few of the characteristics that defined and divided his lot from the Northerners, and the results are still common currency today. 'In the South,' he wrote, 'they are fiery, voluptuary, indolent, unsteady, jealous for their own liberties, but trampling on those of others, generous, candid, without attachment or pretensions to any religion but that of the heart.' Northerners, he reckoned, were more or less the opposite.

As Tyler Jo and I drove back along the trail of the Great Philadelphia Wagon Road, I sat pondering the recent reassessments of Jefferson's credentials for entry into the US hall of fame. Something Tyler Jo said had sparked it. She told me that she'd often thought that one of the root causes of dissatisfaction with the American dream was right there in Jefferson's text for the Declaration of Independence. In the second paragraph, one of the three 'unalienable Rights' claimed to be endowed by man's Creator was the pursuit of happiness. It was a curious thing to include, she thought.

15

Southern Mythology

The distinctive dome on Thomas Jefferson's residence at Monticello was the first to be built on an American house. Jefferson modelled the dome on the temple of Vesta in Rome after falling in love with ancient Roman architecture during his period of office in Europe as a trade commissioner and minister. Meanwhile, George Washington added a portico to his pad at Mount Vernon in the style of the ancient Greeks and a whole classic revivalist architectural trend was launched. It was not a coincidence that this style of architecture should become popular in the newly independent United States of America. The notion that this vigorous new country was the latter day embodiment of the virtues and ideals of ancient Greece and Rome was a strong one, sometimes articulated, perhaps more often subliminal. Either way, it has been a pervasive element in American mythology ever since.

To some extent, such classical mimicry can be found in all the countries of the great European Diaspora, especially in legal, religious, educational and artistic forms, but in many ways the American example is the most pronounced. I had already seen ample evidence of classical architecture's continued vitality in the South, but the legacy was discernible in many other forms. University campuses were plastered with Greek letters to designate fraternal and honorary organisations, there was a profusion of classical forenames still in common use (Homer, Virgil, Cassius, Julius, to name but a few), and what about all those American spacecraft and rocket missile systems that soar into the atmosphere and beyond in the name of ancient gods?

Perhaps the most persuasive evidence for the American's image of himself as the reincarnated Athenian or Roman lies in the phenomenal number of classical place-names all across the country. I had

143

already recognised the American propensity to borrow names from overseas while on the bus journey to Roanoke, but when I came to plan my exit route from Virginia, I was struck by the large numbers of decidedly classical labels. My map was spread out fully this time, to take up most of the floor of Tyler Jo's apartment. I had a week before my next rendezvous which was in Athens, Georgia, but I couldn't immediately see the place on the map, so I had to turn the huge piece of paper over to look it up in the index printed on the reverse. Damn it, there were nine entries for Athens listed, and this map only covered the eastern USA. When I had located the Athens I was heading for, I saw that just in northern Georgia the countryside was liberally sprinkled with classical names and Latinate forms: Rome, Sparta, Cornelia, Augusta and Atlanta. I dug out a more detailed map of the whole state and lots more popped up: Ephesus, Americus, Corinth, Omega, Etna, Juno. There were probably more but I was starting to go cross-eyed in the looking.

When I got back to Britain, I looked into place names in the USA and discovered that there had indeed been a major thrust in the use of classical labels in the immediate post-Revolutionary period, as settlers pushed forward into the unknown regions of their new country, carving fresh places out of the wilderness, pursuing their quest for a new identity and elusive perfection. Of course, there were also plenty of other names from all sorts of origins scattered across my map. I had already passed through places labelled for the topographically obvious (Rocky Mount, North Carolina) and the climatologically important (Frostproof, Florida). Others I saw before me were just as graphic in different ways, like Fairhope (Alabama), Niceville (Florida), and Slaughter (Louisiana). Later in my travels, I spent a whole afternoon criss-crossing the lower Mississippi Delta in a hire car, driving to places just because I liked the sound of their names. I passed through Heads, Panther Burn, Hard Cash, Silver City, Midnight, and Onward, but in every case I rather wished I hadn't because the reality was much less inspiring than the name. I had been aiming to make it as far south as Hot Coffee, but I gave up when I realised that it too would be disappointing.

I suppose that the plethora of exotic names thought up on the spot or borrowed from distant corners of classical history and geography probably reflected, at least in part, the urgent need at the time to conjure up labels quickly. The rapid colonisation of America must have meant that thousands of new settlements had to be named in a very short time. Never before had there been so many new places to label so quickly. Not surprising, therefore, that some of the older maps of US states also show places with names like Niggertown. I'm sure that this mad rush to think up place names must also be related to the distinct lack of imagination shown when it came to labelling streets. All those West 34th streets simply mean that the settlers ran out of inspiration.

For the next part of my itinerary, I eventually decided to hire another car and drive on down into eastern Tennessee. My first stop would be the nicely named Pigeon Forge, home of Dolly Parton's themepark, Dollywood. From there, I'd cross the Smoky Mountains to the Cherokee reservation in North Carolina, dump my car at Asheville, and take a bus to Athens, Georgia.

But not before a trip to Mountain Lake for Sunday brunch. A friend of Tyler Jo, Kathy, had arranged to take us. In the pouring rain, we splashed our way up steep winding roads through thick forests. It had been suggested that I sit up front to see better, but the driving rain tended to obscure most of what was on offer. I found Kathy's selection of car tapes almost as interesting though. They included The Science of Self-Confidence, and The Awakened Life, which made her sound like an unreconstructed hippie. This may not have been that far off the mark, because when I told her where I'd been so far on my travels, she nodded knowingly at the mention of Gainesville, Florida and said, 'It was the weirdo capital of the South in the seventies, lot of transients and hippies sleeping rough downtown.'

'It's a bit different today,' I told her.

'Yeah, they cleaned it up. It's squeaky clean now.'

Kathy told me to look out for the lawn art, and sure enough, every now and again a clearing would emerge to reveal a small wooden house with a lawn in front. Most of the lawns came with interesting collections of ornaments placed on them. There were sea-horses and pink flamingos and angels with wings. There were also ducks like the ones I'd seen on the journey up from Greenville, but here they struck more imaginative poses. The best one featured a small group of mallards deep in conversation with a figure of Jesus Christ.

As we ascended further, small rivulets of rainwater began to stream down the narrow road towards us. The trees on both sides were crowding closer, and the higher we got, the more their leaves were turning. 'It's a pity you're not staying for a few weeks,' Kathy told me, 'when the fall really gets going they singe your eyes when you look at them. It's stunning.' We rounded a bend and she slowed the car. 'When I drove up last week, there was a mother bear crossing the road right here with two cubs. I felt extra special after seeing that.'

The downpour was doing its best to be extra special too. When we finally arrived at Mountain Lake the rainfall had become torrential, and heavy clouds had lowered themselves over the lake so that the view was mostly of a fuzzy white haze. The Mountain Lake resort consisted of a few log cabin outhouses dotted around a large hotel with walls made from chunks of roughly hewn rock set into a crazy paving sort of pattern. Kathy stopped by the steps up to the hotel so that Tyler Jo and I could dash up into shelter. Kathy parked the car and got rather wetter, but she didn't seem to mind.

The hotel did a Sunday buffet brunch that was an eat-all-you-can affair. The tables in the dining room had pink tablecloths and napkins and we found an unoccupied one that overlooked the chill mist on the lake. The food was some of the best I'd tasted so far and I ate myself to a standstill. We all returned to the groaning tables several times, but some people I noticed managed to pile several courses on to a single plate. One elderly woman I saw carried a platter with a thick hunk of prime rib and some vegetables next to a piece of carrot cake, while balanced to one side was a generous lump of blue cheese and a slice of cantaloupe.

The hotel's interior was cavernous and had a rather 1950s feel about it, the sort of place where you would not be surprised to see a young Doris Day having brunch with Rock Hudson before venturing out for an excursion on the lake in a canoe that would no doubt sink at some point. But I also sensed an ominous side to the hotel's ambience, more akin to that remote complex where Jack Nicholson lost it in the *The Shining*. Kathy told me that this hotel also closed down in the winter, which made that feeling stronger. As it happened, the Mountain Lake hotel had a movie pedigree of its own, being the location where *Dirty Dancing* was shot.

As we drove down out of the clouds I thought that the double edged atmosphere at Mountain Lake was appropriately Southern. If the South's mystique as a place apart was as much a myth as reality, both sides of the myth had been aptly reflected in Hollywood's view of the region. On the one hand were the murderous tendencies and serious depravity of the rednecks in *Mississippi Burning* and *Deliverance*, while the matter of fact brutality of Southern prisons was well represented in *Cool Hand Luke*. Then there was always the racial card to play, as in *To Kill a Mockingbird, In the Heat of the Night* and *Paris Trout*. And to balance out the dark side, *Smokey and the Bandit* was the archetypal fun-loving 'good old boy' movie, while *Forrest Gump* proved to the world that Southern family values and heart–warming naivety would always be there to save the day. The South had, of course, also provided America with her quintessential movie, *Gone with the Wind*, perhaps because it had somehow managed to roll most of the Southern themes all into one.

Virginia was an appropriate place for me to have these thoughts, because this was where the myth of the South started, although in actual fact, my thinking was driven by a full belly and the Biblical torrents that deluged from the heavens outside, all spiced by the sight of Kathy's spiritual car tapes. The original strands of the mythical veil were woven by Virginia's earliest publicists. These colonial estate agents, the country's first realtors, portrayed the dangerous wilderness as a 'delicious country' and its fearsome natives as 'noble and angelic'. And so the first misleading layer of mystery was laid down over the enchanted land. The South was born of myth, all Hollywood does is help to propagate it.

That evening, Tyler Jo and I went to the cinema. I can't remember what we saw, but it wasn't a Hollywood offering. After the film, as we were wandering back towards where the car was parked, I stopped to browse in a bookshop window. The display was an interesting one, consisting entirely of books that had been recently challenged or banned according to the 1997 *Banned Books Resource Guide*. More than a dozen titles were on display, each with a small label indicating the place where it had met with disapproval and a quotation to indicate why. I expected to find a good representation of Southern censorship, but to my surprise most of the books had fallen foul of authorities elsewhere.

Racial nerves had been touched in a couple of cases, and one of these was in the South. The Alabama Textbook Committee had denounced Maya Angelou's *I Know Why the Caged Bird Sings* because of its 'bitterness and hatred towards whites', but more extraordinarily, Warren, Indiana opposed *To Kill a Mockingbird* because of its 'psychological damage to the positive integration process' and for its representation of 'institutionalised racism under the guise of "good literature"'.

Sex, violence and bad language were obvious reasons to challenge or ban books, but I wasn't quite prepared for all the titles I saw. The only place that got two mentions in the window was Fairbanks, Alaska where they didn't like *The Bluest Eye* by Toni Morrison ('graphic descriptions and disturbing language'), and they also objected to an 'obscene and pornographic' publication called *The Bible*. Fairbanks' reaction to the Christian good book was reflected in the straight-laced and/or decidedly dated reaction to *Sons and Lovers* in Oklahoma City ('smut'). *The New Joy of Sex* had more predictably been confiscated from bookstores in Lexington, Kentucky, but Hillsborough, New Jersey objected to the 'violence and curse words' in John Grisham's *The Client*. Better still, the *Diary of Anne Frank* was rejected in Wise County, Virginia for being 'sexually offensive', while in Carlsbad, New Mexico *Webster's Dictionary* was dismissed because it 'defined obscene words'.

Some of the other examples were more mystifying still. Boulder, Colorado took exception to *Charlie and the Chocolate Factory* because the 'book exposes a poor philosophy of life', while the objection in Oakland, California to Alice Walker's *The Color Purple* was based on the book's 'sexual and social explicitness'. I stood for some moments trying to work out what they could have meant by 'social explicitness' but had to give up. I still don't know what it means.

The best castigation of all was reserved for one of my childhood favourites, *The Lion, the Witch and the Wardrobe*. According to Howards County, Maryland, the book is totally unsuitable because it's full of 'graphic violence, mysticism and gore'. Perhaps that was why it was one of my favourites. On reflection, the description might also have been applied to the Southern myth, and perhaps this was why I was enjoying my trip so much.

16

Into the Valley of
Country Commercialism

Interstate 81 took me down into the southwestern corner of Virginia where the Appalachian foothills gave the countryside an Alpine feel. Cows grazed the pastures between the hay bales and the trees had started their autumnal displays. As I neared Tennessee, occasional swathes of leaves were laid out across the highway like transient tapestries. Driving through them blasted a storm of vivid yellows, deep fiery reds, and ripe-peach oranges into my rear-view mirror. The only sign of cultivation here was a single tobacco field which they had just begun to harvest, by hand as far as I could tell as I swept past.

I'd been listening to a local music station on the radio, and flicking through the wavebands every now and again to see what else I'd been missing. This time I stopped when I heard a jingle about Spam, 'Good for you and fun to eat, it's the best type of luncheon meat.' The cheery voice went on to rave about such culinary delights as Spam burgers, and Spam and eggs, but the Spam didn't get my full attention because I was just passing a signpost that looked uncannily familiar. It said 28 miles to Abingdon and 43 miles to Bristol.

The Spam commercial was followed by a pretty serious monologue on God and debt. The message was that running up large debts wasn't good for you. 'As Christians,' the man said, 'we have to decide whether having peace in our lives is more important than having things.' If you chose the peace option, the solution to your debt crisis probably lay in cutting back on your spending, he said. It was all very sound, down-to-earth advice. 'Now cutting back is not going to be a lot of fun,' the man pointed out. 'It's a lot of fun to get into debt, it's not going to be a lot of fun to get out of debt.' How right he is.

The Christian debt-buster kept going all the way to the Tennessee state line where a big sign said that the Volunteer State welcomed me. The man had covered a lot of ground on violating basic Biblical principles about money (such as greed) and the need to repent. I had been impressed by the guy's integrity, but just as I pulled off the Interstate to visit the Tennessee Welcome Center his spiel was spoiled. An announcer came on and told listeners that they could find out more about the Biblical principles and how they should be applied by buying the *Complete Guide to Managing your Money*. The hardbound, three-volume set would also make a great gift or an excellent addition to your church library, the announcer said.

I switched off the ignition, killing the radio, climbed out of my car, stretched my arms and ventured into the welcome centre. When I emerged with my own mini-library of promotional literature about Tennessee, I noticed a giant guitar nestling beneath the trees on the opposite side of the highway. The guitar itself was as tall as a tree, even though it was lying on its side, dwarfing what looked like a barn beside it. It was an appropriate symbol of the fact that I was entering 'country' country.

A couple of hours later I turned south, off the Interstate, towards Pigeon Forge. The local weather forecast for northeast Tennessee and southwest Virginia said it was going to be cold tonight, with 49 for low. Tuesday, they were looking for mostly sunny skies and a high of 72. Right now it was 74. A twangy country music song rang out from my radio, followed by an advertisement for a miracle weight loss cure called Metabolite. 'The thing about Metabolite is that you're not going to be dieting,' the man said; in fact they tell you to do just the opposite. 'The only way to lose weight with Metabolite is to eat,' he announced. 'You'll eat less, but you still have to eat. Call 800 968 DIET. You have nothing to lose but weight.'

I passed a homemade sign nailed to a tree. It said 'Jesus is coming', but I couldn't see him. 'Don't worry about it making you sick,' the Metabolite salesman enthused, 'it's all natural.'

I was entering a more built-up area, a garish strip that turned out to continue for miles and miles, all the way up to the start of the Great Smoky Mountains national park. A spattering of fast food restaurants was punctuated with signs for coming attractions. October was Tennessee domestic violence awareness month, said one. 'Don't miss the Action Antique Mall, where the action is', said another. If I turned off at exit 407, it would take me to the world's largest fireworks store. Up ahead, the Smoky Mountains were coming into view. They looked pretty smoky, even in the bright sunshine of the late afternoon.

'I've been talking about it, now's the time for you to try it,' Metabolite man said. 'Call 800 968 DIET. That's 800 968 D-I-E-T.' I crossed a wide river to be met with a giant sized picture of Dolly Parton on a particularly big hair day saying 'Turn me on.' It was an invitation to Dolly's station on 105.5 FM. I couldn't resist it, and anyway I'd heard enough about Metabolite.

The elongate development was becoming increasingly gaudy and by this time the road had widened to five lanes in both directions. I continued driving, half a block, half a block, half a block onward, into the contrived valley of country commercialism. Factory outlet malls to the right of me, resort and convention centres to the left of me, flashing lights and Smoky Mountains helicopter rides in front of me. And all around were the dulcet tones of Dolly's country music.

I passed the Rebel Dish Farm (!) that sold plates and cutlery and stuff. A hoarding for the Dixie Stampede showed a picture of a man on an ostrich. Another hoarding tempted me with 'A day at the beach in the mountains'. I could go ice skating all year round in an enclosed mall, or drop in at the Incredible Christmas Place. Suddenly, every other building was a wedding chapel, and then I saw a flamboyant sign for the Bible Factory Outlet. I could tell I was going to love Pigeon Forge.

My fuel tank gauge looked like it was approaching empty, so I pulled off the road and into a wide gas station forecourt. As I stood holding the nozzle in the gas tank, I gazed in amazement at the Smoky Mountain Trading Post Statuary opposite. It sold a wide range of really gross statues as souvenirs, or at least I think that's what was meant by the word 'sauvieneers'. They had all sorts of fountains, and a selection of animals, mostly dogs, but their most popular item appeared to be a small boy, available in Caucasian or African-American colouring, dressed in red jacket and peaked cap. They looked like little jockeys. Only later did I discover that these little fellows were the Old South's equivalent of garden gnomes. They aren't actually very common any longer due to their racist overtones, having evolved as the lower gentility's answer to the real slave boys employed to tie up visitors' horses in the old days. Everyone I spoke to about them thought they weren't made any more, and none had ever heard of white lawn jockeys, so I told them all to get down to Pigeon Forge.

When I asked the girl behind the gas station counter for a receipt, she said, 'Woah,' which sounded to me like she was trying to stop a horse, but this was probably only because I'd just spent the last few minutes trying to work out the lawn jockeys. 'There's another accent,' she exclaimed. 'Where yawl from?' I told her where we were all from. 'Oh! We had a guy come through here from England, just now,' she replied.

Standing next to her was another server, who said, 'Yeah,' and then drawled something consisting of at least a hundred syllables all coalesced into one long word sentence. I found it completely unintelligible.

'Sorry?'

He did it again. His voice sounded like very thick syrup would sound if it made a noise. I really didn't have a clue what he was saying and the situation was now becoming rather embarrassing. I tried one more time. 'Sorry, I'm not with it, I've been driving for hours. What did you say again?'

The guy wasn't fazed at all by my total lack of understanding of my own language. 'Iluhhh-saayed, y-mait-wannagoan-lukimuuup.' I nodded. I think this translated to 'You might want to go and look him up' but it was a spur of the moment comment and the moment had long passed.

The girl came to my rescue. 'Yeah,' she said, 'he was just leaving, and he had a great time. Welcome to East Tennessee.' I thanked them both and walked out feeling like a simpleton in a mild state of shock.

I'd been driving along the valley of country commercialism for quite a few miles now and as I climbed back into my hire car, I realised that I'd unconsciously been expecting to arrive eventually at some kind of town centre. But as I settled into the seat and turned the key in the ignition, a sense of *déjà vu* came over me. It was that disorientation sickness I'd felt in Gainesville, Florida. I had a nasty feeling that Pigeon Forge was going to be a place that didn't actually have a centre. I switched off the ignition and shuffled through the tourist literature I had picked up at the Tennessee welcome centre until I found one on Pigeon Forge. It included a map. I was right, this was it. State Highway 66 was what human geographers call a suburban freeway corridor, which meant there was no middle. Mildly annoyed, I looked out across the road again at the lawn jockeys, which, in my overtired state, I thought were smiling at me. Either I had been driving too much, or I really was a simpleton.

I looked around me and saw the Mountain Trace Inn motel, so I drove over to it and checked in.

It was only six o'clock and still too early for dinner by the time I had dumped my bag in my room, so I made a beeline for the Bible Factory Outlet. According to my map, it was within easy walking distance from the Mountain Trace Inn, but I gave up on this idea very quickly because it meant crossing a ten-lane crossroads which was a physical impossibility on foot. So I had to get back into my car and drive the few hundred yards.

I wasn't disappointed by the Bible Factory Outlet. It was situated inside a huge concrete bunker that looked like it had been built to survive Armageddon. Inside, it contained everything the committed parishioner might need and quite a lot more besides. There were Bibles galore, including a King James version on 62 CDs, but also T-shirts, bumper stickers, videos, music and all sorts of horrible statu-ettes of angels. There was also a good selection of wall maps showing things like Paul's Journey, and Where Jesus Walked, and the Holy Land Then and Now.

Some of the bumper stickers were first class, such as 'Hangeth in there' and 'Are you closer to this than you are to JESUS?', while others were designed for the rather more serious religious devotee (e.g. 'Only half the patients who enter an abortion clinic come out alive'). Their T-shirt selection was mostly light-hearted, many of the designs being religious mock-ups of more conventional T-shirt logos. One of them came with 'Jesus Christ' written on it in that squiggly Coca-Cola script; another said 'Lord's Gym' in chunky American football style lettering around a picture of a Herculean figure doing press-ups on a bench. On the muscle man's back was a cross with the words 'The sin of the world' engraved upon it.

There were posters too, with all kinds of Biblical quotations written on them, including one that was actually a framed picture with a battery powered luminous green thunderbolt zigzagging down across the simple word 'God' written in bold letters. But my favourite range of religious merchandise was a series of small pebbles measuring about two inches high and four inches long, each with a thought provoking inscription on it. They were The Lord is Good Stones, retailing at $12.99 each. 'Great gifts for many uses,' the packaging declared, 'birthdays, Father's Day, graduations, Christmas.' They weren't even real stones. They were made of plastic.

I was reminded of the plastic stones later that evening after I had eaten in a diner just across the road from my motel. The diner looked real, with original pink Formica tabletops and all sorts of musical memorabilia on the walls. The whole building was long and round like a caravan and decked out in chrome so it was like eating inside a silver cigar tube. I had a Swiss Onion Burger and it took me some time to figure out what it was that made it Swiss. I didn't think it was the onion so I decided it must be the small white splodge of cheese since everybody knows that the Swiss make cheese. But the cheese was processed and utterly tasteless, which would have been a cause of some concern if I'd been Swiss. But I'm not, and the burger itself was very good. It was meaty in the way that fast food burgers never are.

I'd taken my life in my hands getting to the diner. Although it was literally just across the road from my motel, the road in question was six lanes wide and on a bend. I'd nearly been killed dashing across it to get there, but coming back was more dangerous still because I was heavier to the tune of one Swiss Onion Burger and a basketful of fries. I wondered whether this was the sort of activity that helped the US to produce all those great sprinters.

Anyway, when I was safely back in my motel room, I switched on the television and started flicking through the channels. After a brief pause at a game show where the contestants were answering questions on Shakespeare Lite (e.g. What was the name of Juliet's lover?), I became absorbed in an investigative programme about a Southern preacher named Jimmy Swaggart. Like the makers of The Lord is Good Stones, Mr Swaggart was involved in selling religious products to the faithful, but the implication of the piece was that Jimmy Swaggart was not quite as wholesome as he liked to make out. He had fallen from grace some ten years before when an appointment with a call girl turned out to be rather more than just a pastoral visit. He was trying to make a come-back, but there was still some way to go before the guy's television ministry reached its previous heights when half a million dollars in donations poured into the coffers every day. The investigation was full of innuendoes about Mr Swaggart's tax-exempt empire, allegedly dodgy real estate deals and personal extravagances.

The reporter caught up with Mr Swaggart outside a restaurant near Baton Rouge in Louisiana. The TV evangelist looked benignly inoffensive beneath his bouffant hairpiece and denied any wrong doings, suggesting that the reporter could take the Sermon on the Mount and make it look like a plot to overthrow the government. He may well have had a point, but the way in which he claimed his innocence made me think he might at any minute pull out a couple of Gospel albums and try to sell them to the reporter. Later in the programme, there were fresh allegations about Mr Swaggart loitering in a decidedly seedy part of town near where he lived. When questioned by the police, at first he said he was lost, and then later it was stated that he was looking for a radio tower.

Mr Swaggart was no doubt fulfilling some kind of role in Southern society, but it was hard not to view that role in the same light as the guy peddling Metabolite on the radio earlier in the day, or the woman I'd watched in Beaufort promoting soap made from ten different seaweed extracts that made you thin when you washed with it. It wasn't for me to judge whether or not Jimmy Swaggart was a charlatan, but it was easy to see him as just the latest in a long line of salesmen intent on selling another myth to a bewildered Southern populace.

Breakfast was served in room 117 of the Mountain Trace Inn. The bed had been removed and replaced with small round tables and moulded chairs. All the breakfast fare was laid out on a sideboard like a plastic indoor picnic. I hadn't slept particularly well and I was feeling rather grumpy as I walked in to be faced with a room full of old white folks that made me think I'd been transported back to the condominium block in Miami where David lived with his family.

I helped myself to a cup of coffee and popped a muffin into the toaster to brown while I gathered a paper plate, plastic knife, a small container of margarine and another of grape jelly. I sat down at the only vacant round table and buttered my muffin. A scrawny old man with a scrape of grey-black hair and hands like talons sat facing me at the next table. His eyes were large and watery, as was his wife whose skin was as white as the polystyrene foam cup she drank from, only her skin was lumpy and had wrinkles on top, which the cup didn't. The view put me off my muffin.

I briefly thought about feeling guilty because of my ageist attitude, but I hadn't got the energy, so I just concentrated on my coffee. The scrawny old man did the job much more effectively. As he and his wife left, he paused at my table and said, 'Right fair weather today.' It was, indeed, a beautiful day outside.

'Yes,' I said.

'Sure is pretty out there,' he said, and moved on.

Today was the day I was going to visit Dollywood. I'd been looking forward to it in a masochistic kind of way because I thought it would be ghastly. I'd decided to miss out on Disneyland in Florida because I could only cope with one US themepark and I reckoned that Dollywood was more likely to have a Southern flavour. It did, but it wasn't nearly as awful as I'd been expecting.

The place was a short drive from the motel, off the main drag along a road that threaded its way between an electricity relay station and a cemetery on one side and a golf course on the other. I was stung four dollars for parking and boarded an open bus that would take me to the entrance.

'We're all goin' to the front door of Dollywood, every one of us,' claimed the old man who drove the bus. 'Hold tight and remain seated. We're goin' in motion.'

I had thought I'd hate Dollywood because I'd hated Euro Disney in Paris, a place I'd forced myself to visit for a previous travel book. Dollywood was just as commercial as Euro Disney, but it was not quite so plastic and a little less self-consciously clean cut. Indeed, after Euro Disney, Dollywood was small scale and almost quaint. It was still a bit too gushing for my taste, and on the tacky side in places, but here in the US of A it seemed fitting, whereas in Paris, France the whole exercise had been totally inappropriate.

There were all the rides you'd expect from a themepark, including an old merry-go-round of the type that you refuse to ride on when you're a teenager because it's too babyish, but it still wasn't recommended for anyone with back, neck or bone injuries or a recent history of illness. This didn't leave many takers, since most of the visitors were geriatrics like the people who had surrounded me at breakfast that morning. The other thing that might have put people off was the notice at the gate to the carousel declaring that the management had to feel your clothes for wetness before you could ride. This declaration seemed rather at odds with the family atmosphere that otherwise pervaded the park, but the reason was that the antique wooden animals needed protection from damp bottoms. Nevertheless, the notice didn't specifically mention incontinence.

I didn't have a go on the carousel, but I did take a ride on the Dollywood Express, a five mile trip outside the compound on a real coal-burning steam train. The conductor was a wag who was unexpectedly risqué in his warm-up remarks to his passengers. 'Slide up to the right if there's less than five adults on your seat,' he said over the loudspeakers. 'For people from Alabama, the right is the side with the mountain on it.' Everybody laughed, except, I assumed, anyone who happened to be from Alabama, but the conductor was quick to add that he liked kidding folks from Alabama. 'Most of them are real nice people,' he added.

Before the train left the station, a young guy came along the open carriages offering ice-cold drinks for sale. His Dollywood name badge said his name was Kip and I realised that his was the first black face I'd seen since arriving in Tennessee. I think he was also the only non-white face I saw the whole day.

The train took us out into a bit of countryside and initially I was relieved to see that there was some that had escaped the influence of the valley of country commercialism. But my relief was short-lived. Soon after leaving the Dollywood compound the driver asked us to look over to our right, where we saw a stuffed bear. It was the first of a series of Disneyfied objects placed at strategic points along the route to give the driver a structure for his running commentary. The commentary was laced with racy jokes, the bear being an excuse for him to tell us the one about the passenger who got off the train without permission and was chased by a big old bear. 'She hollered at me, "Hello! Hello! Stop the train!" I said I cain't. She said, "Why not?" I said, it states plain and clear in my conductors' handbook that I'm not allowed to let anybody on my train with a bare behind.'

Back inside the compound, I wandered among the old timers, all of whom were carrying huge paper Coca-Cola cups like hand held advertising beacons. Some of the more infirm had taken advantage of the small electric carts that were available from a booth just inside the entrance, although others I saw riding the carts just looked like lazy fat people. The Dollywood compound was surrounded by trees and some had been allowed to remain standing inside. At the foot of each one was a display of pumpkins and squashes, and sometimes a straw scarecrow to give the place a Halloween flavour. But although the trees had obviously begun to shed their foliage, not one leaf was allowed to remain on the smooth black tarmac pathways for more than a minute. A small army of sweepers was ever ready to whisk away any stray leaves that might think otherwise, no doubt to protect against unpleasant lawsuits that could result from a visitor slipping on one.

I bought lunch from Miss Lillian's Chicken House and was surprised by the woman behind the till who said, 'You having a good time today?' It wasn't the question that surprised me so much as the way she asked it. She sounded like she was really concerned about my pursuit of happiness. Mr Jefferson turned up again some minutes later in a conversation I had with a man munching cinnamon bread. We were both eating beside one of the Halloween pumpkin displays, within earshot of a live show of award-winning, hand-clapping Gospel music from the Kingdom Heirs. They sang to a packed audience, many of whom looked relieved just to be sitting in the shade, but most were also enjoying the music and joined in at the clapping parts.

The man gestured towards the pile of pumpkins and said to me,

'Thomas Jefferson said if we ever turned our backs on agriculture we'd be in for a hard time. And if you look at the state of this nation's agricultural industry, sure enough, we're going down the tubes.' The comment had come right out of the blue, and I wasn't sure how to react, but the cinnamon man didn't appear to want a reply. He was obviously in a philosophical frame of mind and he just carried on with another snippet from his outlook on life.

'You ever sit and just watch folks?' he asked rhetorically. 'I do. God must have had a sense of humour. You look at all these people and they're all different, not one of them the same. Yet I see a man looking for his wife, or a child talking to his mother, and I think, Yep, I did that.'

It was a rural, Southern, small-town sort of thing to say, I thought, entirely in keeping with the Dollywood ambience. Although in some ways Dollywood was more commercially aware even than the Disney corporation (the woman behind the till at the chicken place had offered me my change in Dolly dollars, which were of course totally valueless outside the Dollywood area, meaning that you had to spend them before you left, or better still, keep them as souvenirs of your visit), but in other ways, the product on offer seemed more genuine. Part of the reason for this was because Dollywood was rooted in the historical traditions of the Smoky Mountains. Before lunch, I'd walked through a whole zone given over to the preservation of local crafts, where men and women, dressed in dungarees, carved wooden furniture and threw their own pottery, forged tools by hand and made all sorts of things out of leather.

And of course there was Dolly herself. Among the themepark's attractions was a mock-up of her childhood home on Locust Ridge in the Tennessee mountains. I'm not a great fan of country music, and before coming to Dollywood I had no idea what humble stock Miss Parton emerged from. The wooden house consisted of just two rooms, with newspaper instead of wallpaper. One room was a bedroom, the other was for everything else. Dolly was one of twelve children who all slept on the floor on straw pallets.

There was more of her rags to riches story in the Dolly Parton Museum. She was born in the two room shack on Locust Ridge, delivered by the local doctor whose payment was a sack of cornmeal.

I had to bite my tongue when I read a notice that said the family was poor in material things but rich in love, but the tongue biting was my problem because the statement did ring true. Dolly learned to sing in church and recorded her first record when she was ten.

There was the expected collection of musical instruments, awards and mementoes, an original 1977 Dolly Parton doll (a customised Barbie with too much hair and an extra big bust) and a selection of her outfits displayed on headless mannequins also with specially enlarged bosoms. But there was also a large photograph of her hairdresser, and a Bible presented to her by Willie Nelson while on a visit to Texas. Dolly had been married to the same man for decades and had a dog named Mark Spitz. The impression I took away with me was one of a woman who had kept her feet firmly on the ground, despite having hit the dizziest heights. Although Dolly's personal welcome and farewell, shown on video screens at the beginning and end of the museum, were too saccharine sweet for my taste, they did seem genuine even to a cynic like me. Her final words, 'Thank you for coming here today, and do come back. And you remember, that I will always love you', would not have been the way I'd have taken my leave, but then I wasn't a female country music star.

17

Death by Adelgid

There weren't any free tables at all the next morning in room 117. I took as long as I could getting my coffee and muffin, and even loaded a plastic bowl with cereal in the hope that someone would vacate a table in the meantime. No luck. I stood looking forlornly at the sea of elderly faces until a couple on a central table beckoned me over to join them. I thought I was going to have to pay for my uncharitable thoughts the previous morning, but the couple exchanged small talk between themselves until I started a conversation. Then they talked my arm off.

They opened by telling me that they usually stayed at a different hotel, the Hampton. 'It's worth paying that bit extra to get breakfast,' the man said. I wasn't quite sure what to make of this comment. What did they think they were doing here, I wondered, planning a space mission? Then I got this image in my mind of them sitting in the sumptuous Hampton dining room tucking into a serious breakfast consisting of a huge steak with a fried egg on top and hash brown potatoes all over the place, with a side order of pancakes and maple syrup to go with it. Or perhaps they would have it all on the same plate like the old lady I'd seen at the Mountain Lake hotel.

But the image didn't last long. The old man was telling me why they were in Pigeon Forge. They had been visiting their granddaughter in her new place outside Charlotte. She was 25 years old and it was the first time she'd been asked to live without a dishwasher.

'And she's not doin' too well,' said her grandmother.

The elderly couple forged on to give me a blow by blow account of what was wrong with their granddaughter's new accommodation. 'It's a dumb house,' the old man told me, 'and it starts the moment you walk in the front door.'

'Would you believe the light switch is behind the door as you open it?' his wife asked incredulously. She had a funny way of talking, that wasn't entirely due to her syrupy drawl. I couldn't work out what it was until her husband told me she hadn't put her dentures in yet that morning. The old lady smiled, keeping her mouth firmly shut as she did so. I thought she did pretty well without them.

'In the bathroom, the mirror is above the commode,' the man said, 'and light switches are in the wrong rooms.' It certainly did sound like a dumb house.

I'm not good with children or small animals first thing in the morning, but I decided that I could, after all, cope with old people. Their story was harmless enough, if a bit tedious after a while. I could have sat at the next table, where the middle-aged couple who had come in after me were being told a joke by the old guy who had kindly called them over to share his eating space. The joke was about a truck driver running over a cat.

As the catalogue of horrors in the granddaughter's dumb house continued, a young family appeared for breakfast, the mother carrying their own box of cereal for the two small children. A table had just been vacated, so they got one to themselves. As we were getting down to the dumb aspects of the property beneath the house (it was an ideal place for coons to hang out, and they can stink you know), another old gentleman paused on his way out at the young family's table. The old gentleman proceeded to give the young family edited highlights of his life story. I had finished my cereal by this time and had moved on to my muffin. The discourse on my table had turned to plumbing. My informant was pretty handy with a monkey wrench, he told me, which was just as well, because there were a lot of things that needed fixin' in that dumb house, and he proceeded to give me some details.

Over on the young family's table, the old gentleman was finishing up. I heard him say, 'Nice meeting you. We don't know any names here, but it's what's in the heart that counts. As I was passing I looked at you and thought that's a nice Christian family.'

'Oh we are,' replied the bewildered father. It was the first time he had had the chance to say anything at all.

'Now, before I go,' the old gentleman said, 'I want to ask you a favour.' I saw the young father's face freeze for an instant. 'We'd like a photograph of Cecilia who runs this place,' the old gentleman continued. 'Could you take one of us with her?'

I hadn't realised, but the old gentleman had a wife hovering near by.

Clearly relieved that he wasn't being asked to buy a family subscription to the Moonies, the young daddy gladly agreed to take the photograph. The old gentleman positioned himself between Cecilia and his wife in front of the sideboard with the breakfast things on and all three put on broad smiles. A ripple of polite applause rang out from several of the tables after the flash. The old lady on my table forgot herself for a moment and smiled with her mouth open, giving me a brief flash of her gums.

I was driving into the Great Smoky Mountains national park. There was another fine day in the offing as my hire car purred its way along State Highway 66 through the country-style shopping and entertainment resort. I'd thought Pigeon Forge was tacky, but it wasn't a patch on Gatlinburg, the last conglomeration before the park. There was a brief respite between the two, about five miles of forest before the full horror of Gatlinburg hit me right between the eyes. The road had narrowed as the valley sides had closed in which probably enhanced the effect, but there was no doubt that Gatlinburg was in another league when it came to tat.

It was one long line of T-shirts, discount souvenirs, plastic fast food joints, counterfeit candy stores, and art galleries full of appalling pictures. There were baseball caps, cut price wooden signs and all sorts of other futile articles with 'Great Smoky Mountains' written on them. Religious shops sold cuddly toys alongside books of clean church jokes and Bible teaser videos. It was budget this and bargain that, rustic gifts for people with no taste and indoor climate controlled mini-golf for those with time to waste. It was bright lights, big city rural East Tennessee style, and it wasn't a pretty sight. There was even a two-chair ski lift that took punters up the steep valley slopes to give them an aerial view of all the crap.

And then it just stopped.

Suddenly, I was in the park and surrounded by trees. I pulled over to the side of the road, switched off the engine, and drew a deep breath. The air tasted fresh and there was not a sound of 'civilisation' to be heard, just the hint of a breeze rustling the leaves and a few birds twittering somewhere out of sight.

I pulled out my copy of a booklet I'd picked up at the Tennessee Welcome Center. The *Great Smoky Mountains National Park Complete Guide to Planning your Stay* had a fold-out map in the middle. There wasn't an awful lot of choice as to where to go. One road sliced through the middle of the park from northwest to southeast, with a few offshoots to places of interest. I decided just to drive on, certainly to the state line with North Carolina which cut through the middle of the park more or less at right angles to the main road, and maybe beyond.

The road was flanked every so often with parking spots and I stopped in one after about a quarter of an hour and ventured into the forest on foot. Before I did so, however, I read my booklet's safety tips about bears. Like the advice on alligators in Florida, the first tip was do not feed them. There was a lot of stuff on how clever these black bears were, especially when it came to purloining a free lunch. They had been known to open car doors to get at objects they thought may be nourishing, but they obviously weren't that clever because they couldn't read the labels. To a bear, the booklet pointed out, a can of tennis balls might look like a can of potato chips. You were also advised to hide things like cosmetics – because to a bear they might look like food, not because bears like wearing make-up.

I threw a quick glance around the interior of my hire car, trying to do it like a bear would, and decided that there was nothing that even one of average intelligence could interpret as a possible food source. I read on. There was a bit about how to make your campsite bear-proof by hanging all food, toothpaste and cosmetics at least ten feet off the ground. And then the advice ended, with the words: 'If a bear approaches, keep a safe distance and use good judgement.' I looked again. That was all it said. Nothing about running zigzag, or climbing trees, or lying down to play dead, just 'use good judgement'. What was that supposed to mean?

So I locked the car door, and took off into the forest trying my best to think what on earth the booklet had meant by good judgement. Above the section on safety tips had been a photograph of a very large black bear looking straight at the camera. The caption said there were between 400 and 600 of them in the park and you can spot them almost anywhere, which was a great comfort.

The trail I followed led straight into a sun-dappled wilderness of oaks, maples and tulip trees, each trunk coated in a veneer of lichen or a cushion of moss. Carpets of leaves took me through complexes of roots and the delicate filaments of spiders' webs that hung glistening in the sun to catch rather smaller prey. I walked down to a babbling brook of crystal clear water that broke into mini-rapids over rocks smoothed by centuries of flow. Sitting on a mossy perch in a sunny glade, I sucked in great greedy gulps of clean air tinged with subtle forest aromas. Nature was all the more serene after the madness of Gatlinburg, and thankfully there was not a bear in sight.

I drove on, slowly gaining altitude, winding through shadowy stretches where fallen leaves gave a crisp crunch beneath the tyres, and into clearings where the sunlight was momentarily blinding. There were few cars on the road, so it felt like I had the park all to myself. Dolly's radio station told me they were expecting the temperature to hit the upper seventies before I turned it off. Even country music didn't seem appropriate to the setting. I stopped frequently, either to stroll through the trees or just to marvel at the mountain views. The higher I climbed, the more the distant rounded peaks looked woolly with trees, as if you could reach out and run your hand through them like a green sheepskin fleece.

When I reached a lookout named Morton Overlook, the air was blustery and cold and I had to pull on my jacket before striking out, away from the vehicles which had stopped to savour the view. A small notice told me I was at 4837 feet, but the slopes were too precipitous to venture far.

Newfound Gap was at 5048 feet, on the Tennessee/North Carolina state line. There was a much larger area to pull off and park your car here and a long tarmaced walkway overlooking a stunning mountain view. The sun was high, the sky was blue and the Smokies were doing their stuff. I could see for miles before the trees merged with the sky in a faint blue haze.

The USA's approach to its national parks is significantly different to that in Britain. Our parks have towns and pubs and all sorts of other municipal paraphernalia in them, as well as farmers and quarries and goodness knows what else. US parks, by contrast, are a conscious attempt to leave people out of it, unless they're just passing through to have a look. But the difficulties of cordoning off slabs of country-side and keeping them pristine were reflected in one of the public information notices that lined the walkway. It said the bluish haze that gave rise to the Smokies' name, a product of the trees, like a sort of forest perspiration, had got smokier in recent times thanks to air pollution. In 1960, a visitor looking out from this spot could see 22 miles into the distance, but on a clear day nowadays it is just 12 miles before the haze takes over. The airborne pollutants were also thought to be having a retarding effect on tree growth in the park, proving that people can still screw things up even from a great distance. Perhaps they should rename them the Smoggies.

More unfortunate evidence of human blunders was clearer still up at Clingmans Dome, the highest spot in the Smokies. Here, the forest should have been dominated by spruce and fir, a mountain com-munity much like that found in central Canada, fostered by the cool, wet climate. You could see the fir trees all right, but they had a problem. Most of them were dead.

The mountain sides were littered with pallid grey trunks, most devoid of anything green, pointing ramrod straight either up towards the brilliant blue sky or lying at acute angles having finally given up trying. They looked like they were groping the heavens in a desperate last attempt to stay upright. Most of them now made up a ghost forest, just sickly former trees that resembled what I thought a forest X-ray might look like. It surprised me how much the trunks looked like feeble twigs once they had lost their foliage. Was this the result of acid rain, I wondered, or some other deadly cloud of chemicals that had wafted over one day and been blown away, carrying the souls of the trees with it?

No, was the answer. It was nothing to do with poisonous fumes or radioactive fallout. This was the result of the balsam woolly adelgid. The balsam woolly what? I thought to myself as I read the park's service notice. The balsam woolly adelgid, the notice replied, a tiny insect that is particularly partial to a bit of Fraser fir sap. Well, more than just a bit of sap, the notice made clear. These creepy crawlies wanted it all. Up to 50,000 balsam woolly adelgids jump on to a single fir and suck away at it for six to eight years until it's dry. Then they all move on to the next Fraser fir and start all over again. More than 95 per cent of the Fraser firs in the park are dead, having had the life sucked out of them. As if that wasn't enough, the trees are also poisoned by a nasty toxin that the adelgid leaves behind him.

And where did this ridiculous sounding insect come from? It was accidentally introduced to North America from Europe at the turn of the century. Oh dear.

The information board pointed out that nobody knows of a control for the adelgid that is acceptable for application in a national park, where non-destructive insects must be protected. The park authorities had been trying to deal with the little woolly bastards for years apparently. Each summer, the trees are sprayed with a special soap solution that kills adelgids but is completely harmless to every other living thing, or so they reckon. Despite their best efforts, the decimation all around me suggested that there was little doubt about who was winning the fight to save this little piece of Canada in the Smokies. Meanwhile, they're busy collecting seeds from the few trees that are left and trying to raise them in other parts of the park.

I wandered along a path and struck off it into the sad forest remnants. Not all of the trees were dead, just most of them, and the wind through the remaining spruce sounded almost like rushing water. The undergrowth looked fine, and there were healthy ferns everywhere, but the dominant feeling was one of death. Sickly grey trunks had toppled every which way, some spewing up great mounds of earth where their roots had fed, making my progress difficult. The fallen trunks were in various states of decay, most having surrendered their bark to leave a death-coloured wood that snapped with the most brittle crack when I climbed over it. I was clambering through a tree graveyard.

Being the highest point in the Smoky Mountains, Clingmans Dome had been equipped with a surreal concrete viewing tower positioned a short but decidedly uphill walk from the car park. I made my way up to it along the path, through the death throes of the Fraser firs, to ascend a concrete walkway that swirled its way round and up to the top of the concrete tower that looked decidedly like a little piece of

Eastern Europe in the Smokies. From above the tops of the tallest trees, I looked down on the scene of adelgid devastation as a bracing wind pushed and shoved and pulled at my clothes.

When I returned to my car, closed the door against the buffeting wind, and wiped the snot from my runny nose, I let out an involuntary shiver. But it wasn't because I was cold.

18

Cultural Fragments

The pollution problems and the plague of balsam woolly adelgids are, in fact, just the most recent human induced disturbances to hit the Great Smoky Mountains national park. When the park was officially established in 1934, it hardly had any trees because most of them had been cut down.

Europeans began turning up in the Smokies in significant numbers in the late eighteenth century when Scotch-Irish, German, English and other settlers arrived after rolling down the Great Philadelphia Wagon Road. Descendants of these early European pioneers continued to live virtually self-sufficiently into the early twentieth century, growing their own food, raising their own livestock and weaving their own cloth. Their insulated lifestyle and quirky mountain ways earned them their reputation as hillbillies, almost a separate species of high altitude redneck. From the time they first arrived, these settlers chopped down trees, but only to make way for a few crops and to build their log cabins. Although some began to fell trees to sell for lumber in the mid 1800s, it wasn't until the turn of the century that deforestation really got underway on a serious scale.

After clearing large parts of forest in the northeast of the country and around the Great Lakes, lumber companies turned to the southern Appalachians for fresh supplies. By the 1920s, there were fifteen logging company towns inside what is now the national park and many mountain people had turned their backs on ploughing fields and slopping out hogs to cut trees and saw logs for a living. So the park wasn't exactly set up to preserve a pristine wilderness so much as to allow the Smokies to revert to something approaching their natural state.

In order to facilitate this exercise, all the lumber companies were bought out and the hillbillies living within the park's boundaries were asked to leave, although any who didn't want to were allowed life-time residency rights. All pretty benign and forward-looking, you might think. Well yes and no. It was kind to those descendants of the first European settlers, but they weren't the group with the strongest moral claim to be living in the Smokies in the first place. That distinction has to go to the Cherokee Indians, and needless to say they weren't treated quite so kindly.

The Smokies are the sacred ancestral home of the Cherokee nation, originally a breakaway band of Iroquois who probably first arrived in the area around AD 1000. They initially encountered Europeans when the Spanish wanderer Hernando de Soto passed through their territory in 1540, and when the first European settlers appeared about 200 years later, the Cherokee thought they could coexist on relatively friendly terms. In 1721, the Cherokee made their first cession of land to the white man, and in little more than a hundred years they had lost the lot. Their sacred ancestral home, the Smoky Mountains, slipped through their hands in 1819. Agreement to the Treaty of New Echota in 1835 meant that the Cherokee signed away all of their territory east of the Mississippi in exchange for five million dollars and land in the Indian Nation, a concession that ceased to exist in 1889 when it too was opened to white settlement as the Oklahoma Territory.

The Treaty of New Echota was just a formality really because five years before President Andrew Jackson had signed the Removal Act, calling for the forced expulsion of all native people east of the Mississippi river to the new Indian Nation. The Cherokee tried to play the white man at his own game, and appealed against the Removal Act to the US Supreme Court. The Supreme Court found in their favour, but the US president completely ignored the decision. Jackson may be revered by white Southerners as a champion of the common man, but he is viewed somewhat differently by the Indians. They must have rued the day when a Cherokee warrior saved Jackson's life during the Battle of Horseshoe Bend, a skirmish that helped Jackson to reach the White House. Implementation of the Removal Act saw the Cherokee rounded up at bayonet point, loaded on to wagons and forcibly banished. Thousands died along the way. It became known as the Trail of Tears.

A few Cherokee managed to escape the round-up that preceded the Trail of Tears and hid out in the Smokies. Eventually they emerged and managed to lay claim to a few scraps of their former territory that became a reservation called the Qualla Boundary. When the Cherokee first encountered Europeans in 1540, their homeland covered 40,000 square miles. It encompassed virtually all of modern-day Kentucky and Tennessee and bits of six other states. The Qualla Boundary, plus outlying fragments, covers 88 square miles.

For comparison, if a similar thing happened today to the USA, which is 3.6 million square miles, Americans would end up with something about the size of New Jersey to live in. At the height of the Cold War, this is what the boys in the Pentagon were scared of, history repeating itself. US government aides lay awake in their beds at night imagining a nightmare scenario in which the Russians would stroll in and tell the American tribe: 'OK guys, this land is ours now, so you lot have all got to piss off somewhere else. We've set aside New Jersey specially for you. We think you'll be happier there.' The Ruskies would give them a few dollars in compensation, just to make it legal, and then later, after they'd changed the name to New Siberia, they'd claw the dollars back by selling the Americans vodka to drown their sorrows in.

Totally unthinkable, of course, hence the whole arms race thing. And yet this was more or less exactly what happened to the Cherokee, just one of many other similarly dispossessed native tribes. But it was all right because they were only Indians.

I was in the Great Smoky Mountains national park again. I had checked out of the Mountain Trace Inn and was now heading for the Qualla Boundary on the border of the park in North Carolina. I followed the same route as the previous day, but this time stopping only at Newfound Gap on the state line, to look again at the smouldering view.

My eye was caught by something I hadn't seen the day before. It was a wooden noticeboard with the words 'Attention please' burned into its top in barely discernible letters. '"First Amendment" Expression Area' it said below in black and white on a laminated poster. 'This area has been set aside for individuals or groups exercising their constitutional first amendment rights. The National Park Service neither encourages nor discourages, or otherwise endorses, these activities.'

I was completely foxed by this one. I couldn't even remember what the First Amendment was all about. In smaller lettering, the notice added that the site, which was just the walkway, was 'designated for the sale and distribution of printed matter in accordance with the provisions of 36 CFR 2.52 (Permit Required)'. I took a photograph of the notice and showed it to everyone I met during the remainder of my travels through the South. They were all as baffled as I was.

I eventually did discover an explanation care of Tammie, the postgraduate at Greenville, North Carolina who had completed her first degree in Louisiana. She wrote to tell me that they had set up a similarly named spot on campus at Louisiana State University in Baton Rouge. It provided a forum for anyone to express their views on just about anything, she told me. The First Amendment of the US Constitution guarantees freedom of expression, freedom of the press and so on. Having a place set aside for the open practice of that right allowed anyone with very controversial ideas to air them without threat of harassment for disturbing the peace, 'which has happened more than once, especially if they don't like what you are saying', Tammie wrote.

Although I do now understand, I still find it extraordinary that a constitutional right should need a special area in which it can be practised. I would have hoped that one could exercise a supposedly inalienable right anywhere. I thought that was the whole point. The fact that here you seemingly needed a permit to do it made the convoluted system even more bizarre.

At the time, still mystified by the First Amendment Expression Area, I drove on from one little cultural fragment to the next. The Qualla Boundary was hard up against the southern edge of the national park. Cherokee, the main town, wasn't as tacky as Gatlinburg, but it was getting that way. It did have a distinctively Indian flavour, but all this meant was that the horrible pottery consisted of mugs with Cherokee heads on, and the most popular souvenirs for children were shoddy cowboys and Indians outfits like the ones I used to play in as a four year old. There were other items that appeared to be a little more authentic, like spirit sticks with animal skulls stuck on them, ceremonial arrows, and one foot long knives with deer foot handles. But they were tainted and far outnumbered by the influences of the superior American culture. There were galleries full of pictures by the famous artist Kodak, food inspired by the great gourmet McDonald and keepsakes in the manner of that renowned craftsman Disney.

The most depressing sight of all was in a low slung mall complex called the Tepee Village. In front of a large tepee, itself located on the sidewalk in front of an arcade full of exploding video games, was a notice that said: 'Have your picture taken with Chief Henry.' If you used your own camera Chief Henry would pose for tips, but if you used the Chief's camera it would cost you five dollars. Chief Henry himself stood waiting patiently in the bright sunshine dressed in a faded red smock with a huge head-dress of dyed red feathers trailing down his back to rest on his calves. He looked exceedingly bored as he smoked a cigarette and drank ice tea from a large paper cup with Dairy Queen written on it.

The sad scene became tinged with added irony when later I learned that the Cherokees never lived in tepees but in more permanent log cabins. Tepees were designed for quick set-up and take-down and were used by the Plains Indians who followed herds of game. But tepees were what the average punter expected, so that's what the Cherokees gave them.

They also gave them a casino, of course, because as the old timer who had cut my hair in Charleston had rightly pointed out, the Indians weren't as dumb as the white men thought they were. The Tribal Casino was just a large metal hut, like a single-storey warehouse, full of sad white people playing electronic card games because there weren't any real dealers. The Cherokees made do with being cashiers and security men instead while the Cherokee Boys' Club was given over to Gamblers Anonymous for their weekly meeting every Tuesday.

The saving grace of my visit to the Qualla Boundary was a recreation of an eighteenth-century village nestling in the forest on the edge of town. The spot was secluded and quiet apart from the chattering of insects. It was surrounded by trees and rhododendron bushes and wreathed in wisps of smoke from wood fires. The village was staffed by Cherokees doing eighteenth-century things like weaving baskets, making arrowheads and hollowing out canoes, just the sorts of things Andrew Jackson had deemed unsuitable to be practised east of the Mississippi. Interestingly enough, one of the living exhibits was a guy demonstrating a blow pipe, never used in warfare apparently but only on small game. I was shown round as part of a small group by a Cherokee woman with a deep southern accent who sounded as bored as Chief Henry had looked.

As I sped away from Cherokee and out of the Qualla Boundary, I got to wondering about how North America would have turned out if my European forefathers hadn't stumbled upon it. Although it's dangerous automatically to equate indigenous peoples with an harmonious approach to living with their environment, I couldn't really see the Cherokees clearing all the trees from the Smoky Mountains and then having to clear all the people out to let them recuperate. Let alone then messing even that up with industrial pollution and the balsam woolly adelgid. But thoughts like these are pointless exercises and I had a lot of ground to cover if I was going to make it to Asheville before dinner time.

I didn't make it to Asheville. I spent the night in the Maggie Valley instead. Getting this far had been difficult enough because the road was winding, the signposting lousy, and the local pickup drivers distinctly aggressive towards foreigners in hire cars. I'd be doing my best to maintain 30 mph on the tortuous curves when a large motor would appear in my rear-view mirror and sit right on my tail, itching to overtake, but not quite stupid enough to try it until there were at least ten yards of straight road ahead.

As the light was fading, and the mountain road did not appear to be getting any straighter, I pulled over at the top of the valley to let another pickup scream past and decided that if I tried to continue this in the dark I'd certainly be killed. I looked at my map and decided that I was probably an hour or so out of Asheville, and I could still get the hire car back to the airport by 9 a.m. if I got up at six. A little further down the hill, I found a motel and drove in. As I stepped out of the car, a large black cat dressed in a fluorescent green collar came running up to welcome me, confirming that I had made the right decision.

The motel was in a perfect position half-way up the valley. It consisted of a small semi-circle of cabins with round privet hedges and irises growing in front of them and a steep sloping garden that disappeared into trees further up the slope behind the cabins. On the opposite side of the valley, the thickly wooded hills looked untouched and were beginning to haze over with the end of the day. One tiny house poked its nose out from up high, with no apparent way of getting to it.

The lady who ran the motel was originally from Chicago and had a very old dog as well as the friendly cat. The dog was just as friendly, and showed it by giving me a good sniff in the crotch as soon as I stepped through the door into the front room-cum-reception area of the main house. The woman who ran the place smiled and came over to pull the dog away from my genitals.

'He looks like he's been around a while,' I said, as much to divert attention from my crotch as anything.

'Yes,' the woman replied, 'he's gone deaf now. When he was just blind you could at least shoo him away, but now it's a double whammy.'

As the woman was finding a form for me to fill in, I asked her about the signs to a ghost town I'd seen on the road. I'd thought it might be an interesting place to visit. 'Oh it's an amusement park,' she told me, 'the kids love it.'

'I probably don't need to go then,' I thought aloud.

'I don't think so,' she said, handing me the form.

What about places to eat? I wanted to know as I filled in my details. The woman said there was a surprisingly large selection for such a small town. Most of them were down in the bottom of the valley. 'But there's no fast food in Maggie Valley,' she said proudly. 'There used to be a Kentucky's but it burned down and they didn't replace it. When people ask for fast food, I tell them to go to a restaurant. There's less cholesterol, less fat and less garbage.' She said I could do a lot worse than the place just up the road. It was all you can eat and they made the food on the premises. 'It's got a great view too,' she added.

It did have a good view, but it disappeared soon after I got there as the sun dropped behind the mountains to leave a mackerel sky with thick banks of red cloud that looked like furrows of ploughed earth. The food was good too. The place was completely empty when I first walked in, so I just went ahead and helped myself, and I was half-way through my salad before a girl appeared through a brightly varnished wooden door to ask whether I'd like anything to drink. The pace of service was appropriately slow. All the eating places I'd visited in Virginia and East Tennessee had been a little too efficient to be properly Southern.

19

Go Dawgs

The air was mountain fresh and I could see my breath the moment I stepped out of my cabin the following morning. The sun was splashing the mountain tops with amber as I drove down the Maggie Valley away from the motel and I wished I'd spent more time on this side of the Smokies rather than in Pigeon Forge. A few miles beyond the valley the road straightened out and soon I was back in the land of concrete sprawl.

The airport at Asheville, North Carolina was smart, new and empty like every other airport I'd seen on this trip except Miami, which was old and full of people. Like the airports in Charleston, Savannah and Roanoke, this one had round red stickers on its sliding glass doors like the ones saying No Smoking, only these had a silhouette of a gun inside the circle above the words 'No Concealed Handguns'. The implication seemed to be that if you walked in carrying your firearm where everyone could see it, this was OK.

The contrast with the nation's bus and rail stations could not have been more stark. These were always in the seedier parts of town and none had obvious handgun bans, as if the authorities thought you were well advised to carry one if you were stupid enough to travel by bus or train. I spent some time in one of the best examples of the genre while waiting for a connection en route between Asheville and Athens, Georgia. It was in Augusta, and it wasn't a Greyhound station but one belonging to Southeastern Stages Inc. It was situated on a corner, surrounded by wasteland and wooden houses that must have been pretty smart when first built, but this had obviously been some time ago. Now they looked frail and broken like the taxi that a black guy was trying to fix on one of the patches of wasteground.

I was one of twelve people waiting inside the terminal building and all the other faces were black. I'd had a brief conversation with one man who I noticed was wearing two shirts underneath his woolly jacket.

'It's a whole lot different here than up in Hendersonville,' he told me as he unzipped his jacket. 'Damn near froze to death up there. This here's low country. There it's mountain territory; they got hills up there!'

The terminal was divided into two parts, one a waiting area, with the ticket counter where you could also request a token that would open the toilet doors, and the other a sort of cafeteria zone. The cafeteria was self-service down one side, offering one of the least appetising arrays of food I'd seen in a long time, while along the opposite wall stood a series of vending machines with drinks, chewing gum and a selection of brightly coloured rabbits' feet good luck charms.

At one end of the room sat a very large glass case containing souvenirs. The glass case was higher than me and a good five feet wide. Inside it were four dusty glass shelves. On the bottom shelf was a display of knickers and woolly hats. There were three pairs of frilly black and white knickers, each with 'My souvenir of Georgia' written in neat stitching across the crotch, and three flat woolly hats like tam-o'-shanters. Whoever had put these items on display had spaced them out to cover the shelf in an attempt to disguise the fact that they had run low on stock. A similar effort had been made on the shelf above where two necklaces and four bracelets, all in the same cheap black and purple beads, flanked a mug with 'Georgia' written on it. On the top shelf was just one object. It was made of china and had a picture of the state flag on the side. It looked like a hand bell only it didn't have a clanger inside. The third shelf had nothing on it at all except for a dead fly.

It was a sad dislay of cheap merchandise worthy of the poorest African country and it made all the tat on sale in Gatlinburg look attractive. Down on the bottom corner of the glass case I noticed a sticker that said it was protected by an electronic security burglar alarm. I could only think that it was the glass case they were worried about losing.

I was reminded of this collection of souvenirs in the Augusta bus terminal a couple of days later during a conversation I was having about air-conditioning. My hosts in Athens were outlining their theory to explain the resurgence of the South in the post-war years (in this case the Second World War). The saviour of the South, they reckoned, was air-conditioning.

'It made all the difference,' Bonnie's husband Charles told me earnestly, 'and it only became widely available in the home in the 1950s. Before World War Two, Georgia was the equivalent of today's Burkina Faso.'

While air-conditioning obviously hadn't obscured all traces of the area's poorer existence, there was no doubt in Charles' mind that it had brought some major advances. The theory was a new one to me, but it did seem to make some kind of sense. Although where I had just been up in the mountains the climate was definitely less extreme in terms of temperature and humidity, the fact remained that most of the South was low and flat and bloody unpleasant for a large part of the year. I still remembered the searing, muggy heat I'd experienced in Florida and South Carolina, the kind of heat that saps the energy and addles the brain. There was no doubt that whenever I had stepped out of my air-conditioned car, or ventured forth from an air-con building, that hot treacle atmosphere had put the brakes on my pursuit of happiness.

The USA lays claim to perhaps the earliest attempt at air-conditioning, born of a dire emergency after President James Garfield had been shot by a deranged lawyer in 1881. As the president lay dying in the White House in the sweltering July heat, a team of naval engineers was called in to rig up a contraption to relieve his suffering. The engineers came up with a large iron box filled with ice, with a fan at one end to draw air in from outside to pass over the ice and cool the ailing president's quarters. The machine worked after a fashion, but it consumed a lot of ice. When President Garfield passed away about two months later, the device had consumed 250 tons of the stuff.

Less deserving causes couldn't really afford all that ice, and it was another two decades before the first electrical machine was invented, while the term air-conditioner was first coined a few years later by a man in North Carolina. The technology became fairly widely used in municipal buildings like hospitals and cinemas by the 1920s, but it was not until the 1950s that they managed to reduce the size of the unit sufficiently to make it a realistic household accessory. The development of small window models in 1951 suddenly allowed the whole industry to take off.

And with air-conditioning, so the theory goes, the entire South took off. Once the edge had been taken off one of its less pleasant natural assets, there was no stopping the South. Of course it wasn't quite that simple, but it did help to explain why it was that it took a hundred years for the area to recover from 'that war'. Other developments helped, the end of the Jim Crow laws and the whole civil rights movement, the mechanisation of farming, and the rise of jet aircraft and all those dashing regional airports with their bans on concealed weaponry. The ignoble end to the Vietnam war was another factor I heard mentioned. It meant that Southerners were no longer alone in being the only Americans to experience the humiliation of military defeat. All these developments made the South less different; less hot and sweaty, less far away and less intimidating to everyone else. The tide had finally turned, and other Americans started to congregate there in their millions. After fifty years of outward migration, the South began to swell again.

Between 1910 and 1960, Southerners left in unparalleled droves. At least nine million of them, black and white, upped stakes and went north or west. But then the word Sunbelt was coined and Americans flocked towards it like moths. In the period from 1970 to 1990 the eleven states of the Confederacy, plus Kentucky, grew by 40 per cent (more than 20 million people), twice the national growth rate. With the people came wealth and industries and economic well-being. In 1938, Franklin Roosevelt labelled the South as America's 'number one economic problem'; today they call it the country's main engine of economic growth. This leg of my journey was due to end at the biggest jewel in the new crown of the South – Atlanta – but first I had a trip through history to make.

I started more or less at the beginning, at Ocmulgee, where evidence of human occupancy has been found dating back 11,000 years. The area that is now a national monument lies within the city boundaries of Macon, and I drove down there with Bonnie in Charles' shiny red pickup. Most of what you see is of more recent origin, a series of huge flat-topped earth mounds that I found reminiscent of

Aztec and Mayan pyramids in southern Mexico and Central America. They were built when Ocmulgee was an outpost of a culture known to archaeologists as Mississippian because it appeared to crystallise in the Mississippi Valley and spread along rivers throughout much of today's central and eastern USA. The Mississippians thrived here on the floodplain of the Ocmulgee river for about 200 years from AD 900. They built a compact thatched hut town on the bluff overlooking the river and farmed the bottomlands for corn, beans, squash and tobacco, crops that remain as staples of Southern agriculture.

Then they disappeared, leaving no written records or surviving oral legends to tell us why. The archaeologists have tried to find out and have some major artefacts to play with. Bonnie and I wandered through the green pastures to climb the wooden steps to the top of the highest mound. The lush turf on the summit had been kept short, but knee-high grasses covered the mound's flanks where yellow and orange butterflies flicked back and forth across the ancient scene. A notice on the wooden platform at the top said that the archaeologists thought the mound had been built with a million basketfuls of earth. From atop the million basketfuls we gazed through the sunshine one way and saw the treetops of a forest that couldn't have looked much different to the Mississipians. In the other direction stood the city of Macon and it was odd to note that a thousand years of progress meant the mounds were now built of concrete and decorated with satellite dishes and radio towers.

The modern mounds also had people inside, but then so did some of the Mississippian versions. The archaeologists have reconstructed an earth lodge that stood on the north side of the village where twice a year the rising sun shines directly along the 26 foot entrance passage straight at the centre seat on the interior platform. The floor of the lodge is original, clay laid down and smoothed by a little known people while far away the Normans were conquering England. Like the mounds, no one knows what the chamber was used for. Something religious perhaps, or political? The archaeologists think the original was destroyed by fire, maybe in a ceremonial closure, but they're unlikely ever to know for sure.

From the Ocmulgee mounds, we returned towards Athens by a

sinuous route along the backroads. Macon lies at the edge of the coastal plain, though it is 200 miles from the sea, and we were driving away from it into the piedmont, a sloping plateau that stretches up to the Appalachians. You wouldn't think it given all the publicity he gets, but General William Tecumseh Sherman didn't actually burn all of Georgia as he blazed his trail to the sea. One place he seemingly missed was Clinton, or now Old Clinton because it is a shadow of its former self. Back in the 1820s, Clinton was Georgia's fourth largest city but today it's little more than a hamlet of a few hundred people. It never recovered from the Civil War and when the railway avoided it to pass through nearby Gray instead, Clinton's fate was sealed. Old Clinton is now a collection of early nineteenth-century wooden houses resplendent in a leafy solitude that belies the fact that they stand just a hundred yards from a busy road.

The hamlet has more people in its graveyard than in its old houses and Bonnie took me to see the tombstones because she wanted to find an epitaph that she half remembered from a visit many years before. She had tried to find the gravestone again several times in the interim, but had never been successful. She was luckier this time. We found the marble tombstone surrounded by a low stone wall and shaded by towering loblolly pines with bark in chunky sections like armadillo hide. John P Barrow was born in 1830 up the road in Morgan County and died before his 26th birthday. His epitaph struck an appropriate tone for a settlement that time forgot. 'Remember friends as you pass by, you are now so once was I. As I am now so you may be, prepare for death and follow me.'

The pine trees continued north of Old Clinton and there were hay bales in the fields where beef cows from the north wintered. We drove in and out of a Subway and bought sandwiches that looked like each had been stuffed with an entire cow. They were so full of roast beef you could hardly get your mouth open wide enough to eat them. Since we were running late we had to do so in the pickup as we drove. On the outskirts of Eatonton we stopped briefly to look at two old slave cabins that had been reconstructed to house a museum to local boy made good, Joel Chandler Harris. Harris became famous as the author of the Uncle Remus stories of Br'er Rabbit and Br'er Fox and the choice of museum building reflected the fact that he learned his stories from elderly plantation slaves. As Harris declared with a characteristic lack of pretension, all he did was write the fables down.

As the clay soil grew redder and the peach orchards more frequent, we passed through another architectural gem spared by Sherman. The newly painted antebellum houses in Madison were such a pure white they looked unreal, like doll's houses designed for giant children. We crossed emblems of a darker history in Hard Labour creek and Murder creek before we arrived back at the outskirts of Athens, where the hoarding outside a church said: 'If your problems are long-standing, try kneeling.'

The day before I was due to leave for Atlanta was a Saturday, and Charles thought I ought to see something of the University of Georgia Bulldogs football game. He had been building up to it since I'd arrived, with an in-depth anthropological treatise on how local fans prepared for a big match. The 'Dawgs' had an obsessive following, he told me. Real fans got into the right frame of mind the night before a game by eating dog food and sleeping in kennels. Some wore dog collars to the match, he said, their friends walking them by a lead.

It took me a bit of time to decide what to make of Charles. He had the appearance of a laid back radical (with a long thin string of hair tied in a plait down his back), but the seditious side of his nature also came with a curious blend of daintiness. In many ways he was a very meticulous person. For example, he always said 'correct' instead of yes whenever he affirmed something, and when I first arrived, I had to enter the house through the back door because the hall was taken up with an unpacking operation that had lasted more than a month since his return from an overseas trip. But his painstaking attention to detail was most apparent in his approach to cleanliness. I am accustomed to most Americans being physically very clean, people who wash and shower regularly, but in my experience Charles reached new heights of fastidiousness in the hygiene department. I'd never before seen a person sweep the floor around his chair every time he was about to sit down and eat a meal.

I had not met Charles before this visit, and I spent a couple of nervous days trying to gauge whether or not he had a sense of humour. When I had so established (it was a dry one), it took me a while longer before I could tell when he was joking and when he was being serious. His description of the Bulldogs' fans was one such occasion.

They had a fine day for it: bright, hot but not too humid. This was a big game, an all Southern affair against Ole Miss, a team from Oxford, Mississippi. Bonnie took me to it. I think she planned the route carefully because it led us through a world of car parks and what I saw in the car parks was more interesting than what I saw of the game. There weren't any people wearing dog collars, but what there was was just as strange.

A buzz of expectancy accompanied the crowd as it made its way towards the stadium, while far above us small aeroplanes flew back and forth trailing advertising banners across the blue sky. Most people were wearing T-shirts or baseball caps in red and black, the Bulldogs' colours, and carrying red and black cushions to sit on in the 80,000-seat stadium. Some of the women were particulary well dressed, and I recalled the postgraduates in Greenville equating a big football game with dressing up in Sunday best in times gone by. They told me that they had friends who visited the hairdresser before a match, painted their nails and donned their favourite dresses.

The vehicles in the car park all came with bumper stickers saying things like 'This is Bulldog country' and 'Bulldog fan on board'. There were 'Go Dawgs' pennants everywhere and some had cuddly bulldog toys on their dashboards that looked like the bulldog in the *Tom and Jerry* cartoon. One car even had a licence tag that read IAM4UGA. But most extraordinary were the huge recreational vehicles. Some of them were more than 40 feet long, with pullout bits like makeshift bay windows. They resembled the vehicles that corporate outfits bring to fairs in Britain. Some of them could have slept fifteen people inside. They weren't so much mobile homes, as mobile apartment blocks.

The occupants of these movable buildings were obviously set on making a weekend of it. They had brought with them all sorts of equipment to set up, turning the car park into a series of Bulldog shrines designed to make the weekend as comfortable as possible. They had set out red and black deck chairs around their barbecues,

185

they had Bulldog bins for their scraps and Bulldog doormats in front of their vehicle doors. The vehicles themselves were festooned with Bulldog balloons and flags.

As we passed through the car parks, there was less than ten minutes before the game was due to kick off, but many of these makeshift car park patios were still full of people. They were settling down to watch the match, with special Georgia Bulldog things wrapped around their beers to keep them cool. But they weren't going to watch the game in the flesh, they were going to watch it on television. It was all set up. The TV was in a luggage locker and the satellite dish stood on the vehicle roof. I couldn't believe it. The licence tag on one of the monster recreational vehicles indicated that this group had driven all the way from Ohio to watch the game on television in the car park. It was as if they had driven 400 miles only to run out of fuel a hundred yards from the stadium, so they had to break out the TV instead.

When Charles told me about fans eating dog food and sleeping in kennels before a match, I hadn't been sure whether to believe him or not. If he'd told me that some of them drive hundreds of miles just to watch a game on TV in a car park, I'd have definitely thought he was joking.

20

Going Global

Folk argue about whether Atlanta really counts as being in the South or not. The city was founded in 1837 as the midway point on a new rail line linking Augusta and Chattanooga in Tennessee, so it doesn't have the deep historical roots enjoyed by places like Savannah and Charleston. But Atlanta's relatively short existence has still equipped it with a Southern pedigree of sorts. Margaret Mitchell was born here, spent ten years writing her book here, and eventually died here at the intersection of Peachtree and 12th when she was run over by a taxi. Martin Luther King was another Atlanta baby and the city was a focus for the civil rights movement in the 1950s and 1960s. But arguably Atlanta's biggest break came way before any of this, in 1864 when it was burned to the ground.

The half-way point on the rail line had become a big, bustling centre of industry and commerce by the eve of the War between the States and General Sherman knew it was the key to breaking the back of the South. When Atlanta eventually went up in flames, it was like a funeral pyre for the Confederate dream. The South had experienced defeats before, but Atlanta had become the final bastion of resistance. Its incineration marked the end of the illusion of a separate CSA and thereafter the city became the martyred capital of the Lost Cause.

This is at least partly why Atlanta was chosen as the sight for the South's answer to Mount Rushmore. Stone Mountain is a massive granite outcrop a few miles outside Atlanta that rises 825 feet above the surrounding piedmont to loom like an alien spaceship at the end of Highway 78 from Athens. It is a geological oddity and a tourist complex, but it is also the site of a bas relief sculpture that is inevitably claimed to be the world's largest. The carving makes Stone Mountain a Confederate monument because it shows Robert E Lee,

Thomas 'Stonewall' Jackson and Jefferson Davis on horseback holding their hats over their hearts in memory of the Lost Cause.

Bonnie had kindly offered to drive me into Atlanta, seeing as how getting to Stone Mountain without a vehicle would have been a major challenge. So we stopped off to look at the sheer rock face and its mounted riders and decided to take the cable car up to the top of the gigantic outcrop. I noticed that the cable car was of Swiss manufacture, and with a characteristically Swiss regard for completeness, they had equipped it with the most comprehensive No Smoking sign I'd ever seen. It comprised the usual red roundel, but inside it were symbols forbidding the use of matches, cigarettes, cigars and pipes. Perhaps also because it was Swiss, the manufacturers hadn't felt the need to supply any No Concealed Handguns stickers.

A few days later, from an aircraft window, Stone Mountain looked like a small pile of sand beside the neat stack of toy building bricks that were downtown Atlanta, but from its top, I got a better idea of just how big it was. Walking out on to the dun-coloured rock surface I became less doubting of the statistic I'd read claiming that the outcrop was seven miles in circumference. Clinging to its surface, by the cracks left as sheets of rock were peeling off like layers from a giant onion, were stunted pine trees that provided a sweet smell to the air. From here I got my first glimpse of Atlanta and its sprawling suburbs sitting in its own little haze of brown smog down on the plain.

As we descended in the cable car, I gazed out again at the carving of Messrs Lee, Jackson and Davis riding their horses. Although these three characters are undoubtedly Southern demigods, their links with Stone Mountain are tenuous at best. Although the mountain was the site of a minor skirmish prior to the Yankees taking Atlanta, neither General Robert E Lee nor General 'Stonewall' Jackson was involved. In fact, Lee never even saw Stone Mountain, and Jackson was dead by the time the battle took place. And although Jefferson Davis was the first and only president of the Confederacy, he was also a figure of fun throughout Georgia. But what the hell? The mountain is an impressive piece of rock and the bas relief a grand piece of carving. Perhaps it's better to see Stone Mountain as a permanent monument to the Southern myth.

So what is it about Atlanta that makes people doubt its Southern credentials? I began to sense the answer to that one as soon as we hit the city's outskirts and the feeling didn't dissipate as we neared downtown. Atlanta didn't look particularly Southern. With its tall glass buildings, concrete expressways, corporate headquarters and suited executives, it just looked like big cities look anywhere in the US. To add to this impression, it turns out that not many Atlantans are native Southerners (relatively speaking), because an awful lot of the people who flocked to Southern metropolitan areas in the 1980s actually settled in Atlanta and its suburbs, hence further diluting what Southern character it did have. In a sense, however, this was all totally appropriate, because Atlanta is the engine room of the recent, air-conditioned Southern boom, a Dixie bonanza that some suggest actually means that it is the rest of the country that is becoming more like the South, rather than the other way around. The evidence was mounting to support this theory of the Southernisation of America: Southern food and music have seduced the whole country; the Southern Baptist church is the fastest-growing denomination in America; and the South is where the USA's population and economic growth are accelerating. One other little sign pointed in the same direction. When Bill Clinton (Arkansas) won the presidency with Al Gore (Tennessee) as his running mate, it was the first all-Southern White House victory since 1828. That's nine years before Atlanta was born or thought of.

Another of the city's claims to fame is that it was a local man, one Henry Grady, who first coined the phrase the New South. As a label, New South has been around for so long that it has rather lost its meaning, but if it still has any value, it's a term that can be applied to today's Atlanta. When Henry Grady coined the phrase, he was trying to get the South out of a fix. The year was 1886, and Grady was selling a South still crippled by defeat to Northern investors. The South had put racial hatred behind it, he suggested (ha, ha), along with its quarrels with the North (ho, ho). All that was needed for a new South to spring forth was a fistful of Yankee dollars to set the ball in motion. About a century later, this was it. Finally the backwater of the world's most powerful country was rising from the swamps and was on the move. Arguably, Atlanta's crowning glory came exactly one hundred and ten years after Henry Grady talked about the New South, when the Southern city staged the centennial modern Olympic Games of 1996.

So if the South had been rejuvenated and Atlanta was its throbbing heart, and if the city's apparent lack of Southernness reflected the fact that the rest of the country was becoming more like the South, it was logical that Atlanta should play host to two of America's, and therefore the world's, most powerful corporations, CNN and Coca-Cola. This was the side of Atlanta I'd decided to focus upon, so I had booked a room in the Omni Hotel situated inside the CNN Center.

Appropriately enough, the Center was like a city within a city. From my room's balcony I didn't look out across Atlanta but in upon the Center's cavernous atrium, a view of vast climate controlled, smoke free space with moving staircases silently ferrying small people up and down between split-level floors and 'open air' restaurants where it never rained. Ripples of applause wafted up from the audience watching a live Talkback TV show broadcast from the epicentre of the mall, as onlookers gazed down upon the proceedings from aerial walkways en route to the next bank of shopping outlets. See-through bullet shaped lifts with rings of yellow fairy lights at the top and bottom eased up and down between the hotel floors as an aerial mélange of open white boxes and coloured flags were for ever frozen tumbling down from the sky, below the physically highest symbol in the whole building, the stars and stripes. It was an office-cum-shopping mall city, an air-conditioned cathedral to the communications age, capital of a media empire that had stretched its tentacles across the globe. This was the imperial splendour of information technology and global capitalism advancing hand in hand to conquer the planet.

The day after I arrived, I booked myself on a tour of the CNN studios despite the fact that everywhere you walk around the Center you could gaze in, goldfish-bowl-like, on news executives busy in their offices and in one case actually watch the talking heads broadcasting information to the Spanish speaking world. Ted Turner welcomed my group to the global headquarters of Turner Broadcasting ('the world leader in news and entertainment') in a video message before a good-humoured suit named Jay took over for the rest of the tour. Media moguls from New York to Los Angeles laughed at Ted Turner, a Southern boy who grew up down the road in Savannah, when he decided to set up a news network to broadcast out of Atlanta. Cable News Network came into being in 1980, and changed news into a form of 24 hour entertainment, coming of age with those real-time rolling reports from the Gulf War. In less than two decades, as the promotional video delighted in telling me, CNN had become 'the largest provider of news and information on earth'. Along with its sister networks, CNN International and Headline News, it broadcasts from its state-of-the-art newsrooms to more than 116 million homes in over 200 countries around the globe.

The tour took in a pretend studio where the wonders of blue backgrounds were demonstrated to us by Jay giving us a dummy weather forecast, while we had to make do with a description of the teleprompter's magical properties because the demonstration machine had broken down. We visited viewing galleries above a couple of real newsrooms where we saw large numbers of people sat at unnaturally tidy desks surrounded by computer screens. Above these rooms, banks of television sets showed windows on to parts of the world served up via satellite for CNN's own unique brand of mix and match rolling newscasts. The tour ended back at the Turner store where Jay pointed out that you could take part in your very own special guest starring role as a CNN anchor, read the day's headlines and take the experience home with you on a videotape.

I moseyed round the store for a while, marvelling at all the things you could buy with the CNN logo on them. Ted Turner also owns a large number of classic Hollywood movies, and appropriate merchandising was available for some of the best-known, including a boxed set of plastic dolls starring Barbie as Scarlett O'Hara and Ken as Rhett Butler. Local baseball team the Atlanta Braves is another of Mr Turner's possessions, and his store had a special section devoted to Braves equipment. I thought it particularly unfortunate, given the setting, that North American baseball teams compete in what is myopically known as the World Series. How they can call it that when no one else in the world even plays baseball is beyond me, so it can only be put down to that legendary US ignorance of all places foreign. My heart sank further when I came across a CNN paperweight in the form of a small plastic globe on which Tanzania was spelled TANSANIA, and Namibia, a country that celebrated independence from South Africa in 1990, was still labelled SOUTHWEST AFRICA.

Fundamentally depressed by these signs of geographical ignorance right at the heart of the world's largest provider of news and information, I sought solace in another of Ted Turner's products. I had never before seen *Gone with the Wind*, and had resisted the temptation to rent it on video before this trip because I thought that there could be nowhere better for me to have my first viewing than in Atlanta's CNN Center, where it loops continuously as a Scarlett-tinted reminder of times gone by. Needless to say, the CNN Center has a multi-screen cinema complex, and one of the screens is permanently devoted to the all-time classic. I found the entrance, tucked away behind one of the moving escalators, and asked a woman in a glass box what time the next viewing began.

'Sorry,' she said, 'the tape got tangled and all messed up. It's not showing until we can get someone to fix it.'

But the worst was yet to come. After a beer and a mildly disgusting dose of nachos in the Omni Hotel lounge bar, I set forth to stroll the interior streets of the CNN Center to see the focal point of global information gathering at work on the night shift. It was 10.45 p.m. and the place was dead. The set of the live Talkback TV show stood dark and empty, the Turner store had shut down and the cinema complex was closed for business. A few cleaners were just finishing up their rounds of the fast food emporia, and a lone policeman was on his cosy beat, making sure no one was going to steal any news or otherwise cause a disturbance. There wasn't even anywhere open to buy a coffee.

Silly me. I'd had this vision of the CNN Center as a 24-hour hive of activity, a place that never rested. OK, there probably were a couple of guys sitting up in some office somewhere, playing poker while they kept half an eye on those banks of satellite television sets for developments in far-flung parts of the world like Tanzania and Southwest Africa. But if they'd wanted a pizza to keep them going they'd have had to send out for it. The notion I'd had of the CNN Center as an animated hub of all-night action was a complete non-starter. I'd seen more action after 11 o'clock at the 24 hour Huddle House diner beside my Super 8 Motel on the Interstate in North Charleston. I still don't think my expectations of the CNN Center were unreasonable. This was the headquarters of the number one global news network after all.

Essentially unimpressed by my CNN experience, I made my way the following day to the World of Coca-Cola. If the Cable News Network was a child of Atlanta's final coming of age, then Coca-Cola was way before its time in the game of world domination. It was first sold in the same year that Henry Grady came up with the idea of a New South, the year in which, not coincidentally, Atlanta went dry.

Interestingly enough, soft drinks are the South's best known export. While Coca-Cola was invented right here in downtown Atlanta, its biggest rival, Pepsi, originated in North Carolina ten years later. Dr Pepper was first sold in Waco, Texas before either of the colas, while Mountain Dew, a newcomer first concocted in the 1960s, is subject to rival claims from Virginia and Tennessee. But Coca-Cola is the biggest of them all, and claims to be the world's most widely recognised consumer product. Dr John Styth Pemberton invented it in Atlanta and this is where The Coca-Cola Company still has its headquarters. It was a short walk from the CNN Center along Marietta Street, a concrete canyon lined with silver fire hydrants, and right past a bit of flyover, just opposite a reconstructed 12-acre shopping mall known as Underground Atlanta.

Unsurprisingly, the World of Coca-Cola was just one big three-dimensional advertisement for the well known carbonated soft drink. What did surprise me, however, was the expectation that I should pay six dollars for the experience. For this I got corporate videos galore, innumerable reruns of past Coca-Cola commercials, and endless glass cases full of historical paraphernalia. The message throughout was, of course, the familiar one of what a bloody good drink this was and what a bloody good time you're going to have drinking it.

The cabinets and displays all began to look the same after a while (they were, of course, only a lot of objects with the words Coca-Cola and Coke written on them), but I just managed to avoid my boredom threshold by concentrating on a flashing display outside one of the video suites that continuously relayed dazzling statistics concerning the fizzy brown beverage. The display screen was mounted on a wall beside an electronic scoreboard showing a running total of the number of soft drinks served by The Coca-Cola Company since 1886. This was a large number consisting of thirteen digits, the last three of which were moving so fast you couldn't see them.

The Did You Know? type statistics included things like the highest bottling plant in the world (in Bolivia), the world's longest Coca-Cola truck (Swedish – 79 feet long), and information on amazing deliveries (e.g. by helicopter) and consumption patterns. It went on and on with the tallest this and the biggest that, the northernmost consumer and the first trans-Atlantic crossing. But best of all were the demented images The Coca-Cola Company had concocted to give you an idea of just how much Coca-Cola they had produced, and the planet had consumed, since 1886. For example, if all the Coca-Cola ever produced was placed in regular sized bottles and laid end-to-end, they would stretch to the moon and back 1045 times. Similarly, if all the Coca-Cola ever produced were to erupt from Old Faithful at the geyser's normal rate of 15,000 gallons an hour, it would flow continuously for 1577 years on Coca-Cola alone.

Astounding, I thought. Just think if you built a swimming pool to hold all that Coke, I wonder how large that would be? If all the Coca-Cola ever produced was poured into one tremendous swimming pool with an average depth of 6 feet, this pool would be nearly 20 miles long and over 8 miles wide . . . And so it went on, and on, and on. Without doubt, they had come up with some startling facts, but in keeping with the clean-cut image of their product, The Coca-Cola Company had omitted some of the less salubrious aspects of its history, such as the fact that its inventor Dr Pemberton had a morphine addiction and that his original Coca-Cola did contain a cocaine derivative, despite what the company now says.

Reeling from the glut of staggering statistics, I entered the final entertainment area, an all-you-can-drink zone where you could sample both conventional Cokes and a selection of overseas brands. The whole complex was crawling with groups of school children being indoctrinated in the ways of Coca-Cola, but this Tastes of the World interactive exhibit was total bedlam. After saturating myself with global fizzy drinks, I staggered down the stairs to exit through the Coca-Cola retail store, but not before being asked by two Coca-Cola security agents with walkie-talkies whether I had drunk enough. I said I had, but they still reminded me that I could go back for more if I wanted. I'm sure they were just being helpful, but they said it with an almost menacing undertone, as if they had been monitoring my consumption and I hadn't had my quota yet.

In the retail store, the final message was also pretty clear. Having walked into the 3-D advertisement, rubbed shoulders with the product and become familiar with its friendly history, I could now take a piece of it home with me. There was a phenomenal range of red and white merchandise to choose from, including all sorts of amazing objects in the shape of the Coca-Cola bottle. These included skipping ropes with small Coca-Cola bottle handles, Russian dolls in the distinctly non-Russian shape, and binoculars shaped like bottles. I was almost tempted into purchasing a T-shirt simply because I saw the following message on its instruction label: 'Coca-Cola clothes are designed to be worn while having fun and being refreshed with an ice cold Coca-Cola', but I stopped myself just in time. Perhaps more disturbing was the children's Talking Can savings bank that said, 'Gulp, gulp. Gulp, gulp. Aaah Coca-Cola!' when you put money into it.

On the walk back along Marietta Street my head was buzzing with thoughts about this drink that had started out in life as a 'patent medicine' with a distinct cocaine kick and ended up conquering the world as the essence of the American dream that everybody could taste. Like CNN, the propaganda suggested that Coke was enjoyed in over 200 countries ('enjoyed' note, not just drunk), and in all those countries Coca-Cola is the standard bearer for the US brand of a consumer society portrayed by advertising and television as the benchmark to which we should all aspire. Coca-Cola was born of a golden age of quackery that thrived in an America united after the failure of the South to secede. The salesmen who peddled 'patent medicines' were among the first to sell image before product because their products were often worth less than the bottles they came in. Their approach has proved unimaginably successful, so that advertising has become the air Americans breathe and they're busy exporting it all over the globe.

Some observers see Coca-Cola in pseudo-religious terms and the parallels are attractive: Coke as a sacred symbol, its invention like the virgin birth; its salesmen are the missionaries selling a better life and its secret ingredient the holy of holies. As the emblem of all the good things about the USA, it is the secular communion drink. If television is the average American's soul and the supermarket his temple, Coca-Cola is the fuel on which his whole lifestyle runs. Selling the fuel across the globe is producing millions of new converts, a process unlikely to slow until the planet itself is populated entirely by Coca-Cola men and women. And the fact remains that this amazing soft drink is a distinctly Southern product, so perhaps the view of the South as a hundred year old backwater is itself a myth. Coca-Cola succeeded where the Confederate army failed. Less than thirty years after Gettysburg it crossed the Mason-Dixon Line and conquered the whole country. It's just so long ago that everyone's forgotten. Coca-Cola is the ultimate Southern myth, a 99 per cent sugar water drink that was put in a nice bottle and sold as the embodiment of Jefferson's pursuit of happiness. It became so successful that it is now taking over the whole world.

The cab I caught to Atlanta airport was driven by a woman whose main job was in the police department, she told me. It was her last fare of the day and she nearly missed the airport exit because mentally she was already going home. There was an *African Heritage Study Bible* on the passenger seat beside her and Baptist music blaring from the vehicle's cassette player. It was a catchy little number entitled *I got Jesus in my Car.*

There are two versions of a maxim Atlantans tell you about their huge airport. One says that when you go to Heaven you change planes in Atlanta, the second says that even if you go to the other place you'll have to do the same. With Jesus in my taxi, I had no worries about which one I'd end up in if I boarded the wrong flight. And I had a pretty good hunch that I knew which one would be serving Coca-Cola.

21

Elvis

It was January and wet, and the black tarmac on Elvis Presley Boulevard was glistening in the light drizzle. I had borrowed an umbrella from my motel but I wasn't using it. The rain was at just that level of intensity that makes you think a brolly is unnecessary but then gets you wet anyway. By the time I saw the white fairy lights in the small trees on the grassy verge in front of Graceland I was soaked.

Memphis is unfortunate in being famous for two unnatural deaths. Martin Luther King was shot here and Elvis Presley passed away in a lavatory here. The city does have distinction in other fields. It modestly claims to be the world's barbecue capital, and Beale Street is approximately where blues music as we know it was invented, although it really began down on the Mississippi Delta. Memphis is also where the world's first self-service grocery store, and therefore arguably the world's first supermarket, was opened. But the premature demise of these two Southern icons is what most people associate with the place and this was why I made Graceland the first stop on the second leg of my saunter through the Southern states. I'd been obliged to do my travelling in two parts because of teaching commitments at university in England, but now, just a few weeks after Christmas, I was back on the road again. Some four months after the end of my previous trip, the phenomenal global accomplishments of Coca-Cola were still fresh in my mind. Like Coke, Elvis was a Southern success story that had sprung from humble roots and gone on to flourish in all corners of the world.

When I first arrived I wasn't entirely sure that I was in the right place. I had been expecting a house, Graceland, but all I saw was a line of restaurants, Elvis museums and gift shops. I stood beneath the awning outside one of the themed eating joints, brushed rainwater from my hair, and asked a man sitting on a metal chair smoking a cigarette whether I was on the right track.

'Yep,' he said, 'you buy your ticket over yonder.' And he pointed to the far end of the complex of shops and other Elvis attractions. 'Where you from?' he asked, flicking ash on to the wet tarmac.

'England,' I told him.

'My, you've come a long way to see this.' I nodded. 'She's come a long way too,' the man went on, gesturing towards an Asian girl who was approaching to skirt round us to stay out of the rain. 'She's from the Philippines.'

I had been collecting snippets of Elvis memorabilia from newspapers and magazines for a year or so in preparation for this trip. Of course I had a working knowledge of 'the King' due to the fact that he is one of that élite band of people who are known instantly just from their first name alone, but I had still been staggered by the scale of the man and his legend. Although precise figures are hard to come by, particularly for the early years of his career, more than a billion Elvis records have been sold around the globe. After an extensive audit in 1992, his record company RCA posthumously awarded Elvis 110 gold and platinum discs, the largest presentation ever. Number two on the all-time list are The Beatles with just 41.

I walked past the gift shops and saw that Graceland itself sat across the road, beyond the small trees bedecked with fairy lights. Now that I was closer, I could see that the trees were also full of metal crotchets and quavers, adding an appropriately musical note to the foliage.

More than 200 books have been written about Elvis since his death in 1977 and one of the newspaper cuttings I had kept was a review of one of the more obscure. It was entitled *Elvis in the Post: Catalogue and Guide to Elvis Presley International Postage Stamps*. Hardly a light read, I would have thought, but no doubt a key volume for the bookshelves of the most ardent fan. I had kept the review mainly because I thought it totally extraordinary that anyone could find enough material to write a book devoted solely to the appearance of one man on postage stamps. The book contained some great information about the appearance of Elvis on stamps issued in countries that a lot of people have never heard of, like Western Sahara, Chad and Burkina

Faso; Madagascar, Monserrat and Mongolia. When a commemorative stamp of the King was issued in his home country in 1993, it became the most profitable in the history of the US postal service. It had a print run of 500 million, and many fans deliberately put the wrong address on their letters so that they would come back marked 'Return to sender'.

Graceland, the Elvis mansion, is listed on the National Register of Historic Places and is apparently the second most visited place in the USA, only topped by the White House. This made it the most popular house in the South, but perhaps my favourite statistic concerned Elvis' 1973 television special, *Aloha from Hawaii*, which is said to have been watched by more people than the first man walking on the moon. Elvis really was the king. All the rest are peanuts, just pretenders to the crown.

I bought my ticket and joined a short queue of people being issued with headphones and tape recorders and was instructed to wait here for the next bus that would take me across the road to Graceland. 'Can't we just walk over there?' I asked the young woman in charge. The house sat a short way up a drive behind a set of metal gates that looked like an open song sheet with guitar playing Elvises at each end separated by more musical notes. It couldn't have been more than a hundred yards away.

'No Sir,' the woman told me, 'entry to Graceland is allowed only on the official bus.' I suppose they were afraid of being sued if someone got run over crossing the road. So ten of us stood patiently until the bus arrived. Then we all boarded it and were driven the hundred yards across the road and up the drive to the tall white columns of the entrance to the Graceland mansion, where we all disembarked. Getting on and off the bus took longer than the actual journey.

Two lines of poinsettias flanked the staircase that swept away in front of me as I walked in through the front door of the home of Elvis Presley. They matched the Santa-red drapes at the windows and the scarlet baubles on the Christmas tree which was still up. Here was his living room and dining room; beyond was his music room complete with piano. There was carpet on the floor in the kitchen and the tape recorder voice told me that Elvis kept three cooks on his staff. Sometimes he enjoyed eating splurges, like when he ordered meatloaf every night for six months.

Downstairs in the basement was a room done out in yellow and blue with a mirrored ceiling and three television sets lined up along one of the walls. In total, the house had fourteen TV sets. It's common knowledge that Elvis, who also had an interest in guns, sometimes used the TV sets for target practice. Later, in one of the museums back across the road, I saw one with a large bullet hole in one corner of its screen. Apparently, he also fired at other household objects, like the refrigerator and some of his stereo equipment.

Elvis had a pool room, its walls and ceiling covered in printed fabric which made it feel like being inside a huge sewing box. Back up another flight of stairs was his jungle room with a green shagpile carpet and walls covered in short strands of green wool. All this wool was very good at absorbing sound, just like a recording studio, and Elvis cut some records here. Not surprisingly, we weren't shown the lavatory where he died.

Within the grounds were some stables and a trophy building full of those gold and platinum discs and a nine foot glass sculpture from RCA records commemorating 'The greatest recording artist of all time'. The last sight on the self-guided tour was the meditation garden where Elvis is buried alongside his mother and father and a memorial to his stillborn twin brother whose grave remains in their hometown of Tupelo, Mississippi. The graves were surrounded by cards, fresh flowers and wreaths in the shapes of hearts and guitars. A small notice said that floral tributes arrived at Graceland daily from admirers all over the world. It was only when I read the inscription on his tomb that I realised that the following day would have been his 63rd birthday.

I suppose that most people know at least the bare bones of the story of the rise and fall of Elvis Aaron Presley, the boy from a shotgun shack who became the first rock and roll idol to live and die a rock and roll life. His background was classic poor 'white trash'. His mother picked cotton to keep the family from sinking below the breadline, dragging little Elvis along behind her on a gunny sack. When the boy was just three, his father landed up in jail and the

Presleys lost their house. By the time he was 13 the family was too broke to survive in Tupelo so they moved to a public housing complex in Memphis, the big city light at the end of the dark tunnel of poverty that was, and still is, the Mississippi Delta.

Elvis had learned to sing in church and got his first guitar when he was four years old. It was made from a broom handle, a cigar box and a couple of loose strings. In 1953, while studying to become an electrician, he bluffed his way into Memphis Recording Studios, home of Sun Records, and paid four dollars to cut his first record. He said it was for his mother's birthday. Having absorbed the black chants in the cotton fields, the gospel music in the pews of the Assembly of God, and the blues on nearby Beale Street, Elvis had put them all together and come up with rock and roll. Blessed with spectacular genetic advantages, he was good-looking beyond reason and possessed of a pair of legs and hips that appeared to be made from rubber. He sounded and moved like a black man in a white body. America had lost an electrician and found a rock and roll legend.

Sex was Elvis' main selling point and there was no getting away from it. 'Rock and roll' was a black term for intercourse and in his third appearance on the Ed Sullivan Show in 1957 the censors only allowed pictures from the waist up. With his smouldering looks, seductive voice and gyrating hips, this man was new and dangerous. If the postmodern social scientists are to be believed, he was generating a postwar tidal wave of social change, a rebellion of repressed women and an uprising against the forces of racial segregation. Whatever it was, his legions of admirers loved him like they'd never loved anyone before. The pressures of being Elvis Presley were clear in one of the museums across the road from Graceland. One large glass case was filled to knee-depth with envelopes to illustrate the 30,000 fan letters he received every month. On one occasion, two girls had themselves nailed into a large crate and mailed to the King. It was hardly surprising the man shot up a few television sets.

Knowing what to do with all his money must have been almost as stressful. Elvis liked motor cars and he bought a lot of them. Many are housed in the auto museum that begins with a small plaque saying that the first car he bought was second-hand. He loved it so much that he stayed up all night just looking at it from the window of his hotel room. Unfortunately, the next day it caught fire and burned out. Once he had a bit more cash rolling in, he more than made up for it. But he was also generous with his earnings. He used to give money to strangers on the street, and one Christmas he bought all of his thirteen staff a Cadillac each. The impression I was gaining of Elvis as an essentially kind and affectionate character, at times simply bewildered by the greatness he'd achieved, was confirmed when I read a caption in one of the museums about his daughter Lisa Marie. When the little girl was two years old, Elvis gave her a diamond ring and a mink coat for her birthday.

At the end of the string of museums and Elvis emporia sat his very own aeroplane, inevitably named the Lisa Marie. When in light-hearted mood, Elvis also referred to it as his Flying Graceland. To get on to the plane, you had to pass through a mock departure lounge, and visitors were given a boarding pass on which was printed a lot of information about wingspans and fuel capacity. Before boarding, you had to walk through an Elvis fan detector that beeped loudly as you did so. The aircraft's customised interior had leather seats and gold-plated seat-belt buckles. There were even flecks of 24 carat gold in the fabric of the sink. The two redneck guys in front of me were real fascinated by this feature, the ultimate symbol of decadence for someone who had grown up with nothing. 'Gimme the sink,' said one, 'I'm outa here.' This was the plane in which Elvis made his famed sortie to Denver for peanut butter and jelly sandwiches. Twenty-two of the sandwiches were delivered to the plane as it sat waiting on the runway. Elvis ate them all and then flew back to Memphis.

A little while later, I sat licking the grease from my fingers after lunch in one of the diners in the Elvis complex. I had sampled another of the King's favourite sandwiches, this one fried, with peanut butter and banana in the middle. It had been delicious, except that I always prefer crunchy to smooth peanut butter. I was trying to imagine what it must have been like at either end of the spectrum of wealth that Elvis had transcended. For a Southern boy who had been raised on a subsistence diet, much of it foraged from the wild (possum and sweet potatoes, fried squirrel in butter, pigs feet and greens), the lure of eating anything he could possibly have wanted must have been extraordinarily strong. Elvis also loved cheeseburgers because he had been brought up in a household where cheese was a luxury.

Of course it was his conspicuous consumption, of pills as well as food, that eventually killed him in what has become classic rock and roll style. Having never really recovered from the scars left after his mother died, he tried to eat himself to happiness. Instead, he ate himself to a heart attack. In a sense, his death must have been a welcome release from the strain of being Elvis Presley.

But of course he's not dead, is he? Initially I'd been puzzled by two different spellings of Elvis' middle name I'd seen at Graceland. In one case, on his Memphis City Schools Diploma, it was spelt Aron. On his gravestone, the spelling was Aaron. I couldn't imagine that the school authorities would have misspelled one of their pupil's names, but then I suppose whoever had his tombstone engraved was even less likely to have got it wrong.

Unless, that is, he isn't dead.

When I got back to England, I delved a little deeper into the spelling. Nothing was resolved. Not all of my newspaper and magazine cuttings cited his middle name, but those that did were split about equal between Aaron and Aron. In the *Chambers Biographical Dictionary* it was Aron. In five different books about the man, I recorded three Aarons and two Arons. This wasn't getting me anywhere. For a final say on the matter, I found the official Graceland website (www.elvis-presley.com in case you're interested). Their spelling was Aaron. That settled it. He really was buried beneath that slab of granite in the memorial gardens.

No he isn't, I hear you say. What about all the sightings? There have been literally thousands of them in the past twenty years. Elvis has been spotted in supermarkets and at the top of ladders, in helicopters and under tarpaulins. The reports come in from all corners of the globe, from Hull to Haiti. The man's definitely out there, he's just hiding.

And who can blame him? Since his 'death' (I don't know, you must decide for yourself), he has become vilified and deified, the subject of academic conferences and the excuse for international road races. A professor of literature at a university in Finland has even recorded an album of Elvis Presley songs that he has translated into Sumerian, a language of the lower Euphrates valley that died out 4000 years ago. In the foyer of one of the Graceland Elvisabilia shops, a TV production crew was recording interviews with punters asking them how they felt on the eve of his 63rd birthday. Behind the camera, they had to limit the Barbie loves Elvis sets ($79.95 each plus tax) to five collections per person per day because they couldn't manufacture them fast enough. There's even a supposed branch of the Presbyterian church named after him. It's all pretty impressive for a piece of poor white trash from Tupelo, Mississipi. I shouldn't say this, but if he isn't dead I bet he wishes he was.

A couple of days later, talking on the telephone to a friend in Texas, he asked me what I'd done so far. When I told him, he said, 'Pay homage to the King. That's a smart move – give you good karma for your trip.' I think it did.

22

America's Ethiopia

It was miserable and raining again the following morning when I emerged from my room to eat breakfast in the Days Inn breakfast zone. Being just down the road from Graceland it was kitted out like an Elvis shrine. There was a bust of Elvis on the TV, a wall clock in the shape of Elvis with a pendulum modelled as legs that jived back and forth as it ticked, and framed photos of the icon in action all over the rest of the walls. Outside, they had a small swimming pool in the shape of a guitar. It even said Elvis on the doormat.

The place was run by a family of Asian extraction. They provided daily bulletins of news from India printed out from the worldwide web and left on the front desk, giving me a choice of diversions as I waited to pay my bill: the latest from Delhi or an Elvis video that played continuously on a television set behind the counter. Apparently many other motels across the USA are also managed by people originally from the Indian subcontinent. I don't know what proportion of them are US passport holders, but non-Asian Americans sometimes get upset at the idea of their motels being run by these 'foreigners'. Hence in many parts of the South I'd seen notices outside motels declaring them to be 'American-owned'. It was the sort of thing that some might interpret as a covert form of racism.

When I had paid my bill, I asked the receptionist to telephone for a taxi. Half an hour later, I was still waiting for it. This would have annoyed me in England, but I remained calm by reminding myself that I was back in the South. It was probably just par for the course in these parts. However, the receptionist was not so relaxed. She rang the taxi firm again, bawled them out, and told me that her brother would take me wherever it was I wanted to go instead. This is probably the sort of attitude that makes these 'foreigners' successful managers of US motels.

The brother drove me out to a car hire place near Memphis International Airport. It was located along with all the other car hire companies on the appropriately named Rental Road. After a long history of not really bothering with road names, simply giving them numbers instead, there appears to be a move towards labelling them in this no-nonsense fashion. I remembered B's Barbecue Road in Greenville, North Carolina, and when I got to Montgomery in Alabama, the Coca-Cola bottling plant was on Coca-Cola Road. After conducting the formalities, it wasn't long before I was cruising south down Highway 61, the 'Main Street' of the Mississippi Delta, the rich alluvial bottomlands that stretch between the Mississippi and Yazoo rivers.

I was entering the quintessentially Deep South state of Mississippi (the Magnolia State as it said on the sign), and the first county I drove through was named Desoto after the first European to arrive in the area. But if this was the Deep South, where had I been up to now? The Shallow South? It wasn't a phrase I'd come across among the plethora of Souths I'd encountered so far, a glut of labels that had been confusing even to a trained geographer like me. People talked about the Old South and the New South, the Upland South and the Lowland South. The area's northern border was the Mason-Dixon Line or the Smith and Wesson Line (a reference to the South's traditionally high homicide rate). There was the Bible Belt, the Sunbelt, and the Cotton Belt, but of all of the euphemisms, I thought Deep South was the most evocative. It conjured up the images of grand antebellum mansions and sprawling plantations, of Spanish moss streamers and syrupy accents. It's William Faulkner and Tennessee Williams, a place where the past is not dead; it isn't even resting. It's alive and well and living in people's minds.

Actually I'd already spent some time in the Deep South. It's roughly coincident with the Old Cotton Belt, where Mother Nature serves up more than 200 frost free days every year along with at least 43 inches of rain. Georgia and South Carolina are Deep South states, along with Alabama and Louisiana, but Mississippi is supposed to be the deepest and most Southern of them all. It's the South's South. They say that if Mississippi was any more Southern it would be a foreign country.

When some years back Jesse Jackson came to Tunica County, where I was heading, he thought it was. He called it 'America's Ethiopia'.

It was a while before I saw what Jesse Jackson meant. My initial impression was of the space. The landscape was large and flat, but neither of those words came even close to doing it justice. The fields I was passing were themselves the size of small counties and the landscape was so level and so seemingly endless that I thought if I could only get just a bit of a vantage point I'd be able to see all the way back to the British Isles.

The scenery was almost completely without colour, or at least nothing beyond the dark earth and a few dun-coloured trees. When I passed a place selling John Deere tractors, the virulent green of the machines seemed like the visual equivalent of shouting in church. The weather didn't help. It was still raining and some of the fields had patches of standing water on them. If I'd come in the summer, no doubt all would have been tractor green, not with cotton now-adays, but more likely with soya. The centre-pivot irrigation booms would be trundling across the fields spraying water at the crops and the sun would be high and smothering. But in early January the centre-pivot booms just stood motionless beside the road like huge grubby insects and the sun was nowhere to be seen. The panorama just looked vast, drab and dreary. It reminded me of the parts of Siberia I'd seen in winter.

Jessie Jackson's Ethiopia reference came home to me the following day when I drove on down the Delta and saw some poverty. Not charming, honest rural poverty, but the grimy, squalid, no-hope variety you normally associate with urban ghettos. It came in a string of towns with bright and breezy names that mocked their true status: places like Rich, Bobo, Hushpuckena and Merigold. The length of Highway 61 was littered with these depressing apologies for towns hemmed in by deep storm ditches full of crud and garbage. Gruesome shacks with mud drives mixed it with derelict shopfronts and aban-doned filling stations. When I stopped off in Clarksdale at a gas station that was still operational, there was a hand-written note taped to the gas pump saying you had to pay before you filled your tank. In my ignorance of the ways of the poor, I stood there trying to work out how to comply with the instruction when I didn't know how much fuel my tank was going to take. I walked into the gas station shop to enquire and realised what the note meant when the man in front of me asked for three dollars' worth.

The further I drove into the heart of the delta, the worse the road became. It was possible to drive at 55 mph, like the signs said I could, but the regular potholes made the going decidedly uncomfortable. The boom, boom, boom of the bumps was like travelling on an ancient railway line. At Bobo, most of the dilapidated houses sat very close to waterlogged terrain, indicating the importance of minor variations in elevation in such a level land. Just down the road, Alligator just looked small and miserable. If I'd blinked I'd have missed it, which would have been better for all concerned.

More prosaic locations appeared in Shelby and Winstonville, lines of mobile homes, wooden shacks and gutted shells full of the type of junk that not even the poverty stricken can reuse. I passed a signpost to a research demonstration farm and technology transfer centre, just the sort of thing you might expect to find in Ethiopia. People appeared to be living in an old school bus on the outskirts of Mound Bayou, a place that a large hoarding declared was the oldest all-black municipality in the United States. Its smartest building by a long way was the African Methodist Episcopal church, but most of the rest of the place was pretty rundown. At the other end of town was another big notice saying that it was the largest US Negro town, settled on 12 July 1887 by ex-slaves of one Jo Davis (brother of confederate president Jefferson), who conceived the idea before the Civil War. The plan was put into action by Isiah T Montgomery, a resident of nearby Vicksburg who bought several hundred acres and turned it over to the former slaves. The notice stood in front of a hospital that had long ceased to function. On the other side of the road, the former Vacuum Island gas station looked like it hadn't served fuel since the prohibition era.

There isn't much call for fuel in Mound Bayou because nearly half the households don't own a motor vehicle. I was surprised to see a couple of operational gas stations in Shelby, where nearly three-quarters of the black households don't have a car. These proportions are rather higher than the national average, as my reading of the

Nationwide Personal Transportation Survey had informed me when I was in northern Florida. For the country as a whole, just 8 per cent of households are non vehicle owners. But these are the sort of statistics that the Mississippi Delta is renowned for. Winstonville, another all-black town like Mound Bayou, has 66 per cent of its population living below the povery line. This is why this sorry string of spiritless communities looked like the remnants of some terrible holocaust. They were places where the only pleasant buildings were the churches, and virtually the only other properties that weren't falling down were the occasional branch banks which existed solely because of the constant infusion of social security payments. These places were a million miles from the gleaming high-rise New South of Atlanta. They represented a new phenomenon – whole towns that were little more than black ghettos in the countryside.

With a neat irony that somehow typifies the South, they have become so partly in response to the success of the civil rights movement. Ever since the schools became integrated, the Mississippi Delta's whites have been moving out, taking their wealth with them and leaving the poor blacks behind. Historically, Mound Bayou and Winstonville have always been all-black towns, but others have been getting steadily blacker, and steadily poorer, over the past few decades. In 1950, 55 per cent of Alligator's 200-odd residents were black. By 1990, they comprised 75 per cent. In Shelby, the percentage was 62 in 1950, but it passed the 80 per cent mark forty years later. The same pattern has been repeated all over the Delta. Three decades after the end of the Jim Crow era, blacks in the Mississippi Delta are more segregated than they were in 1950.

To account for their poverty, one has to go back a bit further, to trace the cycle of land use in the Delta since its initial clearance for agriculture. King Cotton and his plantations had taken over the Mississippi Delta's fertile soils by the eve of the War Between the States. Emancipation of the slaves didn't do much to alter the agricultural nature of the area. Instead of working the plantations in slave gangs, the Delta's blacks became share-croppers working their individual plots (though most of the land was still owned by the planters). Slowly, share-croppers moved away from their nucleated quarters by the planters' mansions and took up residence in cabins built on the plots that they worked. During the 1930s, a period of dramatic change began in the rural South. Farms and plantations started to become mechanised and reorganised, and so began a mass black exodus from the land. The introduction of tractors in the 1930s was followed by mechanical cotton harvesters in the late 1940s and by the increasing use of herbicides in the following decade. Share-croppers abandoned their cabins and moved into town or out of the South altogether, to the cities of the north and west. The agricultural landscape had come full circle and huge neoplantations, hauntingly reminiscent of their pre-Civil War counterparts, had become the order of the day.

A similar process has been repeated all across the rural South. In 1940, more than seven in ten rural Southern blacks lived on farms. By 1980, the figure fell below three in a hundred. But nowhere have the results been more pronounced than on the Mississippi Delta because Mississippi is the South's South and the Delta is Mississippi's Mississippi. For the share-croppers that ended up in places like Shelby, Alligator and Mound Bayou, there was little in the way of alternative employment. It was a straight swap: share-cropping for a welfare cheque. Some see their plight in similar terms to the cycle that saw the antebellum plantations eventually transformed into neoplantations. From slavery, the Southern black had tasted independence in the form of share-cropping and then been thrust back to rely on federal patronage. Many of those with jobs in the Delta ghetto towns are simply employed in administering their communities' dependence on social security payments. Academics have even come up with a term for it – welfare colonialism. The rural poor stuck in the welfare trap are as unlikely to find work by scanning the help wanted ads as the obituaries. They can't even enjoy the sorts of benefits that you might think were some compensation for being the rural poor. The countryside isn't pretty or accessible, it's just an endless expanse of corporate fields.

Late one afternoon as I was driving back to my hotel, I pulled over to the side of the road in Winstonville to make some notes. There weren't many people about, so I noticed in the rear-view mirror when a young dude in a hooded top walked across the road behind me and came towards my car. He was wearing sunglasses, despite the misty rain and the leaden clouds. When he reached my vehicle, he tried to open the passenger door. I don't know what he wanted, but I didn't stick around to find out. I drove away, in retrospect probably faster than was necessary, leaving the guy just stood there looking. As he receded in my mirror to become just a distant speck, I wondered why he was wearing the dark glasses. I decided it probably wasn't because his future was too bright. More likely because he couldn't bear to look at it at all.

One way out of the economic backwater for the dude in the shades lay up Highway 61 in Tunica County. In the early 1990s this was the setting for an exercise in the bizarre that could only happen in the USA. They started building casinos. The hoardings leading you towards them had started to appear on the outskirts of Memphis like lights on the road to Damascus: 'Jumbo size casino thrills', 'Vegas-style action in a spectacular river setting'. It was Disneyland in Ethiopia.

I spent a couple of nights at Fitzgeralds, a casino and hotel that rose out of the Mississippi floodplain like Camelot in a kingdom of mud. Its entrance was a gateway consisting of two round turrets, one on either side of the new feeder road, in the middle of the vast flat fields. There was no sign of the place itself. It was just a gateway in the mire and the road stretching off into nowhere. After some miles, a series of earnest roadside pledges started: 'Smiles instead of blank looks', 'Respect instead of indifference', 'Attention instead of neglect'. They sounded like the sort of guarantees the people of Mound Bayou could have done with instead of their welfare payments. And then, out of nowhere, loomed a huge mock castle with flags and bright lights and about a thousand acres of car park out front.

The place was surreal. If I had arrived during the hundred-degree summer, I'd have thought it was a mirage. It was as if a group of aliens had landed their space ship on the banks of the Mississippi and left it there while they ventured forth to survey a new planet. Fitzgeralds was like Xanadu in the netherworld. It was Faulkner's Yoknapatawpha County on crack cocaine.

It was also the cheapest hotel I stayed in during either of my trips to the South. For twenty bucks a night I got close to five-star luxury, with quality shampoo and moisturiser, and free bed-time chocolates and fresh roasted coffee. OK, the coffee wasn't up to much. After reading that the complimentary packet was good for four six-ounce cups, I used the entire sachet for half a cup and it still tasted like washing up water. But it's the thought that counts, and the management didn't even charge me for the telephone calls I made to Texas. The food was cheap too. The dinner buffet was $8.59 including tax and you could eat as much as you wanted. On my first night a young black guy named Patrick cut me half a cow and asked if I'd like juice with that Sir (he meant gravy). I splashed out on a glass of house burgundy which wasn't at all bad for another dollar. I was amazed when it arrived in a large glass that must have been designed for fruit juice. Later I was even more amazed when a waitress took away my glass and returned with a free refill. Fitzgeralds can do all this because their guests are supposed to make up for the cheap accommodation and grub in the casino. There's nothing else to do in Tunica County.

I didn't because I didn't know how to play the games. The casino ran training programmes for the uninitiated, but these took place in the mornings when I was already cruising up and down Highway 61 gaping at the poverty. So I had to make do with wandering the cavernous halls of slot machines and green baize crap tables at night, just marvelling at the money people were throwing away in their search for satisfaction. I have to say that most of them looked like they couldn't really afford to lose. Few of them were black. They were the US white peasantry (rednecks to you and me), passionate in their pursuit of happiness.

Punters wandered back and forth, seemingly transfixed by the flashing lights, carrying large plastic cups full of quarters to feed the slot machines. These were arranged in banks around a series of central pedestals on which sat large gleaming consumer products fronted by notices that commanded people to 'Win this truck' or 'Win this drive-yourself lawn mower'. I briefly watched a woman perched on a stool in her nylon lounging suit as she shovelled her coins into three machines simultaneously. After a good five minutes, in which she had received a single payout from her three machines, I moved on. It was like feeding time at the zoo, except that the only one guaranteed to get fat was the casino.

Not all states allow gambling on their territory, which is why the Indian reservations and the few states that welcome casinos do such a thriving business. The Mississippi river has a gambling pedigree that dates back to the riverboats and someone told me that the state only allows the modern stationary versions to be built next to the water, thus maintaining a tenuous link with history. Mississippi reckons on using the huge revenues from its Dixie Vegas for the state's education system. If money raised in a godforsaken spot like Tunica can be spent on such a worthy cause, who can blame them? The casinos also provide some jobs for the local communities, and God knows they need those badly enough. But critics of the casino approach to economic development point to the fragility of the get-rich-quick mentality and the fact that casinos don't actually tend to boost local economies. Gamblers rarely leave the grounds of the casino for a start, the cheap hotels and restaurants help any pre-existing local restaurants and hotels to go under, and a significant proportion of their punters are locals who can't really afford to gamble. After the casino has made its profits and paid taxes, the larger portion of revenues doesn't seep into the community, but is taken out of the state to the casino headquarters. It leaves the local community with a marginal increase in funding, a giant increase in traffic congestion and often a rise in crime and social problems. Enrolment in Gamblers and Alcoholics Anonymous tends to get a boost in consequence.

I suppose you can't blame Fitzgeralds for all that. They were only going about their business, and they did employ a lot of locals. I knew this because all of the staff had been issued with name badges that also gave the name of their home towns. Among the waitresses I noticed Sharlene from Clarksale, Melody from Batesville, Yoland from Tunica, and Lawanda from Hernando. Melody from Batesville brought me a beer in the sports bar one evening and she paused to chat for a while. She worked the evening shift, she told me, 6 p.m. to 2 a.m., and it took her another hour to drive home afterwards.

'It must be tiring,' I said. 'Yeah, but the money's right,' Melody replied. She asked me where I was from and whether I'd had any luck in the casino. I told her I couldn't play any of the games but that it didn't really matter because I was really here to write a book. She looked at me with no expression on her face when I said that. 'That's nice,' she said finally.

We were interrupted by a shout from the casino. 'He's here,' cried a man jubilantly. 'It's Elvis. Elvis is in the house.' And everybody cheered.

I looked around, but I couldn't see the great man. Melody said he was performing on stage in the downstairs section of the casino, so I made my way down the moving staircase, past the framed photographs of past jackpot winners, to listen to his show. Like most Elvis lookalikes, this guy was impersonating the later, mutton-chop sideburn version of the King. I suppose that the earlier Elvis must be impossible to mimic.

The performer looked the part in a white mirror studded jump-suit with rhinestones and a red eagle on the back. Up front, the jump-suit was open all the way down to its huge belt buckle. The guy sweated like a middle-aged Elvis and didn't do a bad mauling of his songs. Old ladies with seriously big hair queued up after the performance to ask him if he would autograph their silk scarves.

23

Grits and Catfish

It rained on and off virtually the whole time I spent in Mississippi and there was widespread flooding in the more southern counties. The ground got so saturated in Hattiesburg that two recently interred coffins floated back to the surface, but the morning I chose to drive to Arkansas was bright and sunny and there wasn't a cloud in the sky. In consequence, I had to scrape the ice from the windscreen of my car before I set off.

It was dull and overcast again by the time I turned off Highway 61, west on Highway 49 towards the mighty Mississippi. The misty rain was blurring the horizon as if the sky was getting greedy and wanted to gobble up a landscape that it already dominated. There were more fields of cotton here, the plants just blackened sticks, some submerged in water, with white bobbly bits still sticking to them. Elsewhere, most of the fields had just been ploughed wet earth. As the road approached the river, it became elevated, a good 15 feet above the surrounding fields, and another batch of casinos appeared as a huge metal girder bridge loomed up out of the haze. A sign said: 'Welcome to Arkansas, the Natural State, home of President Bill Clinton.'

Across the bridge, the small town of Helena didn't look like much. I drove to its tourist information centre (not a visitors' centre here) where a kind woman kept giving me brochures until I had to tell her to stop. They were full of dubious claims about all the globally significant phenomena to be found in southern Arkansas, like the world famous armadillo festival at Hamburg, the world's best-tasting tomato – the Bradley County pink – and the town of Magnolia's world championship steak cook-off.

From the brochure centre, the approach road into town took me through a rundown industrial area of derelict depots, grubby eating places and boarded up wooden houses. They had made an effort to spruce things up nearer the centre of town where many of the wooden houses had been refurbished, but Ohio Street, parallel to and nearest the river, was a dreary stretch of peeling paint and disintegrating brickwork with gaping potholes in the road. On Cherry Street, I stopped to look at a small monument commemorating the first European to cross the Mississippi, that Spanish wanderer Hernando de Soto, who managed it on 18 June 1541. Two years into their quest for gold, which was to remain fruitless to the end, his band of men built four rafts near today's Friars Point just downriver, a place called Quizquiz at the time. The river was also de Soto's final resting place after he died of fever the following year. According to one account, his body was stuffed into a hollow log that was released into the muddy waters and never seen again.

I wanted to take a look at the Mississippi because it really was a feature of world renown. Although Fitzgeralds sat right next to it, it had been impossible to get close to. Its high levee was thick with scrub and I had to make do with staring at a small section of its brown waters through the trees from my hotel room. Helena had only recently resumed diplomatic relations with the river by means of a road that scaled the levee and took me out to the Helena Riverpark established in 1992. In one of my brochures it said that this connection had not been possible since the building of the levees and sea wall in the early 1900s. Although born of the river, Helena was afraid of it. The woman in the tourist information centre had hinted as much of her own volition. 'I'm from Colorado,' she said as she searched for another brochure, 'but my husband's from around here. When I first arrived he told me, "That Mississippi, you got to respect that river."' Respect in Helena took the form of this massive earth bank. It was higher than a two-storey house and it offended my sense of scale, making Helena's buildings look like a set of dilapidated doll's houses.

It wasn't the best time of year for me to visit the Helena Riverpark. It looked drab, like Nature's version of industrial decay. It was just a lot of grey trees, some of which were dead, and grass that was ashen and brown in spite of all the recent rain. There were no animals or birds. I thought I saw a small group of ducks over towards the riverside, but on closer inspection they turned out to be tree stumps.

216

The final stretch, after you had parked your car, was a wooden walkway that took me right to the water's edge. The walkway was greasy and slippery. At its end I stood and looked at the dirty grey-green colour of the water and I thought that it looked more like the ocean than a river. Its eddies and swirls were more like those you'd expect from the sea too.

The Mississippi *is* more like the sea than a river, and it's fitting that it should flow through the USA because it provides a suitably monumental challenge to the most powerful country on earth. Americans have been building great levees along it in an effort to restrain its floodwaters since 1717. The embankment systems now run for more than 2500 miles along the Mississippi valley, but every so often the river hits back, just to prove that no amount of human ingenuity can fully tame its enormous flow. Following the aftermath of a particularly savage flood in 1927, engineers began to tamper in earnest with the very layout of the river. They initiated a mammoth scheme to straighten its channel, to increase the river's gradient and thus the velocity of its flow, thereby allowing the waters to erode and deepen the channel and reduce the likelihood of its flooding. By 1950 the length of the river between Memphis and Baton Rouge in Louisiana – a distance of 340 miles as the crow flies – had been shortened by no less than 170 miles. The stretch of the river on my Rand McNally Mississippi state map was punctuated with truncated meanders left as sickle-shaped pieces of Arkansas stranded on the Mississippi side of the river.

The knock-on effects of all these modifications are felt downstream on the Louisiana coast, helping to transform the natural order of things on coastal marshlands and islands. In some instances, the efforts of mere mortals to control the workings of Nature even make things worse. When the river burst its banks on its upper reaches in 1993, washing over about 10 million acres and seriously damaging more than 40,000 buildings, the period of inundation was prolonged in many places because the levees prevented the return of water to the channel once the peak had passed. The total flood damage was estimated at $12 billion.

The Big Muddy has also inspired more benign acknowledgements of its scale and vigour. Midway through the nineteenth century, it became fashionable for artists to paint the river on colossal stretches of canvas, reproducing its every meander and sandbar to scale along with scenes from the cities, industry, plantations and virgin forest along its course. The painters would spend months charting the river's passage through the landscape, blending artistic endeavour with cartographic attention to detail, before transferring their notes and sketches to their gigantic canvases. These rolls of canvas were exhibited, like precursors of movies, in darkened halls where the illuminated paintings were slowly unfurled between giant spools. For the audience, it was like their very own accelerated steamboat ride up, or down, one of the world's mightiest rivers. One of the longest of these panoramas was produced by a man named Banvard, who took his audience all the way from St Louis through the Southern states to the Gulf of Mexico. His epic canvas was three miles long.

Much of the river's course that formed Arkansas' eastern border must have looked pretty wild on those tremendous canvases. Although the cotton plantations were well established by the 1950s, there were still many backwoods families who were self-sufficient, shooting or raising most of what they needed. Some used dugout canoes into the twentieth century because the roads were so bad. A pulse of deforestation occurred in the aftermath of the War Between the States as lumber men tackled the Delta woods often with the help of the railroads. By the 1930s, ditches ran everywhere and nationally only Florida led Arkansas in the size of area being drained. Even as late as the 1950s, half a million acres of ancient forest were cleared on the Arkansas Delta to make way for soybean fields. Today just a few patches remain of the once great Southern wilderness. Inside a restored building back on the edge of Helena, now the Delta Cultural Center, a black and white photograph from 1915 gave me an idea of the Mississippian dimensions of the trees that are no more. Four men stood at the base of a cypress with pipes in their mouths and axes at their feet. Even with their arms outstretched from shoulder to shoulder they barely managed to encompass half the tree's girth.

That evening I saw Melody from Batesville again. She was serving drinks to the gamblers at the slot machines and crap tables in the downstairs casino this time. She paused to say hello and asked me whether I'd finished my book yet. 'No,' I replied. 'I spent the day in

Helena.' Melody gave me her blank look. 'It's just across the river in Arkansas,' I told her. She shook her head. 'I've never been there,' she said.

I was too early for breakfast at Fitzgeralds the morning I checked out so I stopped at a roadside Popeyes for scrambled eggs, biscuit and grits, a proper Southern breakfast. Grits are about as Southern a food as you can get, and you find them everywhere. In fact, if ice tea can be said to be the South's national drink, then grits is the national dish. Grits are the ultimate all-purpose food, eaten for breakfast, lunch and dinner: with eggs at breakfast, with salt and butter any time, with cheese, garlic, and red-eye gravy. They can be casseroled or topped with shrimp, and leftover grits that have gone hard in the fridge can be sliced and fried. All Southerners love them without exception. If barbecue divides the South, grits glue it back together again.

The first time I ate grits was in New York some years ago. I didn't know what they were so I ordered them to try. They were disgusting. I'd eaten them a few times so far this trip and the jury in my mind was still out. On this occasion I hadn't entered the Popeyes in search of grits but if I wanted to eat there I didn't have much choice. Everything on the menu came with grits. This confirmed a defining story a friend told me when I reached Texas. He said that the South is where they serve you grits in the morning, and the Deep South is where they serve you grits in the morning without being asked.

Grits are tiny round white globules, allegedly made of ground maize, that are cooked in some liquid until they swell and go soft. I say allegedly because the times I've had nasty grits I've wondered whether they might not be pygmy polystyrene balls. The fact that even as I write I'm still undecided on the merits or otherwise of this archetypal Southern food will not, I know, offend Southerners, because like most outsiders I can't be expected to appreciate them properly. Most Yankees don't tend to like grits either. This is because they don't cook them properly, don't put enough butter on them, choose instant or quick grits rather than the regular variety and/or commit any one of numerous other cardinal errors that are all a simple reflection of their misunderstanding of Southern cuisine in

219

particular and Southern culture in general. On this occasion, I have to admit, I couldn't finish them. They came smothered with so much butter that I thought I was going to throw up.

I read somewhere that the idea of grinding corn was another of those things adopted from local Indian populations, but ground corn or maize is a staple food in many parts of Africa and it wouldn't surprise me if the whole idea was brought over by the slaves. In which case, it has come full circle, because maize was introduced to Africa from the Americas. Anyway, lots of other 'typically Southern' food owes its origins to African cuisine – like okra, yams and collard greens – and they became Southern staples simply because most of the workers in the old plantation kichens were slaves. But whatever their origin, grits is now the quintessential Southern foodstuff. Its importance to life below the Mason-Dixon Line is reflected in the following joke, which probably isn't a joke at all. A Northerner is down in the Deep South on business for a few days and the hotel he stays in serves him grits every morning for breakfast. After trying them the first day and deciding that they are not to his taste, the Yankee omits them from his order the second day. The grits appear anyway, so he leaves them on the side of his plate. The same thing happens the following day, and again he leaves them untouched. On the fourth day, he complains to the waitress. 'I don't like grits,' he says. 'In fact, I hate them. So why do you keep bringing them? I don't want them and I won't eat them.' He looks at her sternly. 'You know I don't like them. Why don't you just take them off the plate?' Flustered, the waitress disappears. She returns a few moments later and says, 'I can't take them off the plate Sir. It's against the law.'

As it happens, grits are also a whole lot more than an essential foodstuff. There's an entire branch of Southern folklore, or gritslore, about the stuff simply because they have also been used for so many non-nutritional purposes. Southerners have been known to use grits as emergency cat litter and to put out fires. Wrapped in cheesecloth, grits act like a desiccant if you put them in your closet, and at Christmas, mounds of the stuff can easily be passed off as fake snow in a manger. But perhaps the best known non-culinary application for grits is as a weapon. Folk wisdom recommends them as one of the few successful methods for dealing with fire ants. These unwanted guests arrived in Alabama early this century as stowaways from Brazil and have since spread to cover most of the lower South. In the absence of grits, these insects are virtually indestructible and the problems they raise make the kudzu vine look endearing. The venomous fire ant bite hospitalises tens of thousands of people every year, and kills wildlife and livestock. The ants also chew up air-conditioners, transformers and telephone wires. In fact, you name it, these illegal Brazilian immigrants will chomp their way through it, and their undiscerning palates are their ultimate downfall when it comes to grits. According to the theory, if you sprinkle uncooked grits on these creatures they gobble them up and then explode when the grits expand in their stomachs. Needless to say, scientists deny this, but whether it's true or not, it's a nice piece of Southern folklore.

With the overbuttered grits sitting heavily in my stomach, I drove on. I was heading for Belzoni, a small Delta town that had spearheaded a new Southern attempt to seduce the American public into eating another Dixie speciality. It billed itself as the Catfish Capital of the World.

The sun was still shining as I stopped to fill my tank with gas in Clarksdale again where I exchanged pleasantries with an elderly gentleman who looked as old as his battered pickup. 'Nice day,' he said. 'Real bright and sunny. You staying in town?' 'No,' I told him, 'just passing through.'

Highway 61 ducked under a railway bridge in Clarksdale which made a brief but pleasant change from the unrelenting flatness of the scenery. Otherwise, the only relief from the monotony was the occasional set of grain silos that poked their way into the sky that dominated the landscape. The string of depressing black rural ghettos with their storm drains full of junk looked only slightly less miserable in the sunshine. Before I entered Belzoni's Humphreys County, I passed a couple of air strips with small crop-spraying aircraft, and an anti-smoking hoarding. It showed a beautiful young woman puffing away beside the slogan 'Face of a supermodel, breath of a pitbull'.

A subtle change in the countryside occurred in Humphreys County. It was still a level plain, but increasingly the fields weren't fields at all. They were ponds. I was entering catfish country. I pulled over to the side of the road to make a quick perusal of the tourist literature

I'd accumulated. In rural parts of neighbouring Leflore County, one guidebook told me, people still enjoyed another traditional Southern delicacy – dirt. Eating dirt is called 'geophagy' in more formal terminology, and in these parts the clay-rich snack is baked and seasoned with salt and vinegar, my guidebook said. Needless to say, Southerners have received a fair amount of grief on this score over the years and it makes no difference when they point out that kaolin is a key ingredient to many indigestion cures.

Catfish have also long been associated with the dirt poor. They fed on the bottom of rivers like the Mississippi and were thus on about equal standing in the food chain with those who practised geophagy. But all that has changed since they began raising the catfish in these ponds. They have been transformed from a staple of the impoverished Southerner to a food fit for the tables of yuppie restaurateurs.

When I reached the converted railroad depot in Belzoni that housed a permanent exhibition to the Humphreys County catfish revolution – the Catfish Capitol of the Catfish Capital – I learned how they'd managed to do this. It is a tribute to Southern ingenuity and stealth, with a bit of help from a serious advertising campaign. At first, however, I thought my mission was going to be fruitless. I hammered on the glass door and was about to leave disappointed when a man appeared from inside and hobbled towards me. His appearance caught me off my guard, not because I'd been about to leave but because of the way he walked. He was wearing a contraption on one leg below his knee that was all too familiar to me. It looked like a moon boot, but was actually a post-surgical device consisting of metal supports, Velcro straps and wads of foam, designed to allow its wearer a degee of mobility during convalescence. About a year previously I had snapped my Achilles tendon and had had to wear one of these appliances for six months after the operation to sew it back together again. It wasn't an experience I wanted to be reminded of.

When he opened the door, I asked the guy what he'd done to deserve it and he told me he'd gotten angry with a door he'd bin fixin' and had kicked it harder than his ankle could stand. This made me feel a bit better because it was a slightly more stupid accident than mine, which was the result of playing a football match for the first time in five years. Thanks to our common recent personal histories of limb supports, the man offered to show me round the small exhibition that consisted of catfish inspired artwork interspersed with photographs that came with startling captions concerning the scale of the business here in Humphreys County. The first one I read told me that where I was standing, I was surrounded by over 400 million farm raised catfish.

I was reminded of Ted Turner and his CNN venture when I read that local farmers laughed when one of their number dug his first muddy pond and started raising catfish in the mid 1960s. By 1970, Mississippi was producing just under six million pounds of processed fish a year. Today, the state has 100,000 acres of catfish ponds and it produces 370 million pounds. That's 70 per cent of the nation's output, and one-third of the Mississippi total comes from Humphreys County alone where catfish is the number one agricultural product. This phenomenal rise was due to modern aquacultural methods and careful attention to detail, I was told. The fish were raised in quality controlled environments of clay based ponds filled with pure fresh water pumped from underground wells, but it had also been necessary to recondition the image of the catfish in the minds of the American public. These farm raised catfish were not like their bottom feeding forebears which all too often tasted of mud.

'We taught 'em table manners,' my injured friend told me proudly. 'We feed 'em on a gourmet diet of puffed, high-protein floating pellet food. The fact that those pellets float means they have to come to the surface to feed.' At eighteen months old, the fish were harvested using large seine nets, taken in aerated tank trucks to the factory and within twenty minutes of leaving the pond they'd been processed. The result was a light, white, flaky flesh; just the sort of tasty, low-fat protein source that an increasingly health-conscious America was looking for.

I left the exhibition hall clutching more catfish literature than I knew what to do with. It included a Catfish Institute publication full of recipes from restaurants all over the USA that specialised in the farm raised variety. The recipes included catfish al forno, orange rosemary poached catfish, John Grisham's favourite catfish lafitte, and even catfish tacos al carbon. While grits seemed likely to remain an essentially Southern delicacy, it looked like catfish was following in the footsteps of Elvis and Coca-Cola.

24

The World's Longest Sidewalk

Of course 400 million catfish meant money and jobs for Humphreys County. Amongst the literature I'd been given in Belzoni was a sheet entitled Catfish Facts, on which it was suggested that the total economic impact on the county in 1997 was nearly a billion dollars. I had been prepared to tour one of the processing plants, in the interests of research. I'd read that a typical worker on the 'kill line' would be expected to gut a fish every other second as they sped past on the conveyor belt in one of these plants, hence averaging a staggering 20,000 fish a day. The results of such handiwork were packaged as whole fish, steaks, fillets, nuggets, and strips. Some of them were smoked, breaded, or pre-cooked before being frozen. This would have been something to see, but despite the assurances in the literature that fresh fish do not smell, I had a sneaking feeling that even a flying visit was likely to take the edge off the welcome I could expect at even the friendliest of motels. Hence, a minor sense of relief swept over me when I was told that none of the processing plants were open to the public.

When I left Belzoni, I expected to see some more prosperous places, courtesy of the county's catfish bonanza. Belzoni itself looked like a neat little town, but I couldn't say this for the string of communities I passed as I drove south. The first one, Hard Cash, I missed altogether. It was right there on the road I was following, according to my map, but in reality it wasn't at all. It seemed to have ceased to exist. I did see Silver City, off to the left, a few miles further on. It appeared to be made up solely of gruesome shacks, and silver was about the last word I'd have used to describe them. Most miserable of the three evocatively named settlements was the small town of Midnight. I had to make a short detour to get there along a stretch of road that looked as if it hadn't been repaired since the War Between the States broke out, and it must have been in a pretty sorry state even then. People were still living there, in really rundown trailers overlooking a fetid swamp full of old motor vehicles, but the store and gas station had been boarded up many years before. They must have seen this coming when they built Highway 49 West to bypass the place. Midnight had been cut off, like the truncated meanders on the Mississippi river, and left to die. If these places were anything to go by, that billion dollars hadn't been spread very evenly.

The town of Louise looked like it was faring much better. It had some quite smart brick housing and a new planter's mansion style bank. From here I turned towards the west, giving up on the idea of driving as far as a place named Hot Coffee, despite its having intrigued me since beginning to plan this trip.

I struck off through an area coloured green on my map instead. It was marked Delta National Forest and I thought I might see a few remaining trees. I couldn't manage to get right into the forest because my vehicle wasn't up to it. I drove down a muddy track and stopped at a small wooden building nestling at the edge of the trees to ask how sensible it would be to continue. A huge forest ranger looked me up and down and squelched out into the mud to look at my car. I'd have needed subtitles to understand exactly what he said, but the tone of his statement was clear enough. I wasn't going to get far in that toy.

So I followed the paved road that cut through the Delta National Forest. I did see some trees, but the agricultural fields had penetrated even this forest reserve like the pre-determined rash of progress. I rejoined Highway 61 and although they say the Mississippi Delta ends at Vicksburg, it seemed to me that I effectively left it at Redwood where a big bridge over the Yazoo river re-introduced me to the concept of hills. They looked big after the insipid flatness of the last few days but I don't suppose they were more than about a hundred feet high.

A sign by the road leading into Vicksburg said that it was a certified retirement city, but I wasn't intending to go in search of the blue rinses and white sticks. I wanted to see the National Military Park. When I found it, perched up on a high bluff overlooking the river, it turned out to be quite a size, and because it was so large you could drive through it. I suppose it was inevitable, in a land of drive-through banks and fast food restaurants, that they should have come up with the idea of a drive-through historic battlefield.

The campaign for Vicksburg was a key battle in the War Between the States. Barely a year after the war had begun, the Confederates had lost virtually all of their strongholds on the Mississippi to the Union armies. Vicksburg became the last link between the eastern portion and Texas, Arkansas and most of Louisiana to the west. Union commander General Grant gradually closed in on the bluffs at Vicksburg, and after two unsuccessful assaults on the city, he sat back and decided to starve them out. During the seven week siege, the Confederate troops and Vicksburg civilians were reduced to a prehistoric existence, burrowing their own caves into the hillside to shelter from the shelling. Finally, at 10 a.m. on the 4th of July, 1863, the day Lee began his retreat from Gettysburg, Vicksburg surrendered. The Unionists had gained control of the entire Mississippi, and the Confederacy was cut in two. Vicksburg's bitterness at her eventual humiliation took a long time to seep away into the sands of time. It took more than a century for the city to recover sufficiently to celebrate Independence Day, the other momentous event that occurred on the 4th of July.

The heroic and strategic nature of the Vicksburg campaign is commemorated in the National Military Park with unusual vigour even for the USA. The 16 mile battlefield drive was lined with red and blue markers and plaques with information on Confederate and Union forces respectively. They vied for position with monuments set up by virtually every US state to memorialise their own particular regiments and divisions who took part in the fighting. Some of the obelisks were huge, towering up to fifty feet above the hillsides, while occasionally a state had really gone to town and constructed a marble shrine like a temple to their dead. It wasn't just a few monuments either, there were hundreds of memorials and obelisks. There were literally forests of the things.

With so many tax dollars dedicated to the combatants from both sides, the memory of the 'late unpleasantness' was unlikely to fade because there must have been a lot of tourist bucks to collect on behalf of Vicksburg's tragic past. But the view from the far end of the battlefield park showed a different side to the certified retirement city. Standing in the national cemetery, I watched as the sun sank below a bend in the river, briefly adding a sparkle to the stumpy white marble headstones of the unknown soldiers lined up like sugar lumps in the lush grass. Down below me was a busy wharfside with gigantic cranes and a small fleet of towboats, tugs and barges. Unlike Helena, Vicksburg hadn't tried to hide from the monster river. Quite the opposite, in fact. Thirteen years after the fateful surrender to General Grant, it was the Mississippi that tried to sever its links with Vicksburg when it made a cut-off and left the city high and dry. Vicksburg was having none of this, however. She wanted to remain a port. So with a display of grim determination worthy of people who had starved in caves for seven weeks, they dug a canal to bring the river back. The Yazoo entered the Mississippi ten miles north of the city, but they diverted it to flow along the Mississippi's abandoned stretch. Vicksburg appeared to epitomise the South's heroic dedication to a Lost Cause. Resisting the inevitable had become the city's stock-in-trade.

I made it a few miles across the old Mississippi river and into Louisiana before I stopped for the night at a motel called the Cottonland Inn. There was nothing distinctive about the place except for a small notice beside the headboard in my room saying that a state law forbade me from smoking in bed. The following morning I stopped at a roadside fast food joint for a quick breakfast. A television set mounted on the wall was showing a lengthy news item about the court case against the man thought to be the Unabomber, the DIY bomb enthusiast who had been dubbed America's most wanted serial killer. The reporter was interviewing a former school teacher of the accused and the teacher was saying what a bright boy he'd been.

As I tucked into my non-grits breakfast option (a muffin) and sipped at the polystyrene cup that was said to contain coffee, two elderly black guys came in and took pews at the table adjacent to mine. They were wearing overalls and had taken the first bites from their burgers before they'd sat down. Their eyes had become fixed on the TV screen above us. 'Now he don't want no lawyers,' said one loudly enough for his comment to be addressed to me. 'Wants to defend himself. He'll have to go buy himself a suit.'

The picture had returned to the anchor man in the studio who was telling us about the accused's insanity plea. The other guy at the table next to mine piped up this time.

'What I don't understand,' he said slowly, 'is if he was a genius at school, how come he's insane now?'

Interstate 20 slices across the top of Louisiana. Despite its more elevated status, it was in as bad a state of repair as the Mississippi Delta's Highway 61, so I was glad to take a rest from its juddering concrete and drive south for a short stretch towards Jonesboro. After Ruston, which established its Southern credentials with a Dixie Pawn and Gun store and a cinema bearing the same name, the landscape soon became rolling and wooded, with the occasional swampy bit in between. They were clearing the trees here and there and I passed several lumbering lorries loaded with pine logs. Another feature of the drive was the large number of roadkills. The corpses looked like big rodents, furry creatures similar to giant mice in a way, but it was difficult to say more precisely because they were all roadkills. I marked them down as possums, North America's only species of marsupial, noted for their ability to feign death in the face of danger, hence the phrase 'playing possum'. However, I didn't think that any of the specimens I saw were playing dead. It was pretty clear to me that they'd all been run over.

I'd been noting roadkills as I travelled through the Southern states and they'd made an interesting, if morbid, yardstick of regional differences. Around where my sister lived in northern Florida, they'd all been armadillos, notoriously short-sighted creatures whose armour plating provides little protection against the wheels of a motor vehicle. Like the fire ants, the armadillos were Latino immigrants, but unlike their Brazilian counterparts, the armadillos had invaded the South the hard way. They'd crossed the Rio Grande like the other Mexican wetbacks, only their arrival in the promised land had perhaps been a greater achievement because armadillos can't swim. After thousands had drowned in their dogged quest, one of them must have discovered a highway bridge and then they all started sneaking over at night to avoid the immigration checks. The fact that they'd got as far as Florida was a tribute to their perseverance because there are an awful lot of swamps in between, not to mention the Mississippi and several other serious rivers. I had expected to encounter their flattened brethren all across the South after I saw a back handed tribute to these curious looking creatures in a redneck joke book (God made armadillos to test your braking reflexes). But other than in Texas, I didn't. In rural Georgia the most common faunal road casualties had been deer, closely followed by racoons. Later on in my travels, when I got to Alabama, it was possums again. In the Mississippi Delta I hadn't seen any roadkills at all for several days, but when one did appear, it didn't surprise me that it was a mangy dog. A couple of weeks later, when leaving New Orleans in the south of Louisiana, two more dead dogs turned up on Interstate 10, which reminded me of another sample from the redneck joke book. What's the difference between a dead dog in the road and a dead lawyer in the road? There are skid marks in front of the dog.

Something I'd read before this trip had attracted me to Jonesboro. It said that the town boasted a complete lack of attractions. It had no museums, no historic points of interest, no festivals of any kind, and not one souvenir shop. A place that made a feature of having nothing worth seeing sounded refreshing after so many claims to global fame that in most cases, I suspected, simply reflected ignorance of the existence of a number of other countries on the planet. I often wonder whether the supreme confidence that goes with this short-sighted world view was characteristic of previous global powers. Were the British as myopic when large parts of the world map were coloured red? In the minds of the US people, it was all tied up with the way that they think that their country is two continents. There is something at once rather touching and at the same time rather suspicious about their naivety in this respect. There is also something unnerving about the way this view is adopted outside their native land; even my undergraduate geography students insist on referring to the USA as 'America', despite the widely accepted fact that America comprises two continents, made up of 22 different countries.

Then Jonesboro spoiled it all by adding that what they did have was the world's longest uninterrupted sidewalk. No matter, I went anyway.

To begin with, it was difficult to tell just where the town began. I spotted a stretch of sidewalk and followed it with one eye until it reached a wood processing plant that turned out to be in a place called North Hodge. I noticed there was a big railway siding opposite the wood processing plant, then my attention was diverted by the Christmas decorations that were still up outside some North Hodge residents' homes. In one case, the main feature was Santa dangling at the end of a red and white parachute hanging from a tree on the front lawn.

Jonesboro eventually began with a strip of the usual fast food shrines (Dairy Queen, McDonald's etc.) alongside a place called Nomey's Pawn and Gun. They didn't have sidewalks outside them. I drove on, past quite a lot of houses that also didn't appear to be fronted by sidewalks. I stopped at a fuel station to buy a can of drink and to ask where I might find the legendary walkway, but the man behind the counter was so aggressive that I decided against it at the last minute. I didn't want to give him the satisfaction of knowing that I'd driven all this way just to view his stupid sidewalk.

Then I spotted it, a line of concrete slabs behind a grassy verge. Needless to say, it looked just like all the other sidewalks I'd seen in the South, only longer. Having come this far, I thought I ought to drive round Jonesboro and have a look, so I did. It was a pretty little place on lots of gentle hills. The city hall looked like a low-rise mock plantation house.

I soon found myself driving north back through the pine trees and the squashed possums along Highway 167 towards the Interstate. I passed a sign telling me that this was a hurricane evacuation route. When I reached Interstate 20, I had to break the speed limit for a couple of hours to try and reach Shreveport in time for the rendez-vous I'd arranged with my friend Gordon. What with all the bumps, it was an uncomfortable ride. I still kept him waiting for half an hour, but he seemed unconcerned. 'You're not late by Louisiana standards,' he said. Nonetheless, I didn't let on that it was because I'd been looking at a sidewalk.

25

Small-Scale Texas

Gordon is a Texan, with many of the attributes outsiders normally associate with Texans, the main one being that he was physically large. This didn't mean that he was fat. It meant that he was immensely tall, both because of his long legs and elongated torso, but also because of his head. You don't often see people with tall heads, but Gordon had one. Most of its height came around the forehead area, so that it looked like he might have not one but two brains inside it. This may well have been the case, because his mind was like a computer with superb recall capacity from its data banks, and Gordon stores data like no one else I know.

I remember one occasion when he was staying with me in Oxford and some English friends came round for dinner. One had a doctorate in psychology and she was amazed at Gordon's knowledge of the subject. They had a long and in-depth conversation that ranged across cognitive psychology, child psychology and educational psychology. 'Who is that bloke?' Helen asked me later. 'He knows more about psychology than I do.' The answer was not that Gordon was a psychologist, it was just a topic he'd read a bit about in his spare time.

That same evening, another friend was impressed with Gordon's encyclopaedic knowledge of fine art. Kevin was an artist, so it was his business, but Gordon matched him fact for fact. Kevin was also an unheralded expert on the Kennedy assassination. It was a topic I'd learned to avoid when talking to Kevin because he seemed to know everything there was to know about it and he could talk on the subject at considerable length. As the evening wore on, and everyone else had either left or gone to bed, he and Gordon became locked into a marathon debate on conspiracy theories. As I set to on the washing up, Gordon appeared in the kitchen. 'Nick, do you have any hard liquor?' he enquired. 'I think we're going to need it – we're on the grassy knoll and about to get into some trajectory analysis.' Afterwards, Kevin told me that the whole occasion had been like having dinner with God.

I'm pleased to state that Gordon is a geographer. For a lengthy period, he worked on the US space programme, an enterprise that is very largely based in the Southern states. His job for NASA was to train the space shuttle astronauts how to identify features of the Earth's surface they saw out of the space shuttle windows, to photograph them, to see how they might have changed and to report back to mission control. This helped to explain Gordon's propensity to use a hybrid form of the English language that I think of as NASA-speak. For example, Gordon never did things, he always accomplished them, as in 'I still have a few things to accomplish.' Everything was also a system to Gordon, and he used the word facility a lot. We'd be driving through East Texas and he'd point out of the window and say something like 'That's a playing field facility, part of the Texas schools system.' Gordon's involvement with the space programme had also furnished him with an enigmatic dimension to his character. He tended to disappear for long periods, not responding to communications of any sort for months on end. There had been times when I'd been driven to trying to contact him by telephone, in search of responses to my unanswered letters and faxes. On such occasions, whoever answered the telephone at the Johnson Space Center had denied all knowledge of an employee named Gordon. These events had led some mutual friends in Britain to suggest that perhaps briefing NASA's space shuttle astronauts wasn't the only type of work Gordon did for the US government.

The prospect of meeting Gordon on his home ground was intriguing therefore, although the possibility that he might suddenly vaporise while I was en route to Shreveport had been lurking in the back of my mind for some time. Indeed, my unease grew when he sent me detailed instructions on emergency procedures to be implemented either in the event of his absence or if I was to arrive early, as in the case of hot pursuit, as he put it. Hence, it was with some relief that I found him still waiting at Shreveport when I arrived half an hour late.

The first thing we did after I had handed in the keys to my rental car was to leave Louisiana. Gordon let out a minor sigh of relief when we crossed the state line and said the place always made him a bit nervous. It was a sentiment I was to hear repeatedly during my time in East Texas – everyone appeared to view their Southern neighbour in a somewhat sinister light. We got some lunch in Longview and drove on to his ranch just outside the small town of Mount Enterprise (population: 501, according to the sign).

I suppose when most foreigners ponder Texas, like me they think of cowboys with ten-gallon hats on the High Plains, perhaps of modern day evil aristocrats like JR Ewing, and maybe they even remember the Alamo, but these images don't apply in the east of the state. East Texas is quite different. It's hilly, it has lots of pine trees and everything seemed to be on a human scale, quite unlike the popular image of the state's brashness and wide open spaces. This is what makes the east a bit different and this is why the east is part of the South and the rest isn't.

It's also only relatively recently that it became so. Texas only really became a secure part of the USA in 1848, nearly two and a half centuries after the Jamestown colonists had set up shop on the Virginia coast. While the pioneers were eking out their precarious existence in Jamestown, Spanish gold-diggers like Hernando de Soto had already started wandering around what we now know as Texas, being nasty to the Indians. By the time the descendants of the Jamestown crowd had declared independence from the fatherland, Texas still had fifty years to go as being a part of Spanish Mexico. When the Mexicans got their independence from Spain in 1821, they did a foolish thing. They allowed a few colonists from the USA to settle in Texas. It was the beginning of the end. The Texans rebelled and declared independence. They enjoyed a short period as an independent republic before being annexed by Washington, a move that sparked a war with Mexico which the Mexicans lost. As a result, Mexico ceded two-fifths of her territory to the USA and received an indemnity of $15 million in return.

The early trickle of white settlers had become a deluge as families from the Deep South and from Tennessee and Kentucky poured into Dixie's new outpost. Those who could afford to set up cotton

233

plantations did so, and bought Negroes to work them. When Texas declared independence in 1835, the new republic boasted 700 slaves; by the start of the War Between the States there were nearly a quarter of a million of them.

Gordon took me to see what remained of an old East Texas cotton plantation in Rusk County. 'We're on our way to the end of the South,' he declared as we drove up a hill in the middle of nowhere and stopped at a gateway leading to an isolated mansion. It looked like someone had been doing the place up. The flower beds had recently been replanted and the house itself was newly whitewashed.

'This is the westernmost true plantation in the Old South,' Gordon said proudly. 'Monte Verde. There were between three hundred and four hundred slaves on this property. It belonged to a family that arrived in the 1840s, I believe from South Carolina. They owned about four thousand acres in this area, with this hilltop being the central focus of it.'

Just the main house remained. There would have been outlying dwellings for the household slaves at that time while the field slaves' quarters would have been down the hillside some place. The balance of the 4000 acres, like most of the rest of the whole area, had been covered in cotton. Today, the house had retained a large garden, but the remainder of the hill had reverted to woodland. Maybe the new owners of the westernmost true plantation in the Old South grazed a few cows somewhere, like Gordon did on his ranch, but for the most part, the landscape gave few clues as to its previous farming existence.

Plantation slavery penetrated Texas via its rivers. It came up the Sabine, the Trinity, a bit of the Angelina and up the Brazos about midway, but it never made it up the Colorado or any of the central Texas rivers. It was too dry. The cotton belt was pushed to the edge of its range and stopped where the 43 inch isohyet (a line of equal rainfall) stopped just inside eastern Texas. Beyond it was a different kind of country. The South's plantation slave economy was totally determined by the climate, isolated by its own natural conditions. It was where you could farm cotton, or sugar cane, or rice, or tobacco reliably. Beyond that, it was a different story. When I asked Gordon for his definition of East Texas, he drew a deep breath and began with the natural environment.

'I guess by consciousness East Texas ends where the pine trees end, it's a sort of distinctive vegetative subregion. Then you've got a cultural divide. This was an area that was primarily settled by folks from the lower South, if you go back to the nineteenth century, whereas central Texas was primarily settled by mid-nineteenth-century European immigrants – Germans, Czechoslovaks – who often came straight in after 1848, after the big turnover in Europe in the late 1840s and early 1850s. The other groups who came into central northern Texas were from the northern South, Tennessee specifically. The revolution in Texas was led by Tennesseans. It's a cultural distinction that's pretty deep rooted – upper South versus lower South.'

With characteristic attention to detail, Gordon later sent me the map co-ordinates for the end of the South at the Monte Verde Plantation near the Glenfawn Community in western Rusk County. For the record, they are 30°54'06"N,94°52'15"W. Gordon just thought I could use the exact position.

That evening, we cooked huge juicy steaks on the verandah and ate them gazing across Gordon's land before the sun went down and the horses faded away to be replaced by the sounds of coyotes chasing a rabbit. We drank a bottle of silky smooth Texan red wine, and I realised how much I'd missed the stuff after too many infusions of watery beer and fizzy soft drinks. When we adjourned inside, we cut ourselves off from the immediacy of nature and replaced it with an arm's length version courtesy of some footage shot by the space shuttle astronauts. Gordon's three metre satellite dish offered him a choice of more than 300 different TV stations' outlooks on the world, but he preferred the serenity of the view from Earth obit.

Not all settlers established cotton plantations when they arrived in the East Texas region. In fact, not many of them did because the large majority couldn't afford to. When most of the new arrivals from Georgia, Mississippi, Alabama and Louisiana appeared they simply became absorbed into the forest fabric of the country. They built themselves a log cabin, planted a few crops, and otherwise lived off the land, hunting, trapping and fishing for what they needed.

Wildlife was abundant, so much so in the early days that when a settler wanted deer for dinner he'd just step out on to the verandah and shoot one. All their endeavours were powered by animal and human muscle while the light in their homes came from the sun or resinous 'lighter' pine that burned prodigiously, and only later from kerosene. East Texas looked like one vast primeval forest at that time. The uplands were swathed in the easternmost patch of longleaf pine woodlands, trees I'd seen throughout my Southern sojourn (the vegetative definition of the South), while down in the riverbottoms was a different type of forest, a hardwood world of giant oaks, hickories, magnolias, cypresses and scores of other species. It was deep in these forests that this subsistence lifestyle evolved, a humble, independent existence that in many places continued well into the twentieth century.

Gordon said I ought to see one of the remaining hardwood riverbottoms, and he knew someone who could take me there. We left his ranch bright and early the next morning to drive into Nacogdoches. Three buzzards were circling high above us when we turned off his property and onto the road and Gordon came out with the East Texas equivalent of British magpie counting. 'One for silver, two for gold . . .' he started, but surprisingly he didn't get any further. 'My mother can go up to fourteen or fifteen. I guess there wasn't much entertainment back then, so counting buzzards was big.'

Nacogdoches was originally a Spanish mission settlement that had become the location for the Stephen F Austin State University where Gordon maintained a foothold in the Center for East Texas Studies, despite having recently begun a new job 200 miles away in the state capital of Austin. The original university building had been used as a Confederate hospital during the War Between the States and later as a local headquarters for the Union army, but the modern campus was a quiet and leafy quarter with noble buildings and a surprisingly good library. The atmosphere in Nacogdoches was small-town and tranquil, and I got an inkling of its being an outpost of the Old South when Gordon and I went for coffee in a place just off campus. It was the first restaurant or café I'd been in so far where I was offered black coffee. Everywhere else they had enquired whether I took my coffee with or without milk, for reasons of political correctness. Here it was still black or white.

'Nacogdoches is the buckle of the Bible Belt,' one of Gordon's colleagues told me when I commented on this, 'the last bastion of the Old South.'

'It's still feudal,' said another guy, only half joking. 'And you get kids from rural areas round here who are nine or ten years old before they come into town for the first time.'

There were also cultural throwbacks to what seemed to be a mythical place suspiciously like olde England, I soon learned, indicators that a Southern gentry class was still alive and well and living in East Texas. 'You go up to Smith County, traditionally a big rose growing area, and they still hold a rose festival every year, crown a queen who throws a big tea party in the Tyler Rose Garden.' This from another of Gordon's colleagues, a man named Darrel. 'It's a big social event,' he went on. 'Duchesses flock to it from all over the state. They have dresses specially commissioned. The Queen's dress costs tens of thousands of dollars to make.' He made it sound more like *Alice in Wonderland* than East Texas.

Tom, a postgraduate research associate at the Center for East Texas Studies, told me that fox-hunting was a popular sport hereabouts, as it was in some other rural parts of the South. Participants had all the gear, red tunics and hard black hats, horns and packs of dogs.

Rose garden tea parties? Fox-hunting? These weren't the sorts of pursuits I'd expected to come across in Texas. I wanted to know more.

The fox-hunting, at least, had an identifiably Southern provenance. It must have evolved from the need to hunt down predators when the first backwoodsmen arrived in the region. Bears, wolves and cougars (the latter known as panthers in southeastern Texas) were ever present threats to livestock and had to be controlled. Most backwoodsmen had a pack of vicious hounds used for the purpose. They were trained to run down a predator, until it took refuge in a tree, and keep it there until their master turned up with a gun to shoot it. Black bears were particular targets during the summer months when they would emerge from the hardwood forests to roam the piney wood uplands in search of hogs to dine on. They were also hunted during the winter, when they fed on acorns in the bottom-lands. At this time, bears were a good source of meat and fat. Bear ham and bear bacon were staple foods for the early backwoodsmen, and bear fat was rendered down to produce cooking oil.

Bear hunting ceased in East Texas just after the turn of the century, when they'd run out of bears. It was just one element of a self-sufficient way of life that otherwise survived in some remote eastern corners of the state until as recently as the 1950s. It was down in the riverbottoms that the unsung heroes of the South, the backwoodsmen and women, were located. Their approach to living off the land was based on generations of frontier techniques absorbed originally from the native Indians and developed by their Southern forefathers. The final nail in their subsistence lifestyle came when laws were voted in to abolish the open range. Ever since the first Jamestown settlers had let loose their cattle and pigs into the forest in the early seventeenth century, and found them fat and healthy the following spring, a tradition of open access to large forest areas had persisted all over the South. Livestock were released to roam the woods and live off the fat of the land until their owners set out with their dogs to locate, drive and pen them so that they could use a few. In East Texas, these commons were down in the riverbottoms, and this was where Tom agreed to take me one afternoon.

We drove out of Nacogdoches into small scale East Texas, leaving the paved road near Chireno, a town of no more than 400 residents whose dominant landmark appeared to be a shack with a notice saying 'Rebuilders'. It was surrounded by the dead carcasses of about a hundred motor vehicles. A few miles down a dirt track, Tom stopped at a gate which I opened and we drove across a grassy field past a herd of cows that hardly looked up from their grazing. 'You don't sound your horn to clear cows in East Texas,' Tom told me, 'the cows'll just come to you 'cos they think they're going to get fed.'

Leaving Tom's four-wheel drive vehicle in the field, we ventured forth into the thicket. A marshy trail soon petered out and we were left to wander through a haphazard patchwork of swamp, from one relatively solid patch of clayey ground to another, in search of the river. Tom was confident he knew where it was, but very soon we had backtracked and criss-crossed so frequently in our efforts to avoid any water that was likely to come above our calves that I had completely lost any sense of which way was which. The going was decidedly slow and a constant choice between evils. On the one hand was muddy brown swamp that threatened to suck us into its ooze. Then the relief of a few yards of firm ground was offset by vicious brambles that grabbed a hold and tore at my flesh and clothing. Neither of us had come particularly well prepared for this foray into the primeval swamp and my shoes were soon reduced to a pair of heavy sticky lumps of brown mud.

I asked Tom what the chances were of us meeting a feral hog. He reckoned they were reasonable. Although the open access rules had disappeared from these bottomlands, he knew of people who still released hogs to fend for themselves in the wild, to be tracked down with dogs at a later date. These backwoodsmen also still conducted night hunts for foxes, Tom said. They were quite distinct from the full-kit, red-tunic élite who belonged to the Fox and Hound Club, and needless to say, each dog hunting group held the other in extremely low regard. Passing laws to ban the free range down in the bottom-lands was one thing, but it would take a while longer to change people's attitudes. Although individuals had owned bottomlands like this one since settlers first staked their claims, the unwritten law of the open range had meant that everyone had the right to run livestock and hunt in such areas. In effect, it was an extension of the American Indian idea that the land belonged to everyone. Writing the odd law and putting up a few fences wasn't going to change that belief overnight. I found it odd to think that in a country I'd long associated with private enterprise and ownership, large expanses of countryside had survived effectively as common property for so long.

We forged on, pausing on firm ground carpeted with pine needles and oak leaves to plan our route across the next stretch of mire while caught in a briar's tentacles. I'd choose a fallen tree to guide me across, then place my foot on its wide trunk only to have it sink straight through. The apparently solid logs gave no more resistance than a sponge cake. Tom pointed out various plants of interest as we fought our way through the swamp and bramble maze. There was a thin tree with rings of vicious thorns up its trunk. 'Rednecks strip the bark off and process it 'cos it gets them high,' Tom told me. 'That one's the bull nettle,' he said pointing to an inconspicuous looking little specimen. 'It stings like crazy when it's in leaf. But that's not the worst of it, because the only antidote to a bull nettle sting is urine. So you're hurting real bad and then you've got to piss yourself.'

Eventually the firm ground options ran out and we stood looking at a wide area of chocolate brown water that we decided must be the Attoyac river, a tributary of the Angelina, although it really just looked like deeper swamp. The light was fading and we decided to turn back. For a moment I stood looking at the wetland wilderness and felt lost, which isn't a feeling I get very often. Tom said he knew the way, which was a relief because nightmare images of wandering through this savage underworld for ever had started to appear in my mind. As it grew darker, and the frogs began to screech, it was easy to imagine unpleasant situations involving depraved rednecks, like in a scary Hollywood movie. When we reached the field where Tom had parked, banks of white fog had appeared from nowhere to add to the alien atmosphere of primeval seclusion that was probably best left to itself at night.

26

Paper Cups and Operating Systems

I spent several days driving around with Gordon, looking at sights and reflecting on things Southern and Texan. On one occasion we stopped briefly at a modern historical site of sorts, the oldest Dairy Queen in Texas, which first opened its doors for business in 1950. It was in a place called Henderson. We bought a couple of large paper cups full of ice and soft drink, and had to carry them with us because we had a tight schedule even though it was a Sunday.

'Oh!' Gordon exclaimed when he had climbed back into the car. 'No cup-holders. That's a definite measure of this vehicle's age. It dates from before the outbreak of the cup-holder wars.' I looked around the spacious front seats and dash board. Gordon was right about the absence of cup-holders, but I wasn't sure what to make of his reference to hostilities. 'Have you noticed, Nick, how each new vehicle model comes with more cup-holders these days? Some of the latest models of people-carrier have twenty.' Gordon wedged his cup between his thighs and turned the key in the ignition. 'It's getting out of hand,' he continued as he backed out of the parking lot. 'The motor manufacturers vie with each other to provide more and more cup-holders. They appreciate that people seem to like cup-holders, so they say "Let's give 'em some more!" Every available space is now taken up with cup-holders.'

It was an interesting point, and in tune with a theory I'd been developing during my time in the South. Southerners appeared to be inseparable from these huge paper cups. Everywhere I'd been I'd seen people walking along the streets carrying them, and sitting in their cars in traffic jams sipping from them. Gordon himself did. After leaving the Dairy Queen, we drove to a Walmart to buy a few groceries and he walked right into the store holding his paper cup as if this was a quite normal way to behave. I'd finished my drink before entering the Walmart and deposited my cup in a bin because there's something deep rooted inside me that acts like a brake on my eating or drinking while mobile, except on rare occasions due to the influence of alcohol. But not Gordon. By the time he had collected his purchases in a basket and paid for them at the check-out, he was still holding his paper cup. The drink had gone, but he was now chewing the ice cubes. This put me in mind of another aspect of the visit Gordon made to Oxford, the time he had impressed my friends with his extensive knowledge of various diverse subjects. I'd been compelled to buy two new ice cube trays for my freezer because Gordon consumed ice in such alarming quantities. Perhaps in his case it was just to keep his brain from overheating.

As we drove away from the Walmart, I ran through my new theory in my mind. I didn't think it was simply that the lives of the paper cup people were too busy for them to drink in more conventional locations. The way they paraded everywhere with them, almost as if they were fashion statements, made me think it was more deep-seated than that. It seemed to me that just as cigarettes were fading in popularity as accessories that were acceptable to be seen with in public, so paper cups full of soft drink and ice cubes were taking their place. Paper cups served many of the same purposes that amateur psychologists put forward to explain people's addiction to cigarettes, other than the nicotine that is. Paper cups provided something to do with your hands and a sip was a convenient way of playing for time in a situation that demanded conversation. Paper cups had become the nation's new obsession. I had begun to see people carrying paper cups as addicts and I'd started feeling sorry for them. Later in my travels, while driving through Alabama, I passed an advertising hoarding for Winston cigarettes saying 'At least you can still smoke in your own car.' Well unless Winston have made contact with the motor manufacturers, even that possibility may soon be phased out. The space currently used as an ashtray in most vehicles is likely to make way for another cup-holder in the not too distant future.

As we motored through the rolling hills of East Texas, it even crossed my mind to wonder how long it might be before hypnotists caught on to the trend and started offering treatment for paper cup syndrome, or whether one day in the state of California the carrying of paper cups in public places would be made illegal.

Gordon brought me out of my reverie when he commenced his brief on the place we were heading towards. It was Kilgore, a town with a slightly stronger claim to fame than Henderson. Kilgore was situated on the East Texas oil field, discovered in the early 1930s, the oil strike that put Texas on the world map. It was like going home for Gordon since his father had been in the oil business and this was where Gordon had been brought up as a child.

It seemed like a normal enough little place. It had brick buildings in the downtown area and they had a slightly forgotten air about them, although the fact that it was a Sunday probably had something to do with this. What did mark out Kilgore from a hundred other little East Texas towns, however, was a piece of downtown that a substantial metal sign declared to be the World's Richest Acre. It was bristling with steel oil derricks, literally a small forest of the things. It looked like a storage compound for electricity pylons.

'This should give you some idea of what Kilgore was like when I grew up here,' Gordon said. 'At the height of the oil boom, there were more than a thousand derricks in the downtown area.'

The derricks on this particular acre had been preserved from those days before well-spacing rules were introduced. Looking across Kilgore's modern skyline, it was still punctuated with dozens of operational derricks, but they were now much more widely spaced. When they struck oil here, a small railway junction with fewer than a thousand inhabitants was turned virtually overnight into a boomtown of more than 30,000 people as wildcatters, lease hounds, speculators, con men and cabaret girls flocked in to enjoy the fantastic riches. Most pictures you see of present day oil wells show rigs in the middle of nowhere, in the North Sea or surrounded by sand in the Arabian desert, but this wasn't what it was like in Kilgore. People erected derricks and sank wells in their backyards, the town's Presbyterian church set one up right next to the church building. Anyone who owned a plot of land, no matter how small, could become an oil millionaire. Black gold fever had come to East Texas.

The Texas Historical Commission sign told me that this block was the most densely drilled tract in the world, with 24 wells on 10 lots owned by six different operators. Since it began production, this little acre alone had produced more than two and a half million barrels of crude oil. The whole East Texas field has yielded nearly four billion barrels to date, and it's still producing. For Texas, the oil strike was made at an appropriate time. While most of the rest of the country was suffering the deprivations brought by the Great Depression, the black golden triangle of Tyler, Temple and Longview was making whoopee. When World War II came along, the Texan oilmen saw that it was going to be a rather different affair from previous armed conflicts. This war was going to be fought largely with machines, and those machines would be dependent on oil. They set to and built a pipeline across the United States to take their East Texas crude to where it was needed most, to the refineries on the New Jersey coast. The Big Inch, as they called it, was supposed to take five years to build, but they finished it in less than 12 months.

In a sense, then, Hitler's Germany was finally defeated right here in East Texas. The honourable nature of the ends served by Texan oil was echoed in Kilgore's East Texas Oil Museum where a plaque on the wall inside the entrance declared that the concept, design and installation of exhibits were dedicated to the glory of God. But when the oil bonanza really took hold, the inhabitants of this last notch in the Bible Belt relegated the spirit of temperance to a back seat. New wells were coming on-line at a phenomenal rate in the early thirties. From seven wells every fortnight, the pace increased to seven a day. At its peak, oil was spurting from more than a hundred new wells every 24 hours. Bars, saloons and honky-tonks sprang up at an almost similar rate. Fortunes were won and lost in an evening on the gaming tables. Roughnecks and camp followers, middlemen and con men materialised in their droves. For a period insanity ruled, until the National Guard was called in to restore the peace. They chained people to trees and took six weeks to sort things out.

Not even the National Guard could save the man that started it all though. He was Columbus Marion 'Dad' Joiner, a seventy year old Choctaw Indian wildcatter from Oklahoma. Old Dad Joiner had already drilled two dry holes in East Texas before he spudded a third on a farm in Rusk County in 1929. More than a year later, a production test was carried out on the well and it gushed. Most of the history books say that Joiner sold his interest in the strike for $8 million, but if the truth be told, swindled out of it might be a more appropriate phrase to use. He lost his claim in an unfriendly poker game to one Haroldson Lafayette Hunt. Hunt later paid Dad Joiner the eight million to salve his conscience. It was a lot of money, of course, but HL Hunt made an awful lot more. Joiner blew the cash looking for more gushers, and Hunt went on to become the richest oilman in US history.

The East Texas oil field's shyster spirit of fast practice and occasional oversights when it comes to the law continues to colour several aspects of life in the area. Some of the foremost modern-day patrons of this noble artform, or operating system as Gordon might call it, can be found among the state's political representatives who come from the east. One of the most imaginative recent members of the Texas legislature hailed from Longview, at the apex of the oil triangle. Mike Martin really made a name for himself when he came up with his own unique spin on the sympathy vote to ensure his re-election in 1981. He hired his cousin to shoot him in the arm with a shotgun and then claimed that the incident had been inspired by a shadowy cult named the Guardian Angels of the Underworld. This group, Martin asserted, drew its fiendish inspiration from satanism and communism. It was out to get him because he was such a strong supporter of family values and the great American dream in general. Unfortunately for Representative Martin, however, his cousin confessed and Martin was called before a grand jury to explain himself. But he vanished before he could make his deposition, so the Texas Rangers were dispatched to try and find him. They eventually tracked him down to his mom's trailer in Kilgore, where a thorough search of the premises revealed him to be hiding in the stereo cabinet. As one columnist said at the time, Martin had always wanted to be the speaker.

In the end, Mike Martin was fined $2000 for lying to the grand jury investigating the case. Annoyed by such unfriendly chastisement, he then sued his cousin for shooting him.

Another interesting view on the law and order debate was reflected in a more recent case that was in the news while I was in East Texas.

One of the state senators, a character called Drew Nixon of Carthage, just down the road from Mount Enterprise, had been arrested in the state capital of Austin on charges of soliciting for prostitution and carrying an unregistered handgun. In his defence, Senator Nixon, a Republican, claimed to have been lost and asking for directions. Unfortunately, the woman he stopped in front of a church was an undercover officer of the law who taped the conversation. Nixon's poor sense of direction plea seemed unlikely because no one could find any record of two Texas communities named Intercourse and Blowjob. When questioned about his unregistered firearm, the senator declared that it was for his personal protection against threats from the same sorts of civilian militia groups that had been originally implicated in the Mike Martin shooting. Nixon's understanding of Texan law was as lamentable as his knowledge of state geography. Apparently he hadn't realised that a licensed handgun would be equally effective against coup attempts. 'I was just stupid' seemed to be the most sensible comment Senator Nixon made at his trial. Nonetheless, he got off with probation on the prostitution charge, although the weapons misdemeanour earned him 180 days in jail. The sentence wasn't too tiresome, however, because the judge said he only need serve it at weekends.

Despite calls for his resignation, Nixon refused, so probably becoming the only state senator to serve a jail term while remaining in office.

After a few days, Gordon had to make the five hour drive back to the heart of the state's body politic in Austin where his new job was. Strictly speaking, Austin was off limits to me since it was beyond the bounds of East Texas and thus outside my Southern remit, but Gordon reckoned I ought to have at least a quick look at the city so I went along with him for the ride.

Gordon's new job was managing the state's digital mapping and imagery operations. You might think that Texans already have enough maps of their state, but you'd be wrong. They needed more and Gordon was the man to do it for them. Like many other avenues in the modern world, computers have taken over the business of making maps. These days, a lot of cartography is based on imagery taken from space and manipulated using something called a Geographical Information System, or GIS for short. Both Gordon and I shared the same doctoral supervisor at Oxford who used to sneer at the new-fangled GIS when it first appeared on the scene. He called it electronic tracing paper. He was right, it doesn't really do much more than that, but it does allow you to produce maps rather faster than before. Either way, GIS has become all the rage. It has also become a hugely specialised vocation, which, like other academic sub-disciplines, has constructed a whole new vocabulary along the way. It was a vocabulary that Gordon was entirely familiar with, needless to say, but not one in which I am particularly well versed. So when my Texan friend began to tell me about his new assignment en route to Austin, I found it difficult enough to follow. Coming on top of Gordon's propensity to talk in NASA-speak, there were times when it was like listening to a foreign language.

After a quick run through the basics of metadata (data about data), orthoimagery (I missed that one) and fuzzy foot problems (I was punch-drunk by then), Gordon had me completely lost. But he had moved on to explain the importance of commencing his work with an industrial strength computer operating system, which made it sound like he might after all be dealing with weapons grade material rather than just pretty pictures from space.

There were certain systems, Gordon told me, that offered you the facility to discover the root cause of their own problems, while others did not. That sounded OK to me, I was back on track. Manipulation of very large files caused some systems to burst apart on you, breaking down in ways that were unpredictable, he continued. I was still with him.

'It's sort of like running UNIX,' Gordon said. I didn't know what a UNIX was, but I let that one pass. 'You know UNIX'll dump cores on you,' he continued. (Dump cores? No idea.) 'Certainly when you're doing high end stuff, like image processing or surface model generation, but you can go back in and explore that core dump and find out where things got dodgy. So you can sort it for next time.' I wasn't sure of all the details, but I was still hanging on.

'What I've always found with NT especially, trying to do things there, is that you get error messages that are never the same.' (NT? Don't know; another system or facility no doubt.) 'And you don't have a core that dumps out that you can explore, it's just a mystery. It's a problem that PR had in China, setting up a GIS on the NT to do the kinds of things that we were doing here routinely.' (PR was a person, I'd met him.) 'Just routine stuff. And it was just too unstable to handle it.'

We were on to the benefits of industrial strength operating systems. 'When you write code on top of it, you know what it's doing and why it's failing. And it will fail. It's inevitable, especially when you start writing AMLs and different software, customised features and things.'

All this high-tech gadgetry was a million miles from the subsistence lifestyle of the backwoodsmen in the hardwood bottomlands and I was in danger of tuning Gordon out. Consequently, I nearly missed a point of interest on the roadside. 'There's Alligator Annie's right there,' he said suddenly. I just turned my head in time to see a track leading off the main road. For a moment, I'd thought it was just another piece of GIS jargon that I'd never heard of. 'Alligator Annie is a septic specialist. She does constructive wetlands, that's the alligator part.' This was a character Gordon had told me about a couple of days before, a woman who dealt in reconstructing marshlands to treat sewage, thus dealing with a waste disposal problem in an environmentally friendly way. The passing of her establishment had brought me back from the edge of oblivion.

Gordon got straight back to telling me about the sort of person he needed to deal with the problems of core dumping and system failures. 'You know the guy who gets that right the first time is probably not the person you want to work for you because they're too narrowly focused,' he said. 'You need the guy that can sit down and be creative and pin it down in six or seven attempts. That's what I tell grad students, you know. Some of them come in and I start teaching them how to programme in GIS, and they'll do a kind of patch job. They'll come up to a stage when they say OK I could go back and reiterate, get a much finer tuned fix to what I'm attempting to do. BUT I don't want to do all that work, so instead I'll just take a little side step here and run this other routine on top.' I was in danger of losing it again, but I furrowed my brow and concentrated hard. I'm glad I did.

'So they do that five or six times,' Gordon went on, 'and I'll tell them it's like the Donner party going up the Sierra Nevadas. And you can start making wrong turns, and you'll be OK, 'cos everybody takes a wrong turn or two. But eventually you're half-way up the mountain in the deep snow and you're eating each other. There's no way back. If that's the way you wanna live your life, keep making those wrong turns. Sooner or later, you're going to have to eat somebody, or they're going to eat you. Think about it. That'll cost you.' The way he put it, Gordon's training programme was probably a matter of life or death to these people.

Texas might have come a long way from the self-sufficient back-woods, but it was comforting to hear from Gordon's description that in one sense it didn't sound like mankind had really advanced very much at all. It was getting late and we stopped at a roadside eating joint to feed on some native cuisine. I had chicken-fried steak, a Texan speciality which turned out to be like a Wiener schnitzel that hadn't been hammered. The operating system I used was a knife and fork. Then we drove on, through the night and into Austin, with Gordon talking all the way.

When in Georgia, I'd asked a man who had lived most of his life in Tennessee what traits he thought most characterised the South. After lengthy consideration, he came out with two things. 'First,' he said, 'you can get ice tea all the year round here, while up north it's seasonal. Second, the pace of life is slower in the South.'

Although Austin wasn't in the South, Gordon told me that both of these defining qualities used to apply to the state capital of Texas. But that was the Austin of yesteryear, he added. Things had changed seriously since he had first lived here as a student at the University of Texas back in the mellow seventies. 'It first hit me when I went into Quacks on the drag and ordered an ice tea. They offered me a *choice* of three different varieties!' Completely stunned by the incident, Gordon had quickly started to notice some more startling differences. 'Another unsettling event was when I saw a woman in a smart suit shoot through a revolving door clutching her briefcase and dash off down the street. When I first lived here, they'd have got out the hypodermic, sedated that woman, and put her under observation for a few days. Twenty years ago, no one moved that fast in Austin. Now it's commonplace.'

The transformations that had occurred in Austin were all part and parcel of a broader shift affecting the whole state, one in which Texas was moving away from a resource based economy towards one based on brains. It was bye-bye bottomlands and hello GIS operating systems. They still had the oil and the longhorns, but Austin had become the second biggest producer of microchips after Silicon Valley. It was now a boomtown with more Porsche Boxsters per capita than any place outside Santa Monica. Kilgore had had its day, now it was Austin's turn.

Gordon and I were sitting in a restaurant on the edge of town, an old favourite apparently, having just finished a farewell dinner. It had involved very large quantities of meat, the sort of meal that was still widely available despite all the changes. I had spent the day in the library at the University of Texas reading up on the Southern states. The sheer volume of literature available had amazed me. There were books and articles on virtually every aspect imaginable, which had been a testament to the vitality of the South as a region worthy of study if nothing else. They had covered the New South, the Old South, the future of the South and the disappearing South. There had been journal articles on blacks and whites and every possible shade of grey. My attention had been caught by one suggesting that kudzu might spread northwards under the influence of global warming, crossing the Mason-Dixon Line in a renewed Southern attempt to invade the North more than 130 years after Gettysburg. This had led me into a number of books on how Southern values were shaping American life and how the South was becoming more northernised.

With these latter themes in mind, and given the recent changes that had taken place in Austin, I thought perhaps I might have a chance of getting a decent cup of coffee, so I asked for an espresso. The waiter apologised, saying they only served regular coffee.

'They tried to introduce espresso and cappuccino here a while back,' said Gordon, 'but they had to give up due to a lack of interest.' He smiled. 'It was just a bit too early.'

I'd booked a flight to New Orleans for the following day. With its supposedly more obvious European influence, I thought perhaps I'd have better luck there.

27

The Big Easy

I'd become a bit nervous about returning to Louisiana. Several of Gordon's colleagues had left a pregnant pause in the air after I'd told them I was heading there next. The pause was usually followed with a question like 'What are you going there for?' delivered in a voice laden with thinly disguised incredulity. Next came a story of unexpected goings-on in the state, often involving a friend of a friend who had either been the victim of an assault or had been locked up in jail for a lengthy stretch on a trumped up charge. East Texas wisdom held that the Louisiana police force didn't like people from out of state. The cops seemed to go on the premise that most outsiders were guilty until proven innocent of whatever unsolved crime they had on the books that day, and if they didn't have an unsolved crime to hand, they could just as easily make one up. Other than being unnerving, these comments surprised me because I hadn't come across any animosity between Southern states until now. All the venom had been reserved for the Yankees.

I had toyed with the idea of hiring another car and driving from Austin to New Orleans, but it already felt like I'd driven round the world a couple of times so I flew instead. The bus into town at the other end gave me an introduction to a strange city. We passed a store selling guns, cigars and magazines, which to my mind seemed like an odd combination of merchandise, and then the highway cut through a series of sprawling cemeteries. The elderly graveyards flanked both sides of the road for a considerable stretch, giving the impression that most of the city's inhabitants had frequented the gun, cigar and magazine store and had wound up dead as a result.

When we reached downtown, the impressions changed. Snatches of jazz music began to throb on the heavy air as we drove down streets in need of urban regeneration. They were punctuated here and there with soaring towerblocks that indicated how the city authorities would have it done when they got around to the task. Canal Street was wide and in need of some cosmetic attention, but all of a sudden it was gone and we were in the French Quarter. Here I was in the famed narrow streets passing small wooden houses with shutters at their windows and lacy cast-iron galleries adorned with hanging baskets and coloured flags. By now, I should have been used to the sharp contrasts that characterise North American cities, but the abrupt change still surprised me. It was like tucking into a pecan pie and finding a steak au poivre underneath.

Having been struck by the cemeteries on the drive into town, I pushed Gordon's colleagues' warnings to the back of my mind and decided to go and have a look at one after I'd checked into my hotel. St Louis Cemetery Number 1 was just a short walk away, on the western edge of the French Quarter where the freshly painted wooden cottages sat looking across a freeway at some prime urban decay. It was the tail-end of the afternoon but the sun was still high and there was not a cloud to be seen. I wandered in and out of Louis Armstrong Park, which seemed strangely deserted beneath such a perfect blue sky, before strolling along N Rampart Street to the small cemetery entrance.

Being so close to the Mississippi river, New Orleans has always buried her dead above ground because almost as soon as you start digging you hit water. So St Louis Cemetery Number 1 looked like a small walled city for the deceased with narrow streets laid out in a gridiron pattern. As in life, its inhabitants had been allotted premises in accordance with their wealth. Some of the family vaults, fenced off by iron railings, resembled miniature mansions for the rich, while multiple burial facilities like apartment blocks catered for the less well-off. The 'apartments' were set in long stone walls and are historically rented for a year and a day, after which the remains are pushed to the rear of the narrow vault and the coffin burnt to make way for the next tenant.

More than two hundred years after it was first established by the Spanish in 1789, the cementery is still in use today. The most recent tomb I saw was dated 1993 and among the rows of apartment vaults were some newly polished grey granite frontstones ready and waiting for someone to die. But despite the occasional fresh tombstone and one or two healthy young palm trees, the entire mini-metropolis had an air of faded grandeur about it. Not many people had responded to the discreet advertisements for perpetual care contracts ('a one-time investment obligating the cemetery always to keep your family memorial in good condition and repair'). The narrow streets between the tombs were pockmarked with potholes of neglect, many of the vaults needed a lick of whitewash, and most of the brickwork badly needed repointing. The whole place had been allowed to run down, like the deceaseds' version of urban decay. It was, in effect, a ghetto for the dead.

Unsurprisingly, the personal histories of the cemetery's occupants mirrored the annals of New Orleans and to some extent Louisiana itself. Some of the inscriptions were in English, others in French. I paused to read one tomb that said it held the city's first mayor after France acquired Louisiana from Spain in 1801 (almost 40 years after the Spanish had themselves taken it over from the French). The man was also the first successfully to granulate sugar commercially. There were several headstones for combatants who died in the Battle of New Orleans against the British in 1815, by which time Thomas Jefferson had purchased the Louisiana Territory to add to his collection of united states. Many others had died in the Yellow Fever epidemics that swept through the city in the eighteenth and nineteenth centuries. Later I learned that one end of the cemetery was a separate non-Catholic section, echoing the state's division between its Catholic southern parts and its Protestant north.

Two other tombs aptly reflected the position of southern Louisiana as an integral part of the South but also as one with a distinctive twist. The first was a smoothly weathered edifice with a spray of faded red material roses tucked into a corner of its broken stone cladding. It was that of Homer Adolph Plessy, whose defiance in 1892 of a state law designed to segregate people on the basis of race led to a landmark decision in the US Supreme Court that paved the way for the whole Jim Crow era. Plessy was a so-called 'octoroon' (one-eighth black) which meant that he was nearly pale enough to sit in a whites only railway carriage, but not quite. So when he tried it, he was arrested. His act of civil disobedience marked one of the first legal challenges to the separation of races in the South following the postwar Reconstruction period. He lost, and the ruling in his case, *Plessy v Ferguson*, upheld the constitutionality of Louisiana law. The idea of 'separate but equal' facilities was deemed to be a legal one, and states all across Dixie rushed to place appropriate statutes on the books. It wasn't until 1954 that the Supreme Court overturned *Plessy v Ferguson* by ruling in the case of *Brown v Board of Education* that the segregation of public schools was unconstitutional.

The South Louisiana twist came at the nearby tomb of Marie Laveau, voodoo queen extraordinaire, who was actually two people, or at least a mother and daughter partnership. Appropriately enough, they're not even sure that this is Marie senior's final resting place, but just in case it was, a lot of voodoo pilgrims had chalked red X's all over the unkempt sentry box-style vault and others had forced one cent pieces into cracks where the plaster had started to come away. The newer donations were still twinkling in the sunshine beside small patches of bright green moss. The ground in front of the tomb was littered with an interesting assortment of offerings. They were all single objects, including a small pomegranate, a string of white plastic beads, a similar string of beads in yellow, and a luminous blue sweet in its cellophane wrapper. There was a single red plastic rose and a solitary red real carnation that had only been there a few days. Beside the faded fresh flower was the only double presentation: two shiny brown cockroaches sunning themselves in the afternoon heat. Interestingly enough, the largest single offering was a paper cup from the fast food chain Krystal, indicating that perhaps even in the afterlife people like Marie Laveau could contract paper cup syndrome.

Voodoo was brought to Louisiana by black immigrants who arrived after the uprising in Haiti, in which the French were kicked out of their Saint Domingue colony by means of the only successful slave revolt in history. The mystical cult adds a dark dimension to the frisson of being in New Orleans, although all the voodoo dolls I saw on sale in the city's French Quarter were made in China. Despite the nearby commercialisation of what is an essentially serious religion, Marie Laveau's tomb still provided a vaguely sinister air to the already morbid ghetto of the dead.

It was only after I'd returned to my hotel that I read up about the cemetery and its environs in a guidebook. In the book's safety section it advised me not to stray across N Rampart Street at any time, and at the end of the entry on St Louis Cemetery Number 1 came some more unequivocal advice: 'Do not enter this cemetery alone!' Apparently, even the guided tours came with disclaimers absolving them of responsibility should anything unpleasant happen to you. They weren't referring to the danger of bumping into a zombie. Like any other urban ghetto, this place was well known for its muggings and murders. I counted myself lucky that I'd come through the experience unscathed, and decided that perhaps Gordon's colleagues had been on to something after all.

Having said that, I've never met anyone who doesn't like the French Quarter. It's a 24 hour party zone, a laid back pleasure centre with good food, lots of music and plenty of booze, the sort of place where no one looks at you sideways if you order a beer to go with your beignets at breakfast. It was easy to while away a couple of days and nights just hanging out listening to the impromptu jazz bands and watching the world go by. Louisiana's hub of hedonism catered to customers from all walks of life. From a balcony vantage point, over a dinner of blackened redfish, I looked on one evening as teams of white college boys clutching 'go cups' full of Dixie beer meandered from bar to bar along Bourbon Street in their button-down collars. Some stopped to marvel for a moment at a squad of small black kids, one with a spinning bicycle wheel on his head, tap-dancing for pennies on the sidewalk opposite. Others paused to jeer at a transvestite street performer who didn't stand a chance of holding his statuesque pose in the face of such gibes. Half an hour later, the college boys returned. They were slightly subdued, probably because they'd ventured as far as the lower Quarter, a zone of carefully ironed white shirts and earrings, where every other reveller wears a hard hat and male strippers perform above the bars.

Down by the riverside one morning, I listened to a man with a greying beard playing his saxophone alone on the wharf while a black-bearded white man searched the bins for his breakfast. Behind the saxophonist, the wooden walkway was being slapped by significant waves from a tug pushing what looked like two giant plates piled with gravel and broken rock. Anywhere else in the world and the haunting tones of the sax would have seemed totally inappropriate outside in the fresh air at 8.30 in the morning.

In Jackson Square, beneath the pointy spires of the white cathedral, respectable elderly couples mixed with the weirdos, freaks and bohemians to have their palms or tarot cards read by experts sitting behind their collapsible tables in the shade of wobbly parasols. And if you didn't want to look into the future you could simply enjoy the present in the form of an unlikely collection of musicians whose tunes had little to do with their dress sense. Two sax players in baseball caps and beat-up trainers flanked a man in an old T-shirt whose huge presence was nonetheless dwarfed by his tuba. Behind him stood a dude with a trumpet and a youth in dark glasses holding a banjo, the case of which lay open, brimming with donations, at the front of the band. The only white guy in the frame sat hunched on a bar stool in a hooded sweat top plucking a double base swathed in masking tape all up one side. This motley crew took turns to perform solos on their battered instruments and sing old favourites in voices made of gravel seasoned with the effects of smoking two packs a day. One lunchtime as I sat and listened, they were joined by an elderly gent in dark glasses, black beret and a dinner jacket who was wheeling a small drum on what looked like a shopping trolley. He paused on passing through to sing a few lines of 'Who's sorry now?' before continuing on his way.

Quieter spots were also in plentiful supply for those visitors who just wanted to take time out and reflect on life or drink themselves into oblivion. Late one afternoon I dropped in on Lafitte's Blacksmith Shop, a single storey wood and brick shack that looked from the outside like the most decrepit hole in the city. The only artificial light inside the place came from the candles flickering in bowls on the rickety tables and I was just beginning to let my imagination loose on New Orleans' legendary pirates and illicit smuggling deals when I noticed the surveillance camera on a black rafter and the Automatic Teller Machine in one corner. These ATMs featured in every bar and restaurant in the French Quarter because nobody wanted you to spoil the party by running out of cash midway through.

That evening I found myself in Kaldi's Coffeehouse opposite the waterfront on Decatur Street. I'd entered the place thinking it looked a good bet for some more live jazz and found myself in the midst of a group self-expression session run by the local young black community. I should have realised what I was getting myself into when a grubby dude on the door asked if I was a poet, but I just said no and assumed it was a case of mistaken identity. Kaldi's was in a former bank building with a classical façade involving fluted columns built into the exterior walls. It claimed to double as a coffee museum but in practice this just meant that the place was strewn with a few old sacks of coffee beans, and a couple of ancient grinders positioned in discreet corners. It was the sort of alternative venue where the characters serving behind the bar wore woolly hats pulled down over their ears and sported earrings in unusual places. Old brown fans whirred away high on the ceiling and there were nicotine stains on the whitewashed walls. No one had swept the floor in at least a month and they'd probably last emptied the ashtrays at about the same time. Nevertheless, the coffee was good and strong and I was fortunate to find myself a table against one wall where I could observe most of the action unnoticed.

I thought my luck was in when a group of guys started setting up on a low wooden stage. They jammed for a while in a way that might have been a tune-up but equally could have been an avant-garde piece of performance art. They were all young and black, dressed in an unofficial uniform consisting of trainers, baggy denims and hooded sweat tops. They looked like the type of characters I'd have given a wide berth to if I'd seen them outside St Louis Cemetery Number 1 without their brass instruments, but the sounds they made in Kaldi's Coffeehouse were so dreamy and rhythmic they'd have soothed the souls of even the living dead.

After about half an hour of this, I was on my second espresso when the compère for the evening took up the microphone and started the ball rolling by telling us that this was the best open mike this side of the Desire Housing Development.

'Put your hands together for Brother Fred Flintstone who wants a rap beat on the double bass and drums behind him.' I had an inkling that this wasn't going to be my sort of evening as soon as Brother Flintstone began with the words 'Who am I?' but I stuck with it for another hour before making my exit just as a dude named P (Pea?)

struck up with his number entitled 'Don't smoke that rock'. It had all become a bit too self-conscious for my liking.

Before the impromptu jazz had started in Kaldi's Coffeehouse, I'd fallen into a brief conversation with one of the only other white faces in the house. The guy had moved over to where I was sitting and crouched down against the wall beside me. He had looked rather nervous and I'd put this down to our minority status, but after we'd exchanged a few bits of small talk, it became clear that I'd been mistaken. The guy was killing time, he told me, trying to relax before going to bed and getting a good night's rest because tomorrow he was running in a marathon. When I expressed an interest, he took it as his cue to tell me all about his training regime. Twenty miles a day here and thirty a day there, endurance weights and special diets to fuel the system. He went on and on about how he'd been doing ten mile 'sprints' before lunch and two or three miles every night before bedtime. It was like talking to a car.

I didn't immediately make the connection the next morning when I saw what I thought were a couple of joggers in the Warehouse District. Then I saw another gaggle of runners and I realised that this was probably it. I paused outside the New Orleans Zen Temple to ask a man watching for confirmation.

'What's the race?'

The guy shook his head. 'I dunno brother,' he replied world-wearily. 'All I know is, it's a marathon. What they're running *for* I dunno.'

It wasn't surprising to find such an attitude in a city known as the Big Easy. A bit further up the street, inside a small shop looking at some shirts, I thought I'd try some conversation with the chap behind the counter. 'You're not running?' I asked him. 'No man,' he replied, 'when I got out of the army that was it. I don't run any more, unless someone calls me for dinner.'

I was making my way to the oldest museum in Louisiana, the Confederate Memorial Hall which looked like a small fortress in brown brick with a large iron cannon outside. The cavernous hall was where, at the end of the last century, the one and only Confederate president, Jefferson Davis, lay in state for a couple of days before being moved to Richmond, Virginia for burial. They had a selection of Davis memorabilia on display in their exhibition cases which I perused to a muzak version of the South's unofficial national anthem, 'Dixie Land', playing over the tannoy. The song predates the use of Dixie as a term for the whole South, and Southerners argue over the origin of the word itself. Those among the people of New Orleans who care about such things claim it was invented in their city and the reason why was also on display in a case full of Confederate bank notes. The story goes that the enterprising Citizens' Bank printed bilingual $10 notes for a city divided along a border that ran down Canal Street between English speaking Americans and francophone Creoles. With the denomination written as Ten on one side and Dix on the other, Southerners began referring to them as Dixies.

As a label for the South Dixie is supposed to be fading in its popularity, although from what I'd seen its use was still fairly widespread. Going from some of the other exhibits in the Confederate Memorial Hall, feelings about that little North–South conflict also still ran fairly high. The Sons of Confederate Veterans were still awarding posthumous medals to honour Confederate soldiers (the most recent certificate I saw was dated 1991) and at the entrance to the museum a large Confederate flag had been mounted behind a glass screen beneath a slogan saying Adopt a Flag Program. The glass had been divided up into a grid of small squares and people paid to buy a star to stick on a grid square. The donations had come from all over the Southern states and some had managed to squeeze a comment in addition to their names on the small stars. 'For all our sons and daughters who fought so valiantly,' wrote Sheila Reno from Biloxi, Mississippi. Daryl Robertson of the 3rd Louisiana Cavalry, Camp #133, Sons of Confederate Veterans had dedicated his star 'To our brave hearts'.

Meandering my way back towards the French Quarter, I stopped at a small café to buy another shot of espresso because I didn't think I'd find one again in what remained of my tour of the South. I sat and sipped it at a table on the street watching the marathon men as they continued to struggle by. I counted forty white runners before the first black one passed me and I guessed that most of his counterparts were more concerned with playing jazz than with running a road race.

Back on the crummy fringes of Canal Street, I stopped for a quick snack at a greasy spoon run by two friendly middle-aged ladies. They were both dark, and spoke with accents that were difficult to place. They had a Southern drawling element to them, but there was something else about their voices that evoked the flavour of the Mediterranean. One of them spread my burger bun with margarine from an industrial sized tub while the other flung the compressed meat onto the grill.

When I came to pay, the woman who had cooked my burger looked intently at the hand I'd outstretched for my change. Rather than giving me my money, she took hold of my wrist. 'Your hand always that red?' she asked studiously. 'Yes,' I replied.

'You've got a lot of wisdom,' she said. It was a simple statement, just as if she was saying my shirt was grey. Then she lost interest and gave me the change. It wasn't the sort of after-dinner service I could expect to find anywhere else in the South.

28

Heart of Dixie

My route to Alabama, the last stop on my tour of the eleven Confederate states, took me across the bottom end of Mississippi. I'd hired another car and left New Orleans driving in a north-easterly direction on Interstate 10. Soon after leaving Louisiana, I turned on to Highway 90 because it ran right along the coastline of the Gulf of Mexico. The road was like a long tarmac corridor that ran for miles and miles between a neat strip of white sandy beach on one side and a long stretch of elegant antebellum houses on the other. These Gulf coast mansions sprung up with the invention of the steam boat which allowed the more affluent residents of New Orleans to get out of town whenever the Yellow Fever epidemics raged, leaving the Big Easy's poorer inhabitants to stay put and fill the graveyards. It was a string of plush coastal bolt-holes from the heat and fever of the metropolis, serving the same purpose as Beaufort had for South Carolina's back-country plantation owners. But the view from the broad front porches that looked out over the sea in those days was not that which they enjoy today. The strip of pristine white sand that runs for 26 miles west of Biloxi wasn't created until the 1950s. Sure enough, it is the longest man-made beach in the world.

I stopped at Pass Christian to stretch my legs on the artificial wonder, and was struck immediately by another similarity between this place and Beaufort. A signpost erected by the Harrison County Beach Department echoed the Stalinist approach to law and order I'd seen in the South Carolina Low Country. It was a Beach Ordinance list that declared:

> No Dogs
> No Littering
> No Tents
> No Camping

No Glass, China or Pottery
No Motor Vehicles
No Horses or Livestock
No Firearms or Air Guns
No Fireworks without Permit
No Fire without Permit
No Molesting of Wildlife

They certainly intended to take good care of their counterfeit coastline.

At the Biloxi end of the world's longest made-made beach was another rash of Mississippi casinos. I could tell they were approaching because of the sudden outbreak of pawn shops and the advertising hoardings designed to get you into the right mood. The casinos were glitzy and outlandish in the same way as their counterparts in the Delta, but although they stood in stark contrast to the antebellum mansions, here on the coast the gambling joints didn't look as surreal and out of place as they had further north. One was called Treasure Bay and was built to look like a 400 foot replica of an eighteenth-century pirate galleon. It had three masts and according to one of the hoardings, the loosest slots on the coast, although somebody had scrubbed out the top part of the O in slots to make it look like a U.

It wasn't the loose slots that tempted me to stay the night just outside Biloxi. I was more interested in an historic attraction, an old planter's house called Beauvoir where Jefferson Davis played out his final years penning his memoirs about the Lost Cause. The following morning I found the place on Highway 90 with the help of a forthright brown signpost that pointed to The Jefferson Davis Shrine. I drove in under a Confederate battle flag draped over the entrance.

In the time following his two year incarceration without trial in a Virginia jailhouse after his side lost the war, the former president of the Confederacy hadn't yet become the martyr of the Lost Cause. He was more of a lost soul. Stripped of his US citizenship, he spent a decade looking for somewhere permanent to live before accepting an invitation to Beauvoir where he stayed until his death 12 years later. The fact that the place is now regarded as a shrine is a tribute both to his resurrection as the honourable leader of the Cause and to the Mississippi Division of the United Sons of Confederate Veterans Inc.

who run the place. The vitality of this cult of the dead was plain for all to see in the form of a new Jefferson Davis library and museum under construction beside the car park.

The main house was a single-storey cottage, raised up from the ground against flooding and to improve ventilation. It was a glorified version of the dogtrot house, a design found all over the South in which two rooms are separated by an interior breezeway where the dogs could roam. In this case the central run had been enclosed and turned into a hall, and a couple more rooms had been tacked on at the back. A prominent feature of the extensive grounds behind the house was a huge live oak under which the ex-president used to read his Bible. Beyond this was a small Confederate cemetery. The engraving on a monument stone read: 'No nation rose so white and fair, none fell so pure of crime.' A few of the graves were marked with small Confederate battle flags.

One particular set of exhibits in the small museum housed in a former veteran's home indicated one of the many reasons why the noble cause was lost. Beside a display of Confederate banknotes was a short explanation of how the Confederacy had financed its holy war. Aside from a bit of taxation and a few loans, they had issued a lot of paper money. Any economist will tell you that this is not the way to go about buying yourself out of a crisis, and the explanatory note here in Beauvoir was surprisingly candid in describing the Confederate monetary system as unworkable. It was refreshing to see such a realistic appraisal after a similar display in the New Orleans Confederate Memorial Hall which had just made do with a few uncritical facts about the banknotes it displayed.

Between 1861 and 1864, no fewer than 72 different types of Confederate currency were produced, and a shortage of suitable paper meant that many of the new notes were printed on the backs of other currency. Although historians have since called the war between the Confederates and the Unionists the first modern, or industrial war, most of the industry was in the North. Down South the signatures on all but four sorts of their new currency were done by hand. Each treasury official had to hire 200 special clerks to sign the notes for them in brown ink because otherwise the men at the top wouldn't have had any time to run the Confederate economy. They'd have spent the entire war signing banknotes. As a consequence, there were literally thousands of signatory combinations. Add to this the fact that the Confederate government also allowed the circulation of notes issued by individual states, cities and private corporations (such as banks and railroad companies), and the variety must have been truly bewildering. As the war dragged on, coins became so scarce in some parts of the South that even small businesses got in on the act. They began creating their own paper money for regular customers. The result must have been Kafkaesque.

Kafka might also have been amused at the length of time it took for Jefferson Davis to have his US citizenship posthumously restored. Congress didn't pass the appropriate bill until 1978, which was 89 years after his death.

I continued skirting the Gulf of Mexico along Highway 90 and stopped for some lunch before the Alabama state line at a fast food joint nestling among the pine trees. I'd been on the look-out for a Krystal for some time because it is a distinctly Southern chain out of Chattanooga, Tennessee. The Krystal speciality is a tiny hamburger, similar to the fare produced by White Castle in the Midwest. One's not enough so you buy them by the boxful and they're real cheap. The people who know about these things say that these Krystal miniburgers are as Southern as Coke, and that their best known connoisseur was Elvis. I don't eat a lot of junk food at home, but I'd downed a fair amount during my time in the South, and wherever I am, when I feel like a fast food burger, I really want one. This was one of those occasions. I bought a pack of four miniburgers that came in a small red cardboard presentation box with the Krystal logo on it. The logo looked like it had been designed in the 1950s, and when combined with the fact that the restaurant badly needed a refit, this made my lunch seem like a scene from Buck Rogers in the twenty-first century on TV. Looking back, I'd have to say that Krystal's hand-held rations tasted like the result of an experiment to manufacture a food product out of cotton wool, but at the time they were just what I needed.

Although the South in general is often characterised by its small-

265

town, rural flavour, these features are supposed to be particularly pronounced in Alabama, hence its catch-phrase 'the Heart of Dixie' which appears on the licence plates of all vehicles registered in the state. The first place I was aiming for as I skirted round the city of Mobile, and a hoarding advertising a money-back guarantee for microsurgery vasectomy reversal, was Monroeville. On the map, Monroeville was just a small dot more or less in the middle of Monroe County, itself just a squarish patch of land mostly on the east side of the Alabama river. The reason for going there was that this was the birthplace and home town of Harper Lee, and reputedly the model for Maycomb where Atticus Finch defended a black man on a rape charge in *To Kill a Mockingbird*.

North of Mobile, the highway soared over a maze of rivers, at one point the 'central reservation' between the two sides of the road becoming 200ft of brown water flanked by brown swamp forest with no leaves. The trees were draped in brown creepers instead and I thought it might be dead kudzu. I turned off towards Uriah and entered an agricultural landscape where bulls were grazing in the pastures between blocks of pine forest. I passed a Beagle Club and a hand made notice saying Turnips for Sale. The plants in a cotton field had been cut short so that they looked like little sticks, making for a neat contrast with the tall, arrow straight pine trees. A pole and timber company was making the most of Nature's bounty, turning out immense logs that were ready-made telegraph poles. Some of the trees were so tall they probably got two out of each one.

The countryside became more rolling as I crossed a bridge over a creek that took me into Monroe County. Signs beside the road indicated the locations of Adopt a Mile litter control programmes whereas in most of the other states I'd driven through they were known as Adopt a Highway schemes. Either way all the ones I passed were run by local community groups, schools or businesses, and I never saw any evidence to confirm something I'd read about outfits like the Ku Klux Klan getting in on the act. In parts of North Florida they'd used jailbirds to keep the highway verges clean and tidy. Big fluorescent orange triangles emblazoned with the words State Prisoners Working had alerted oncoming traffic to their presence. The penalties to discourage people from dropping litter along the highways in the first place had varied widely between states. In the Lone Star state, typically straightforward messages said Don't Mess with Texas, Fine: $4000. Previously the lowest penalty I'd seen for the litter misdemeanour was $200, and unsurprisingly, this was in Mississippi. Here in rural Alabama it was $100.

Pecan orchards lined the road between Uriah and Frisco City, both neat little towns, although the houses on the other side of the railroad tracks slicing through Frisco City were a bit dilapidated. Coming into Monroeville from the south, the road was hemmed in by the usual fast food, supermarket and motel suspects. They hadn't quite sucked all the lifeblood out of the one storey shops that ringed the court-house square in the middle of town but it looked like it might only be a matter of time. The courthouse itself no longer functioned as a courthouse, because they put up a new one in the 1960s. The turn of the century original was still there all right, but it was surrounded by historic markers. When the surrounding shops finally go under, the heart of this county seat will just be another downtown historic district to go with all the other Southern towns and cities I'd seen that had turned their centres into museums.

Monroeville had a lot going for it in this respect. Not many other Southern towns can lay claim to being the setting for one of the world's best known novels, but there didn't appear to be much interest in maximising the commercial potential. One of the historic markers proclaimed the fame of the very solid looking red brick building in a Romanesque style with a Georgian influence and mentioned the famous courtroom scene. On the opposite side of the building, beneath an oak tree swathed in ferns, was an Alabama State Bar legal milestone that paid tribute to Atticus Finch 'lawyer hero'. But that was about it. Here was an unmistakable contrast to the relentless promotion of *Midnight in the Garden of Good and Evil* in Savannah, Georgia. There 'The Book', as they called it, was on display in every shop window, and newspaper cuttings about the movie were pasted up all over the historic downtown district. I even saw a tobacco blend named after the book in a tobacconist's. That wasn't the way they did things in Monroeville. Harper Lee still lives there, and she values her privacy. She's never written another book, she does no publicity and she doesn't give interviews. Her home town seemed to respect that and was just getting on with being a small county seat in the rural Deep South.

I got a similar impression a couple of days later when I visited Marion, county seat of Perry County just to the northeast of Selma. Marion also came with a well groomed courthouse square surrounded on all sides by Mom and Pop shops and the local post office. Marion could have pushed itself a lot further too, if it had wanted, but it didn't appear to be that way. They'd put a slab of marble on the lawn outside the courthouse to commemorate one of their local heroes, a man named Nicola Marschall who designed the Stars and Bars, the first official flag of the Confederacy, as well as the Confederate uniform. I did a double-take when I read that Nicola Marschall was a he. Remembering the confusion over the spelling of Elvis' middle name at Graceland, I thought they must have got it wrong, but later I saw a picture of Nicola and he was definitely a man.

Also prominent outside Marion's Perry County courthouse was a small cannon cast at Tuscaloosa in the early days of the 'Civil War' (the plaque's quote marks), along with evidence that the town was forward looking too, in the form of two time capsules that had been buried beneath the lawn. But Marion also had an important black history. It was an incident here that provided the impetus for the famous civil rights march from nearby Selma to the state capital at Montgomery and most of those who marched were residents of Marion. The incident in question was the death of a protestor, shot by state troopers for trying to protect his mother from being beaten in a local café after a mass church meeting had been broken up. The leader of the Selma to Montgomery march was remembered on a stretch of the road that ran along one side of the courthouse square where a green sign indicated that it had one of the longest names ever given to a stretch of road. It was the Dr Martin Luther King Jr Jan 15 1929–April 4 1968 Memorial Highway. It was the first thoroughfare I'd seen named after King that wasn't a boulevard.

Despite these historic Southern credentials, Marion wasn't flaunting them. Many of the old stores surrounding the courthouse square sold antiques and collectibles but none of them offered reproductions of the Stars and Bars or model Johnny Rebs made of crushed pecan shells. The only postcards I found showed the courthouse and views of Judson College, one of the oldest women's educational establishments in the country. They were in a general store where the black man in front of me in the queue spent several minutes enquiring after the white cashier's mother. When I'd purchased my cards, I ambled across to the post office that stood opposite a faded marines' recruitment poster on a rusting stand. I passed three people on the way, and they all said good morning. Inside the small post office building, the man behind the counter had to look up the price of a postcard to England and the black woman behind me asked where I was from after she heard my voice. When I told her, she looked at me with genuine surprise on her face and said, 'What are you doing here in Marion?' It was all very refreshing after the longest, tallest, biggest mentality I'd found in so many other places in the South.

My journey up from Monroeville towards Marion had been a passage through the small-town, rural South of Atticus Finch, Br'er Rabbit, Huckleberry Finn and so many other fictional characters thrown up by the region's unpretentious backwoods. The roads were wooded and winding and the soil almost unnaturally red until I hit the Black Belt, so-called not for the colour of people's skin but because of the raven black earth. I passed occasional signposts to places that processed venison and a few trucks carrying loads of cut logs, but most of the way it was just standing trees and a string of sleepy little hamlets minding their own business. One I drove through, Bell's Landing, had two wooden churches on the right-hand side of the road, one for the Methodist community and another for the Presbyterians. On the other side of the road were two whitewashed wooden houses. That was it. That was Bell's Landing. I'm sure there wasn't any more to the place because I was so astonished at the ratio of houses to places of worship that I stopped a little way up the road and drove back to make sure. A mile further on was yet another church. This time it was Baptist and there wasn't a house anywhere near it as far as I could see.

I side-stepped the middle of Camden but passed through its outskirts which I thought looked pretty dire. It wasn't really poor, although it clearly wasn't rich either. It just looked unkempt, as if no one here worried about finished edges. I stopped to buy a can of soft drink at a Piggly Wiggly supermarket on the edge of town and was immediately spotted by a kindly assistant who approached to ask whether I needed any help.

'Where you from, Sir?' she asked when she heard my voice, and when I told her, 'Are you staying in town or just passing through?' She looked truly disappointed when I said I wouldn't be stopping.

29

Strange Fruit

I spent a day in Selma because I wanted to see where that march had taken place. Of all the things that define the South, the racial issue is still probably the most important and there was no doubt that the 1965 Selma to Montgomery voting rights march had been a landmark in the civil rights era. I arrived in the evening and bisected the city from north to south looking for accommodation along the length of Broad Street. I soon found myself crossing the Alabama river on the Edmund Pettus Bridge, the spot where the marchers had been beaten back by law enforcement officers all those years before. On the other side of the bridge was a strip of car dealerships, a dead laundromat, and a place selling agricultural machinery. Just beyond a dead car tyre dump sat a seedy looking motel, and beyond this the countryside began. I pulled over to the side of the highway to take stock as the golden rose glow of sunset was splashed across a cotton field. I hadn't liked the look of the seedy motel next to the tyre dump, so I decided to try to find somewhere else. I re-crossed the bridge as the shadows lengthened and drove the length of Broad Street once more, past the red brick Presbyterian church with a tall tower next to it that looked like an elegant minaret. Back on the northern edge of town, I finally found a more salubrious motel that I'd missed on my first reconnaissance.

I asked the man behind the desk, who was of Asian extraction, if he could recommend somewhere to eat and he pointed behind me to a display of brochures. Among these I found two leaflets for places that were close.

'Which is best?' I asked him. 'This steak house or the Tally-Ho restaurant?' The man looked at the two leaflets I was holding up with a distinct lack of interest and told me he didn't know because he didn't eat meat.

I plumped for the Tally-Ho because it wasn't a name I'd expected to find in deepest Alabama. It was in an old hunting lodge, now completely surrounded by a residential district. The waitress who served me was very chatty. She was originally from Arkansas, she told me, but had attended school at a convent in Vicksburg, Mississippi. She couldn't tell me why the proprietors had chosen such an English sounding name for their restaurant, however.

'Oh gosh,' she said, 'I can never remember, I'm supposed to know.' She wasn't much good in helping me choose my dinner either, because she too was a vegetarian. I went for salmon. It was fresh and succulent and tasted like it had recently inhabited a river rather than an artificial pond, but the béarnaise sauce was straight out of a bottle and the special baked potato was a mistake because the cheese on it was more closely related to a space ship than a cow. But the most curious aspect about this dinner was the garnish. When the plate first arrived I assumed it was a piece of lettuce, but on closer inspection it turned out to be a cabbage leaf.

The following morning was clear, bright and sunny. I grabbed a couple of small doughnuts from the motel foyer and filled a cup with coffee so that I too could partake of the ritual of sitting in a traffic jam while sipping a drink from a large paper cup. The Selma rush hour didn't last long enough for me to finish the coffee so I did it sitting in a church car park on the corner of Jeff Davis Avenue and Martin Luther King Jr Street. I was at the starting point of an historic walking tour, established here because this was where the voting rights march had begun.

Actually there were three marches, or at least two attempts, before the protesters managed to make it all the way to Montgomery. A bust of Martin Luther King Jr sat astride a monument to his dream outside the Brown Chapel African Methodist Episcopal Church, a twin spired red brick building trimmed in white whence the marchers set out one Sunday in March 1965. Dr King wasn't involved in the first attempt to reach Montgomery. He was called upon to lead the subsequent marches after the first was turned back by state troopers and a sheriff's posse just outside the city limits on the far side of the Edmund Pettus Bridge. To say they were 'turned back' is understating it somewhat. When the 500-odd marchers, carefully briefed in the techniques of non-violent demonstration, reached the first traffic light outside the city limits, they were told that their assembly was unlawful and were ordered to disperse. The marchers didn't move, so the troopers edged towards them, pushing them back with their billy clubs before a full-scale attack broke out, in which tear gas was fired and marchers beaten. The city's two hospitals that admitted blacks reported 65 injuries from the attack and the day went down in the annals of civil rights history as Bloody Sunday.

Footage of the scene was broadcast on network television that night and many Americans were horrified by the spectacle of law enforcement officers attacking peaceful citizens. A couple of days later, the second march, led by Dr King, stopped at the site of the attack, offered prayers and returned to Brown Chapel. That night, an out of town minister who had come to Selma to show his support for the voting rights struggle was attacked and murdered outside a café by four white men. The incident led to an influx of more activists and two weeks after Bloody Sunday, 3000 marchers set out from Selma and made it all the way to Montgomery.

When history is written, words like 'activist' and 'marcher' can conjure up the wrong images of organised protest. This is not to say that the Selma to Montgomery march wasn't organised. It was, and carefully so, with participants properly briefed on the techniques of non-violence. But what sometimes gets lost in the telling, and in the use of this collective terminology, is the fact that most of the marchers were ordinary men and women who were simply fed up with the injustice of living in a country where their skin colour meant they were denied basic rights of citizenship. It was the ordinariness of the setting that struck me more than anything else as I strolled down Martin Luther King Jr Street in the bright sunshine. It was just an average street with traffic-calming bumps and low cost houses with air-conditioning units on their sides and barbecues set up out back, much too mundane a place to be the starting point for such an historic event.

The sense that ordinary people had made history happen was captured perfectly in the nearby National Voting Rights Museum and Institute. Just inside the museum, to the left as I walked in, one wall was entirely covered by a black and white photograph of the Edmund

Pettus Bridge that had gone all grainy because it had been blown up so much. It was called the I Was There wall and was covered in post-its, an idea that was similar to the Adopt a Flag Program in the Confederate Memorial Hall in New Orleans. Some people had just signed their names on the post-its to record their presence at the historic occasion, while others had left comments like 'What a difference Selma has made' and 'God's speed'. My eye was caught by the only offering that was type written. It was from the mayor at the time of Bloody Sunday, JT Smitherman, and his comments were strangely factual. 'I was the mayor of Selma in 1965 when Dr Martin Luther King led massive voters' rights demonstrations which were climaxed by the march across Edmund Pettus Bridge which is now referred to as Bloody Sunday. This demonstration led to the passage of the national Voting Rights Act.'

The post-it I found most moving was also factual, but the straightforward, hand-written summary perfectly caught the essence of a people's struggle. In a laboured hand of largely unjoined-up writing, a man named George H Kimbrough summed up the feelings and motivations of a people who calmly rose up to demonstrate against such a simple injustice. 'I was the first black person to go in the Trailways bus station. There were helicopters overhead protecting us from harm. I was 20 years old and impressionable. We had to pick cotton and Homer said come on over so we can vote. My mother wanted to vote real bad so I'd rather march than pick cotton.'

Further in, the museum was a series of rooms dedicated to various aspects of the civil rights struggle. There was a memorial room full of pictures and case histories of people who had died for the cause, including that of Jimmie Lee Jackson, the man from Marion whose death at the hands of state troopers, while trying to protect his mother, had sparked the Selma–Montgomery march. The short description of these events noted that no one had ever been charged with his shooting.

A long corridor lined with photographs of black senators and representatives under the heading Fruits of the Labour led to the rear of the premises where the walls of a small lecture room were lined with more old photographs from times gone by. There was a picture of an area of the city of Birmingham, where so many bombs had exploded during the civil rights era that for a time it had become known as Bombingham. Another, older photograph that caught my eye showed two black men hanging by their necks from the branch of a tree. The notes below the caption explained that between 1889 and 1918 at least 3211 black men, women and children had been lynched in the South. Justification for this type of action had ranged from suspected poisoning of wells to paying attention to a white girl. Mob members openly flaunted their identity, the notes went on, and many people dressed up in their Sunday best for such special events, referred to here as 'lynching bees'. The black and white photographs, apart from the appropriate irony of their two-colour tones, had the effect of firmly confining the images to history. But they also made them more powerful. What depressed me most about them was their symbolism of man's inhumanity to man. OK, it was white man's inhumanity to black man, but it was still man's inhumanity to man. The caption that went with the picture of the two men hanging from the tree was apt. It said 'Strange Fruit'.

Back towards the entrance, I picked up an information sheet entitled Voting Rights Milestones. Towards the bottom of the sheet the adoption of the 1965 Voting Rights Act was noted. Then President Lyndon Johnson had responded directly to the barbaric scenes of Bloody Sunday and he signed the act into law five months later. But what surprised me was the last entry on the list. It was for 1982 and it said: 'Extension of the Voting Rights Act – after one extension in 1975, the Act was strengthened and extended for 25 additional years to the year 2007.' I'd thought that the issue was closed, that the right of all US citizens to vote, regardless of race, colour, sex, education or any other let out clause, had been finally granted, without any qualifications, in perpetuity. I said as much to the black lady behind the counter, who I'd seen earlier talking to a group of school children in one of the museum's rooms.

'The 1965 Act was just an act,' she told me. 'During the Reagan administration it was strengthened. It was like the Old Testament and the New Testament, if the Old Testament had been sufficient we wouldn't need a new one.' She paused, 'Now, as we approach the year

2000, I'm sure it'll occur to somebody to launch a campaign hopefully to make it ironclad, part of the Constitution or in the very least make it a law.'

It was only later that I remembered the Fifteenth Amendment to the US Constitution, ratified after the War Between the States, in 1870. When I looked it up, I found it said: 'The right of citizens of the United States to vote shall not be denied or abridged by the United States or any state on account of race, color, or previous condition of servitude.' They already had the right to vote enshrined in the Constitution, it was just that the South had taken no notice of it for well nigh a hundred years.

I asked the woman what it was like now living in Alabama, and in the South in general. She drew a deep breath before she answered.

'Most people have this perception of what the South is when they come,' she said, 'that not much has changed. It has to be slow, you know. But a lot has changed. We have a long way to go now but a lot has changed.' A smile came over her face. 'Like this lady told me yesterday, her son moved to Montgomery from the north and they followed him down and they came over to visit the museum. She said she told him, "Don't you do anything to make these people kill you."'

I laughed loudly because she'd said it with a smirk on her face. 'Good advice,' I said.

'Well I guess you got a point there,' she told me, 'but I don't think we have to worry about lynching today, you know. It wouldn't be high on my list anyway. It's possible, but he's more likely to be killed by someone he knows, than for it to come from the other side. At this stage in time anyway. So we've come a long way, we just got a long way to go.'

She paused, and then changed tack. 'In England they don't have much racism do they? Because the population of blacks must be very small.'

'It's certainly not as large a proportion as it is here,' I told her, 'but racism is still in a lot of people's heads, and there is racial violence as well.'

'Oh yeah?' She sounded genuinely surprised. 'There was some stirrings when I was in Germany, that skinhead movement . . .' She trailed off, thinking for a moment about German skinheads. Then she came back on-line. 'Here in the United States, we don't call ourselves Ku Klux Klan anymore, we call ourselves "militia".' I thought it was interesting that she said 'we' and not 'they'.

'Just changed the name?'

'Yeah. Same old people, same old beliefs, just change the name.' She paused again. 'They're not as strong as they were in the heyday of the KKK, but they're still out there.' I nodded. 'And we will never ever have another non-violent period,' she said categorically.

'You think not?'

'I know not. Because our children, they've gone into an age of violence. Particularly towards each other and if they were ever organised enough to realise that they're their own worst enemies, that I shouldn't hate you because you're just as oppressed as I am. And if they ever get to that point and it's not channelled correctly, it would be a violent revolution.'

She said it was the more subtle forms of racism that needed to be faced now because the ones that come out and slap you in the face had been dealt with. But her fears that the next generation of Southern blacks might not try to solve the reasons for their malcontent as peaceably as their forebears echoed those that Bill, the retired air force man and motel minibus driver, had mentioned to me in Charleston. He'd been worried about the young black kids today who had no legitimate reasons for the anger in their rap music.

I'd seen many of the fruits of the civil rights era during my time in the South, but they hadn't all been positive. As the lady in the Voting Rights Museum had said, they'd come a long way, but there was still a long way to go. Memories run deep in the South and attitudes don't change overnight. During the first leg of my journey, I'd been saddened when one of the postgraduate women at the dinner party I attended in Ayden, North Carolina had said that the Ku Klux Klan was still active in the area. On a Saturday night, she still saw pickups with crosses on the back shooting past her father's house in a white area bound for the nearby black suburb. Later, while flicking through the channels on the TV in a hotel room one night, my attention had been held by a documentary about a former Grand Dragon of the KKK and co-proprietor of The Redneck Shop full of Klan paraphernalia in Lauren, South Carolina. The moment I switched to the programme

I was met with a greasy haired, ferrety individual who declared in the broadest Southern drawl, 'I grew up hating Mexicans, blacks, Puerto Ricans, Chinese, Japanese, Hondurans. You name it, I didn't like 'em. If they weren't white, I didn't care for 'em.' The irony of the programme was that the man, having fallen on hard times, had been helped by a local black Baptist minister. They had become firm friends, but in so doing the white former Klan member had been cut off by his parents and many of his white acquaintances.

The programme appeared to confirm part of the old adage suggesting that while whites in the North love the black race and hate the individual, in the South they love the individual and hate the race. It was just that in some cases they hated both the race and the individual. They say that although blacks and whites in the South often work or go to school together, they rarely live or worship side by side. I'd seen some clear examples of the lack of residential integration. Memories of the derelict, virtually all-black settlements in the Mississippi Delta would stay with me for a long time, and I also remembered the almost complete absence of black faces in Pigeon Forge, Tennessee.

And when it came to long memories, it struck me that the whole civil rights era must have played a significant part in helping to rekindle memories of the War Between the States. Once the Yankees had won the war the Reconstruction period was built upon the emancipation of the slaves, but the Southern states had turned back the clock for nearly another hundred years with the Jim Crow laws. In one sense the fruits of the civil rights era, the end of Jim Crow, had been the final defeat of the Confederacy. The Voting Rights Act was signed into law 100 years after Lee's surrender at Appomattox in 1865.

In that respect, perhaps it was understandable that in some parts of the South Martin Luther King Day was also known as Robert E Lee Day. Tyler Jo had told me that this was the case in Virginia, for example. It was a neat compromise enabling Southerners to take their holiday in honour of whichever Southern hero they chose, depending on their proclivities. The birthdays of King and Lee were within a few days of each other which was very convenient. The holiday in question had passed a few days previously and the news had been full of stories of rallies and parades. TV reporters roved through the masses asking what the captions described as 'eclectic residents' whether or not Dr King's dream was still alive. Wall Street had closed for the first time on the occasion of Martin Luther King Day, but I saw one report from the small Alabama town of Tallassee where the town's government had been working as usual, despite the closure of its schools. The Tallassee mayor told the reporter that nobody had ever asked to dedicate this day to either King's or Lee's birthday. Anyway, race relations in his town were just fine, he added. An ominous confirmation of the point made by the lady in the Voting Rights Museum came from Baton Rouge, Louisiana where someone had been shot dead at a Martin Luther King Day rally. A report from Baton Rouge said that the dead man had been the victim of a disagreement between rival groups of black teenagers.

Several of the 'eclectic residents' I saw interviewed on that day said that Martin Luther King's dream was really the American dream, and was therefore relevant to everyone. The comments were in tune with the theory that equates the black civil rights era with the Lost Cause of the Confederacy. They were both distinctly Southern phenomena, but both very American at the same time. The logic behind the ironic compromise of offering the option to honour General Lee or Dr King was brought home to me when I strolled the streets of Montgomery a few days later. From the top of the marble steps leading up to the Greek revival state capitol, I looked down the wide boulevard of Dexter Avenue. I was standing on the small six-point bronze star inlaid to mark the spot where Jefferson Davis took the oath as the first and only president of the Confederate States of America. It was along this concourse, then known as Market Street, that his inaugural parade processed to the tune of the South's unofficial national anthem, 'Dixie Land', played as a band arrangement for the first time.

As the words of the song have it, the world was made in just six days, and finished off in various ways, God made Dixie trim and nice, but Adam called it Paradise. Dr King managed a glimpse of Paradise himself when that march from Selma ended with a rally on these very same steps. The opportunity for Southern citizens to celebrate the achievements of two such different dreams was an appropriate modern day demonstration of the Janus-faced Southern culture. The

South is as much black as it is white. Their history is a common one, stretching from the old plantations to the manifestation of Elvis as a black man in a white skin.

When I walked into the lovingly preserved First White House of the Confederacy, I shouldn't have been surprised when the woman behind the counter in the small gift shop offered me a piece of a huge Robert E Lee birthday cake stuck with Confederate flags. Only in the South could I have eaten a birthday cake made for someone who died more than a hundred years ago. I'm sure if I'd looked hard enough I'd have found an equivalent made for Dr King. It was just another of the strange fruits that have sprung up from the fertile earth of the Southern states.

30

Lost Luggage

That image of Paradise kept coming back to me during the last few days I spent in the South. I drove north from Montgomery to evade the severe thunderstorms that were forecast for the southern half of Alabama, but the high winds and torrential rain followed me up Interstate 65. Although it was midday, visibility was reduced to about a hundred yards. Spray from the vehicles in front of me obscured my view in the fading light and it became difficult to see the white lines on the highway. The low, dark clouds looked like massive bruising on the sky and they took on a touch of evil when I passed a hoarding that said 'Go to church or the devil will get you'. This part of Alabama didn't look like Paradise, and now I understood why.

I skirted round Birmingham hoping to catch a glimpse of the city's famous landmark, a huge cast-iron statue of Vulcan stood up on a hilltop, but the weather put paid to that. I veered off towards a town called Boaz instead because I'd seen an advertisement for the place as one of the nation's top factory outlet centres. For those that couldn't climb aboard the casino bandwagon, factory outlet centres seemed to be the latest approach to that pursuit of happiness thing. I'd already seen a number of variations on this interpretation of the American dream, the feeding frenzy in casino land in the Mississippi Delta and the special angle on the problem taken in the French Quarter in New Orleans. I knew by now that I could take the instant route to happiness via the simple infusion of a fizzy brown soft drink invented in Atlanta, Georgia, but I wanted to take a closer look at a place that was being hyped as a shoppers' Paradise. I'd passed signposts to these factory outlet centres several times on my travels, but had stopped to look only once, in Pigeon Forge, Tennessee. Fascinated by the Bible Factory Outlet there, I was hopeful that Boaz, an otherwise unprepossessing little town in a rolling landscape of pasture and trees, might throw up something equally remarkable.

It did, and it came in the form of the Unclaimed Baggage Center, an entire department store stocked with goods lost during air travel. It sat amongst a vast series of warehouses, all selling discount goods and all virtually empty of customers. I wandered through a few of them before I found the Unclaimed Baggage Center. They were all staffed by North Alabama robots who were programmed to speak the words 'How are you today?' on entry, and 'You come back now and have a great day' on exit. The trouble was, most of them said it with such conviction that I felt a pang of guilt every time I walked out without buying anything.

I spent longer in the Unclaimed Baggage Center because it had all the excitement generated by the potential bargains you find in a second-hand shop combined with an unparalleled fascination at the sorts of things people take with them on aeroplanes. And then leave behind. There were aisles of shoes, gloves, cassettes, Walkmans, headrests and blow-up pillows, along with an extensive series of shelves devoted to spectacles and spectacle cases. There was a small, rather sad cuddly toy section and row upon row of clothing, as well as a good selection of bags, holdalls, briefcases and suitcases. All these items I expected to find in a store specialising in unclaimed lost luggage, but the merchandise didn't end there. There was a short but significant shelf devoted to laptop computers, all in full working order. 'Oh damn!' I could hear their owners saying. 'I've lost my laptop. Now where could I have left it? . . . Dunno, guess I better buy another one.'

In the sports department, a wide range of tennis rackets was on display. Next to these were the skis and ski boots, and then the bowling ball section. Can you imagine going on a skiing holiday and forgetting that you'd brought your skis? No, neither can I. Coming home from a skiing holiday and forgetting them? Slightly more feasible, but still highly unlikely. Even if I broke both my legs and never wanted to ski again, I'd want to sell them, or ceremoniously burn them at the very least. But it got better. Over in the corner of the sports department was a hang-glider. Not a missing piece of a hang-glider that had fallen off in transit, not a broken wing that was too damaged to bother picking up from the conveyor belt. It was an entire, fully functioning, almost brand new hang-glider. Explain that one if you can. And when you've done so, what about the industrial size knitting machine in the upholstery department?

With the heavens still relieving themselves outside in a big way, I spent half an hour trying on raincoats and left with a bargain Burberry for $50. I made it to a nondescript motel on the edge of Boaz and was greeted by a young woman who asked me how I'd enjoyed my shopping today.

The following morning, my last day in Alabama, I drove across country to take a quick look at Cullman because someone I'd met a couple of days previously, in Montgomery, had said it was interesting. I'd had trouble finding the place because to my ear he'd pronounced it Coleman. I should have realised earlier given the difficulties I'd already faced in telling a number of people that I'd be flying home from Birmingham. No one understood what I was talking about until it dawned on me that they called the place Birming*ham*.

Cullman was unhurried and small-townish. It was also very white and rather European looking, with a double spired Sacred Heart of Jesus Catholic church. The settlement was founded in the late nineteenth century by a German colonel as a colony for his countrymen. Its attractions were advertised at the time as 'No malaria, no swamps, no grasshoppers, no hurricanes and no blizzards.' What Colonel Cullman neglected to mention was that there was no fertile land either. But somehow his town had survived. It was just another example in the long line of tales I'd come across showing how the south has been mis-sold to newcomers as a promised land. The English had been at it since the very start of their colonial settlements in Virginia, advertising the hazardous territory as a delicious country and its fearsome natives as noble and angelic. The French had done it as well, with the earliest promoters of Louisiana portraying it as a new world paradise, leaving it for the unsuspecting immigrants to find flood prone swamps rife with Yellow Fever. The Spanish too had been driven by the lure of gold that had never come to fruition.

As I drove south towards Birming*ham* airport, I considered how a veil of mystery had been woven from these original strands of mythical imagery, eventually to cover an entire enchanted land. The South was not a geographical place but an emotional idea, one steeped in heat and history. It was a way of life developed in a region where a day was 24 hours long like it was everywhere else, only here each hour seemed to last a little longer. I'd seen some sobering sights in the South, but nothing really approaching the Heart of Darkness images I'd been half expecting. The American dream had taken some unexpected turns down in Dixie and I rather suspected that these could be related to the inbuilt fallibility of the notion that the South was Paradise. The idea was based on myths from the start, but because the advertising that said it was a promised land was wrong, Southerners immediately set out to prove it right. To the literal minded, a myth is simply something that isn't true; in the South they'd managed to turn it into something truer than fact. And having fought and lost a war to preserve the honour of their promised land, these down-to-earth Southerners have defied the unprincipled superiority of the outsider ever since.

My hire car still splashing its way southwards, I got to thinking of a bizarre, very Southern conversation I'd had a few days earlier in my hotel in Montgomery. I'd spotted a cut-price coupon for the Holiday Inn in the downtown area in a give away tabloid type publication I'd picked up at the Alabama visitor's centre. These freebies were available at state visitors' centres all across the South. Printed on the sort of cheap paper I normally associate with comics, they were full of advertisements and cut-price coupons for motels, hotels and restaurants. In most other states I'd picked up these publications and then forgotten to use them, but in this case I'd been struck by an unusual fit of efficient behaviour, and actually managed to ring up in advance and book a room.

When I arrived in the foyer, I was met with a scene of organised chaos. A lot of people in suits were checking in and there was only one young woman behind the desk to deal with us all. As I waited, I noticed that I was the only guest who wasn't wearing a tie and that my rather world weary holdall stood out somewhat from the assortment of smart overnight bags and suit-carriers all around me. Many of the men inside the suits appeared to know each other, and none of them looked like the sort of people who would spend any time cutting discount coupons out of comics.

After what must have been nearly half an hour, the not too flustered woman behind the counter finally took my coupon and credit card details and allotted me room 421. She handed me a small paper wallet with the number written on it and a plastic card inside to open the door with. The hotel was designed in such a way that the room doors all faced inwards to a central atrium. There was only one lift and room 421 was directly opposite, so I had to lug my bag the longest possible distance. When I got there the door was ajar and I could see a man's jacket on a hanger through the opening. I checked the number on the door and on my small paper wallet. My heart sank. I knocked and went in.

The voice of a television announcer was talking about the weather prospects for tomorrow and I saw a suitcase open on the sideboard to reveal some pressed shirts and a wash bag. Around the corner, sitting on the nearer of two beds, was an elderly man in shirt sleeves chewing some gum.

'Hello,' I said, 'am I in the wrong room or is it you?'

The man on the bed looked at me for a moment longer than I thought was necessary and said, 'They've given you the wrong room.' He chewed his gum some more and added, 'They know me here, I bin stopping here for years.'

I started to turn but he went on, 'Why don't you phone down to reception and letum sort it out? Dial zero.'

The telephone was on my side of the bed and I followed his advice. I recognised the voice of the vaguely hassled woman at the desk downstairs. 'Hello, my name's Middleton. I just checked in and you gave me room 421 which is where I'm ringing from, but there's a gentleman already in it.' I don't often use the word gentleman, but it seemed appropriate since he was sitting right next to me. The faint sound of computer keys being tapped came over the telephone. The woman apologised and said I should come down to get another key.

'Leave your bag here if you like,' the man said amiably, 'I'll look out for it.'

Back at the reception desk, the queue was a bit shorter. The young woman had been joined by a colleague. He told me their computer system was down, but he was pretty sure that room 218 was empty.

The way the plastic card key worked was you put it into the slot in your door and a little green light flashed to indicate that you were in. Except that in the case of room 218 I wasn't. The handle turned, but the door wouldn't open. I tried a couple of times before returning to the front desk again. It seemed like they were making me pay for using the discount coupon.

'I think there's someone in that room too,' I told the man on the desk. 'It won't open. Must be locked from the inside.' The man did his best to hide the mild look of alarm that had appeared on his face. 'You too huh?' came a voice from my elbow. I turned to see a suit beside me. 'Someone in my room as well,' the suit added. Although somewhat relieved that it wasn't just me that was being given the run-around, I was getting pretty annoyed, but everyone else was still surprisingly calm given the reputation American consumers are supposed to have for demanding efficiency. Southern consumers were obviously a little more patient.

'Wait a moment,' the man behind the desk said to me suddenly. 'What room number is that?'

'218.'

'OK, turn the door handle up. There's only one room in the hotel with an up handle, and that's it.' His advice seemed just unlikely enough to be true, and it was.

Back at room 421 again, the door was still half open. I knocked as I walked in to collect my bag. The old guy with the chewing gum had been joined by two other characters who were sitting on the other bed. The older of the two men on the far bed was also in shirt-sleeves, but the younger man next to him wore a dark suit with his tie pulled down to reveal a top button that was undone. His legs were crossed and he was wearing fancy cowboy boots. All three men were holding very large red plastic cups which made them look faintly ridiculous.

'Thanks for looking after my bag,' I said.

'They sort you out?' asked the gum-chewing man.

'Yes thanks.' I stooped to pick up my holdall, conscious of the three sets of eyes on me.

'Where you from?' asked the chewing gum man.

'England.'

There was a brief pause while the gum was chewed some more. Then the man said, 'England,' as if he was evaluating the truth of my statement. 'Never bin to England. I was in the marines and travelled a lot, but I never went to England.' It was almost tantamount to him saying that he didn't think my country existed.

'I worked with an Englishman once,' piped up the older of his two friends. 'He sounded like you. Came here to live. When his brother came over to visit, even he couldn't understand him.' All three men had their eyes fixed on me, as if they were testing to see whether I might rise to their challenge concerning the Southern accent. I didn't. I just smiled in what I hoped was a friendly way.

'He was in the Air Force,' the other old guy went on, 'he flew in that mission to blow up that dam. He was in the only plane that came back.' I raised my eyebrows and nodded some more and the old guy on the opposite bed kept going. 'People from up north speak strange too. When they come here they're Yankees, when they stay they're damn Yankees.' It was the type of comment that might have been construed as a joke, but it was delivered in a deadpan voice and none of them laughed.

The younger man, the one with the cowboy boots, took a sip from his large red plastic cup and turned to look at the television set. For some reason I'd assumed the red cups to contain hard liquor of some kind, but their weight and the soft rattle of ice cubes suggested it was a more voluminous drink, like ice tea. It was time for the weather report again. Over to Cyndee O'Quinn the meteorologist.

If this meeting had come earlier in one of my visits to the South, I'd have probably made my exit at this point, but I sensed that the conversation hadn't finished. It was like the communication equivalent of playing chess. You make your move and your opponent has three minutes in which to respond. I thought hard for something to say, but the gum-chewing man beat me to it.

'What are you doing here?' he asked me. That one was easy, but I silently counted to three before answering. 'Writing a book,' I replied.

The guy didn't react. He just sat there staring at me. The only part

287

of his anatomy that moved was his jaw as he methodically chewed his gum, but his eyes were boring deep into my head. For a moment I was transported all the way back to the alligators in the St Augustine alligator farm. The man hadn't even batted an eyelid, but he hadn't needed to. His eyes said it all: what you doing that for? On the television, Cyndee O'Quinn was saying that tomorrow was likely to be fine, but there was a 20 per cent chance of thundery showers.

'This your first book?' he asked finally. A little bit of me wanted to say yes. Their unhurried demeanour could have been intimidating, but most of me was quite enjoying the encounter. 'No, I've written a dozen or so.'

I don't think any of them knew how to react to this piece of information. My statement was met with silence from all except Cyndee O'Quinn who was talking about the meteorological prospects for the weekend. They included the strong possibility of thunderstorms in the south of the state. It was the turn of the gum-chewer to take a sip of ice tea from his red cup. Everything he did was slow and supremely unruffled. I could imagine how he'd react if his hair was on fire. He'd sit there for a moment or two, chewing his gum and pondering the options before ambling over to the bathroom door.

'This book's about the South,' I told him, 'it's a travel book, about people and places.'

'Where you bin in Alabama?' the gum-chewer asked, almost quickly for him. If I'd been writing up the conversation as a film script, I'd have added 'boy?' to the end of his question.

'I only just arrived, I came through Monroeville, Selma and Marion.'

'There's a lot of history in Selma,' said the man with cowboy boots, turning away from the television again. 'I like them houses.' He looked at me with no expression on his face and then said, 'You oughta come on up to Coleman. That's where I'm from. Lot of folks with German roots settled in Coleman.' I managed a 'That's interesting' before gum-chewer chipped in. 'Used to be a sign,' he said. 'Niggers don't let the sun set on your ass in Coleman.'

Cowboy boots gave me the hint of a smile. 'Still very few of 'em there,' he mused.

There was another pause, during which I noted that this was the first time I'd heard the N word used during my time in the South. Then the old man who had worked with an Englishman said, 'I was up in Montreal once. They speak French there. I was driving round, looking for a motel, and stopped to ask. This woman started talking French at me at first, then changed to English. She said that's a motel over there, looks real shabby from the outside but it's right clean inside, and it was.'

I nodded. It was another tricky one to respond to, but the three of them had turned towards the TV set once more, indicating that I had the full three minutes in which to reply. It was like being in another time zone, where everything was in slow motion. I was glad for the time to think, and for the diversion from the N word.

'What line of work are you gentlemen in?' I asked finally. There was that other unfamiliar word again. It felt strange in my mouth, but I was playing safe because I sensed that it might be advisable to mind my Ps and Qs. I'd also just remembered that old adage about Southerners being real polite up until the point at which they pull out their gun and shoot you.

'We're here to watch the state legislators,' gum-chewer said without taking his eyes off the TV screen. 'When they get together nobody's safe.' The other two almost sniggered.

'Are you observers of some kind?' I asked after an appropriate delay.

'Yeah, you could call us *observers* of some kind. We're the Plumbers and Gas Fitters Examining Board.' He reached into his pocket with his free hand and produced a card. Still chewing, he handed the card to me. On the card it said 'State of Alabama Plumbers and Gas Fitters Examining Board'. The gum-chewer's name was below in bold and below that were the words 'Executive Director'. It was my turn not to know how to react. My brain worked furiously on something appropriate to say and came up with nothing. It was one of those occasions when the only comment that comes forth is 'Interesting', but I'd already used that one, and besides I wasn't confident that I could utter the word with any conviction. I applied a gentle pressure to my tongue with my teeth instead. The guy turned towards the TV set again. It wasn't a dismissive gesture, he was just calling time out in the conversation. I hesitated, then went for my holdall. I really couldn't think of anything at all to say and my three minutes were up.

'Well, I'll be getting along to my room then. Thanks again for looking after my bag.' The gum-chewing Executive Director of the State of Alabama Plumbers and Gas Fitters Examining Board fixed me with his eyes one final time.

'You'd get on with my son-in-law,' he told me. 'He's in the entertainment business too. He's bin to England. He writes songs.' He paused to chew a bit more. 'He thinks of the lines while he's cooking breakfast.' Then he raised his plastic cup to his lips to take another pull on his iced tea.

At Birmingham airport I returned my hire car. Once inside the terminal building I bought a newspaper for the flight home and walked towards the departure gate, leaving the South in all its variations behind me.